D1489028

Praise for *Win When They Say You Won't*

Winning is realized at the end of a battle, but it is first conceived in the beginning of the battle . . . in the mind. Daphne E. Jones focuses the reader's mind on seeing personal setbacks as business problems or growth opportunities, using business tools and methods to overcome those challenges and win! Daphne "keeps it real" through her stories of women's injustice, experiences, and triumphs.

— **REVEREND AL SHARPTON**, President and Founder
  of National Action Network

I had the good fortune to work with Daphne for several years during my tenure at GE. This front row seat allowed me to see not only her incredible work—strategic, creative, and disciplined—but also the strength of her character and leadership skills. I learned from Daphne at every step of the way, and her compelling new book continues that journey. With important tools and a focus on mindset, this guide can be used by anyone who has ever felt the wind in their face.

— **JOHN FLANNERY**, CEO of General Electric (ret.),
  CEO of GE Healthcare (ret.), and Managing Director
  at Charlesbank Capital Partners

There is something wonderful about the way an engineer thinks, especially a female engineer. As a woman advocate and mentor, I have seen many books, many that resonate emotionally and are a respite in a storm of injustice. Daphne does connect to the injustice of her otherness, but she connects her sisters to tools that successful managers in tech and business use. This book is so different because she has created a system that uses the best management tools for you to work on your most important endeavor: you.

— **GERALDINE LAYBOURNE**, first President of Nickelodeon,
  Cofounder and Chairwoman of Oxygen Media, Vice Chairman
  of Vital Voices, and Cofounder of Day One Early Learning
  Community

Daphne's story of her journey from secretary to senior vice president and beyond is inspiring and will excite, ignite, and empower readers. The playing field for women is not level, and Daphne's methodology helps women win in spite of barriers that can block their success. I love her ambition, perseverance, and stories of transformation.

—SHELLYE ARCHAMBEAU, author of *Unapologetically*
Ambitious and CEO of Metric Stream (ret.)

It's evident from her steep ascent into senior corporate leadership, Daphne clearly learned how to play the game that was not designed for her to win. As a Black woman, of immigrant parents, born and raised in poverty, she shows that no matter your background, you have the power to define your own narrative and win using her EDIT methodology.

—GAIL EVANS, author, *Play Like a Man, Win Like a Woman*
and EVP, CNN Newsgroup (ret.)

"Yes I can!" are the words that came to me as I read the book *Win When They Say You Won't* by Daphne E. Jones. Daphne's book is a story of triumph and adversity, which serves as an inspiration to never give up on your dreams despite being told that they are not possible. Chronicling her personal and professional journey, the book is a tangible reminder of what can be achieved through sheer grit, tenacity, and determination. The personal accounts and the stories of other women makes the book relatable. However, the absolute value is highlighted by her desire to assist others in achieving their dreams through the creation of her four-step EDIT strategy, which guides the reader through the transformation of their mindset to one of optimism and possibilities.

As Jamaica's Ambassador to the United States, I am always extremely proud of my Americans with Jamaican roots who make their mark in their adopted home, setting positive examples for others who choose to follow their footsteps and demonstrating the positive contribution of immigrants to the American society. As an entrepreneur who was never deterred by a closed door and as Jamaica's first female Ambassador to the United States, I know the importance of self-belief and perseverance.

For these reasons, I commend Daphne for using her journey and lessons learnt to encourage and guide others. I am certain that this book will serve as a beacon for individuals aiming to achieve their true potential.

—**H. E. AUDREY P. MARKS**, Jamaican Ambassador to the USA, Permanent Representative to the OAS, Embassy of Jamaica

Great leaders are often diamonds in the rough. They need guidance, encouragement, and direction to shine. Race and gender biases often add layers of dirt and crust that smother one's radiance. Daphne Jones has provided personal insights and a technologist's systems approach to success that will empower readers to realize their full potential.

—**MICHAEL K. POWELL**, President and CEO, NCTA—The Internet & Television Association and Former Chairman of the FCC

I have read many books directly, and I have been exposed to many others indirectly by a plethora of quotes. However, the expression of multiple aspects of Daphne's encounters outstrips the other works of this literary type.

What we have in this work is personal development, professional aspiration and achievement, friends, and family relationships. We have a smorgasbord of her philosophies, ideas, insights, and sagacious directives, which is a recipe for any readers' success.

I somehow hear Daphne saying, "If you take my advice, you will never envy my achievements." This is a great read!

—**BISHOP NOEL JONES**, City of Refuge, Los Angeles, CA

I love this book! It's the playbook that equips you with the mindset, skill-set, and willset to WIN. The EDIT methodology is simple to understand and implement personally and professionally. I am buying this book for nine specific people who are destined to be in the winner's circle, and I am recommending it to everyone I know in Corporate America.

—**SIMON T. BAILEY**, author of *Ignite the Power of Women in Your Life—a Guide for Men*

Win When They Say You Won't is the prescription for today's working woman and future leaders. In fact, it should be required reading in high school curriculum and college syllabuses.

Over the course of my 32 years as an attorney and senior government executive, I know and experienced firsthand the challenges that all too often hamper the advancement of women and People of Color in work environments be they public, private, or not-for-profit institutions. As a state Chief Diversity Officer and a member of the Chief women's professional network, I have had the opportunity to interface with women leaders and C-Suite executives from diverse backgrounds ranging from Fortune 500 companies to successful startups. The refrain from these amazing accomplished women is largely the same: "I am not being paid or valued the same as my male colleague irrespective of seniority or experience." Oftentimes these women suffer in silence or move on to another opportunity only to find themselves bumping against a new glass ceiling.

Fortunately, this book offers a paradigm shift for success. I would encourage any woman/leader ready to reset their trajectory to learn the "EDIT" process and be a part of the movement that "wins when they say you won't."

    —HESTER AGUDOSI, ESQ., former Chief Diversity Officer,
    New Jersey Office of Diversity and Inclusion

WIN

WHEN THEY
SAY YOU
WON'T

**BREAK THROUGH BARRIERS and
KEEP LEVELING UP YOUR *SUCCESS***

DAPHNE E. JONES

New York | Chicago | San Francisco | Athens | London | Madrid
Mexico City | Milan | New Delhi | Singapore | Sydney | Toronto

1 2 3 4 5 6 7 8 9   LCR   27 26 25 24 23 22

ISBN   978-1-264-27799-5
MHID   1-264-27799-7

e-ISBN   978-1-264-27800-8
e-MHID   1-264-27800-4

Library of Congress Cataloging-in-Publication Data

Names: Jones, Daphne E., author.
Title: Win when they say you won't / Daphne E. Jones.
Description: New York : McGraw Hill Education, [2022] | Includes
   bibliographical references and index.
Identifiers: LCCN 2022028479 (print) | LCCN 2022028480 (ebook) |
   ISBN 9781264277995 (hardback) | ISBN 9781264278008 (ebook)
Subjects: LCSH: Success in business. | Success. | Women—Vocational
   guidance. | Career development.
Classification: LCC HF5386 .J774 2022 (print) | LCC HF5386 (ebook) |
   DDC 658.4/09—dc23/eng/20220616
LC record available at https://lccn.loc.gov/2022028479
LC ebook record available at https://lccn.loc.gov/2022028480

McGraw Hill books are available at special quantity discounts to use as premiums and sales promotions or for use in corporate training programs. To contact a representative, please visit the Contact Us pages at www.mhprofessional.com.

McGraw Hill is committed to making our products accessible to all learners. To learn more about the available support and accommodations we offer, please contact us at accessibility@mheducation.com. We also participate in the Access Text Network (www.accesstext.org), and ATN members may submit requests through ATN.

CONTENTS

STEP IV: Transform

INTRODUCTION

Have you ever heard comments like these?

- "You're a woman—why do you want this global job?"

- "You don't have enough gray hair to be a senior vice president!"

- "You are so aggressive; you should try to be more likable."

Have you ever met all the required qualifications for a project or a promotion, but you still do not feel qualified enough to take on a new role?

Have you ever been in a meeting when a male colleague repeated what you just said—and he then received great feedback on the idea that everyone ignored when you said the same thing?

I have. Often. Throughout my career.

I was born in Phoenix, Illinois, a town so poor and small we didn't even have our own post office, bank, or grocery store. My parents had emigrated from Jamaica and wanted me and my three siblings to have all the opportunities America could afford us. I wanted those opportunities, too, but I had no idea what they were. Many folks in our town commuted to larger towns to work blue-collar jobs. Nonetheless, I prepared for something better than that. White kids were bused into our neighborhood to attend Coolidge Elementary School, and then for high school the tables were turned. I was bused to an all-white high school and was quite proud of my 4.0 grade point average. When I asked my guidance counselor about applying to college, he said, "Oh,

Daphne, girls like *you* don't go to college. They become secretaries. You will not get in, and if you do get in, you won't graduate." I got the message: I should know my place. College and good careers were only for white girls and boys.

So I followed my guidance counselor's advice and enrolled in a two-week secretarial course. I had already learned, in high school, how to type well and take dictation, so I was a top candidate for a great secretarial job. The college placed me at *Women's Day* magazine in downtown Chicago. I had a desk job in a big city. The people back in Phoenix thought I had made it. I was one of only two women of color working for an entirely white male staff. Yes, an all-male staff running a woman's magazine! But I soon realized, "I shouldn't *be* a secretary; I should *have* a secretary. I know I can do more; I just need some education!" I said that to myself, even though I had no women of color in my life, anywhere, to show or tell me this was possible.

"I don't care what that guidance counselor said I can't do; I'm going to go to college anyway," I told myself. And the rest, as they say, is "herstory."

Through many examples in my life, in the lives of my family members, and in my friends' lives, I was continually reminded—through people's words and actions—that I wasn't good enough, or "right" enough, to win.

Millions of people suffer social injustice because of their gender, race, and other visible "differences," and that injustice leads them to feel they cannot win. The conditioning to not believe in ourselves begins early. When we are first called the "N" word by little kids that may have first heard that term by an adult, we are conditioned to believe we should be grateful for whatever job we are given, whatever salary is awarded. That conditioning follows us all the way to adulthood, when it transforms itself into imposter syndrome. I experienced the subtle and not so subtle messages and actions directed at me that told me that I couldn't and wouldn't win.

In spite of those messages and behaviors I've lived through, I've achieved a lot, and I am grateful for my victories. Not only did I *go* to college, but I received my bachelor's degree in three years instead of the usual four years. I went on to get my MBA, receiving it in one year instead of the usual two years. So I was able to take the negative energy of my counselor's predictions and biases and use it as an agitant to spur me on to achieve. I've worked for some of the world's most recognizable companies—IBM, Johnson & Johnson, Hospira (now part of Pfizer), and General Electric. Although I started my career in an entry-level position of systems engineer at IBM, I rose to director, executive director, and vice president. From there, my titles included corporate officer, chief information officer, senior vice president, and senior executive. I have traveled to every continent in the world except Antarctica, and I have run global teams in those same continents, delivering countless millions of dollars of value for those corporations.

Starting out as a young Black woman in STEM (science, technology, engineering, and math) wasn't easy. I was often not just the only Black—but the only female. A unicorn. But I got invited into those rooms because I decided and designed my career to spend my professional life using and implementing digital technologies to help companies differentiate and transform their business models, distribution channels, and products—enabling the companies to win in their respective markets. I found that when I could help companies win and simultaneously design a winning career for myself, I was unstoppable. Even though others would try to stop me. It is the strategies that helped me win and be unstoppable that I share in this book. I want *you* to win when people say you won't. And if a little Black J'American girl from Phoenix, Illinois, can win, so will you!

I was inspired to write this book and share my experiences and those of others because being a winner wasn't always clear for me, and I want this book to create a movement of winning, a movement of continuous improvement. We don't want to only *hope* to win; we want to *know how* to win. Every woman has the capability to be able to win, and I want to show you how.

I knew how to win as a little girl because my mom set goals in my mind and told me what to do—whether it was learning math or reading a set number of Nancy Drew mystery books each month. When I achieved those things, she told me I did a good job, although it wasn't with much fanfare: she expected me to do what she said, so there was not much to celebrate. My first objectives were education-oriented.

Then I realized that having an objective and achieving it means you have won! Getting As in school, being promoted to the next grade, and graduating from college two years early were all signs of forward progress and success. However, when I looked at those achievements from a higher level, I realized that to continue being a winner meant I had to achieve and improve *continuously*. It meant never resting on my laurels. Winning is a continual journey, one that I never quite complete, but I do get placed in the "winner's circle" for my profession or my business! I felt I understood that. Life is fair: just set a goal, and life will be there to help you achieve it. Right? Not necessarily . . .

On my journey to the C-suite, I discovered a new reality: that too often, my color, my gender, or both caused me to be disrespected, underpaid, underpromoted, undervalued, and overlooked. But I also found out that didn't happen only to me. One of my friends was an SVP of HR at a Fortune 100 company who recalled a compensation meeting with the top leaders of the company where she heard justifications on why a man should receive more compensation than a woman. "Jack has a family of three kids at home to support, so he needs to get a bigger bonus than Jen." The fact that Jen's husband was laid off and that Jen was supporting her sick mom (or whatever Jen's story was) didn't matter. Enabling Jack to have a better home situation was prioritized over meeting Jen's needs. What about performance, potential, and leadership as the real differentiators?

As a director, or executive director, or VP, I was often cut off in mid-sentence or treated as an "other"—as though I weren't as experienced, as wise, or as capable as others younger and whiter than me. I was told and treated as though I couldn't and wouldn't win. And like many of my protégés and friends did, I began to listen to that crap; and from time to time, I told myself that I wouldn't win. That I was not good enough. Not global enough, not expert enough, etc. I learned through my own career, and from the thousands of people over the years who reported to me, that we need to teach women and people of color from the bottom up to systematically deconstruct for themselves the momentum that has been set against them.

These challenges are not new, but the Covid-19 pandemic has had an outsized negative impact on women in what many are calling not a recession, but a "she-cession." According to a 2021 *McKinsey Report*, this she-cession is resulting in more obstacles for women who are already struggling for representation in the workplace. Women, as a whole, have lost 5.4 million jobs since February 2020, which comprises over half of all net US job losses in that time period. While some women have found work, more than 2 million women have vanished from the paid workforce altogether.

A large portion of job losses for women stemmed from working mothers who have succumbed to simultaneously being mom, teacher, daycare and eldercare provider, housekeeper, cook, therapist, and so many other roles, all while working full-time. They are burned out and stressed out. The stats are even worse for Black working moms who are leaving the workforce at twice the rate of their white counterparts.

All told, according to the US Bureau of Labor Statistics, "The pandemic has set working women back by more than three decades . . . to levels of labor force participation last seen in 1988"—and it's had a disproportionate impact on women of color.

The reckoning of the Black Lives Matter movement has been painful for us as a nation, and I am fortunate to have achieved another level in corporate America—to sit on the board of directors for three separate multibillion-dollar public corporations. I've seen inside the upper echelons of corporate America and am witnessing the time and energy that is being put into finding solutions to the enormous disparities between opportunities given to white employees and those given to nonwhite employees, and also between opportunities offered to men and those offered to women. In my work as a board member, I see the efforts being made at the top to overhaul the Five Ps—policies, pay equity, pipeline, procurement, and philanthropy—the areas that have disproportionately negatively affected women and people of color in the workforce. But that is not enough.

Initially, I wrote this book for women, women of color, and people of color, because data has shown that those groups tend to have micro-inequities and blatant discrimination thrust upon them. Society doesn't seem to value or expect as much from us as it does from the majority. And doesn't consistently seem to give the benefit of the doubt, or assistance, that the majority may receive. Therefore, my goal was to share how I, a J'American woman, succeeded when society didn't expect much from me—and showed me as much—so I could help other women win. But in reality, anyone can want to win, and anyone can learn to win. As a technologist, I believe in systematizing processes, as much as possible, to help drive speed and efficiency. So I decided that as I won continually, there had to be a way to capture the process so it could be replicated not only by me, but by others—any demographic. So I took a "wash, rinse, repeat" approach. Although we are all different, and we have to allow for the context that is different among us, I believed my basic approach could be applied to nearly anyone. And I wanted to share it.

This book can be used by leaders as a personal/professional development life cycle approach to coach women or others in their organization on how to systematically win. It can be used by men who may want to read examples of the challenges a woman has and may inspire a change in their mindset or behavior. It can be used by those who want to transform their mindset and subsequent behaviors to have a winning one. My four-step approach can be applied by anyone who wants to win and is motivated to invest the energy to walk through four steps to winning when "they" say you won't.

I wrote this book to show you that wherever we do find systemic and top-down racism or sexism, it can be combated and defeated when we set our minds and use the tools that are at our disposal to treat these issues as a business problem, and not get caught in the trap of responding only emotionally or without a strategy. I am committed to showing you that we can set our sights on our objectives and win when others say we won't. You don't have to rely on what women, especially women of color, have needed to do for many, many years—that is, to work twice as hard to get half as far. We can work twice as smart, just like businesses do, and go further than you ever imagined. You don't have to wait for change to come from above; you can use my strategies to advance *right now*, even in seemingly impossible situations.

How? By using a process I think of as a personal/professional development life cycle, which I call EDIT. Its steps consist of *E*nvision, *D*esign, *I*terate, and *T*ransform. Figure I.1 provides an overview to this process. This process comes from a similar technical process that app developers use to develop apps we know and use everyday.

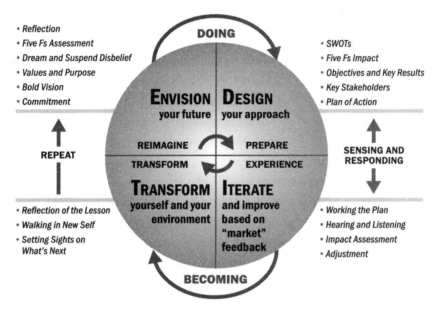

FIGURE I.1   The EDIT process

EDIT means *change*. People can change their minds, change their lives, change their expectations, and change their outcomes. In this book, I help you learn how to apply the EDIT process to your goal of improvement and advancement. Just as you have seen continuous improvement and new versions of products and services you use—whether that be your iPhone iOS software (at Version 15+ now), your car, advances in healthcare, and more, you, too, can see yourself as a product and can change or create a new version of yourself. EDIT helps you change and grow through advancing yourself to a new level of capability.

You don't have to stay at the current version you are now. What do you think a new version of you could look like? Even in environments where you may be the only person of color (POC), or the only woman, or where people of color or women haven't yet broken through to the level of their organization that they want to attain, you can be that one to create a new version of yourself and transform those around you.

When businesses run into issues like declining market share or a product portfolio of many unprofitable products, for example, they do at least four things: use tools to assess the situation, decide outcomes they want to achieve, design and execute their strategy by running a proof of concept or pilot test, and then measure the outcomes and determine if they need to refine their strategy to hit or exceed their target. When finished, they will have transformed their business from losing market share to neutralizing the loss and then on to gaining share. Or they've gone from having too many unprofitable products to a more rationalized portfolio of products with gross margins that beat the competition. That doesn't happen overnight, but it gets done. When winning businesses discover a challenge or a new direction they want to go in, they don't get emotional about it, and they don't quit. The business leaders dispassionately but intently and earnestly use the information and tools available to them to move the company to a better place. That is the same thing you will do.

Win When They Say You Won't presents the EDIT methodology broken down into chapters where each one is a step with a clear goal. Whether you want a promotion, a pay raise, more responsibility, or a better seat at the table, by achieving so many wins along the way, you will be able to build on that feeling of accomplishment all the way to your big win. A journey is not done in one giant leap, but in a series of steps that go forward. And for me, each step forward, no matter how big or small, was a win. In each chapter, I provide guidance on how you can start concretizing your ambitions; I also illustrate with my own stories of succeeding in impossible situations, as well as stories from people I have mentored or worked side by side with. To show how EDIT is applied at each juncture of an upward journey, I've included various stories of how I, my protégés, my family, and my peers faced challenges in our lives, and how the EDIT principles and business tools were used for the win. (These stories appear in italics, to make them easier to read and learn from.)

Step I addresses the critical and challenging work of envisioning where we want to go. As underrepresented people in the corridors of power and influence, we may not have any template from our families or friends for how to achieve what it is we want. Which is why a technology framework like EDIT is going to be so helpful—it is a proven and concrete iterative process for making small and big leaps.

As you dream, you will apply critical thinking to what is and isn't working in your career, so that you can be strategic and specific about your goal. And then use the metric of what I call the Five Fs—faith, family, fitness, finances, and furthering career—to ensure that you have thought through the impact of your goal on every key area of life. This way, you won't make the mistake of attaining a goal that fulfills one area but capsizes all the others. It's not worth getting a higher-paying job (*furthering career*) if you are then blindsided that your *fitness* and *family* are suffering. You will work solutions and interventions into your process. You then leave Step I by making a commitment to yourself to meet this newly identified goal, even if and when it gets challenging.

In Step II, Design, I illustrate how to prioritize your objectives, because you may have several, and you will apply a bit of agile and design thinking to your objective. When I ran large tech divisions, we accomplished our big goals by breaking them up into small sprints and mapping out exactly what would be required in terms of resources to attain them. Here you will do the same. By performing your due diligence, you will be prepared to leverage tailwinds and withstand headwinds that come your way.

By the time we reach Step III, Iterate, you are ready to launch. Here you run the play that you designed in Step II, and you will tweak your action steps, or your overall plan, based on feedback from your marketplace, be that your boss, your colleagues, or your family. Maybe you didn't demonstrate enough leadership potential with your first big project. You will learn to ask for another opportunity, to iterate, and get closer to your win by understanding what you may have overlooked, so you can try again. If you keep iterating, which includes working the plan, soliciting feedback, altering strategy, and trying again, you inevitably will get closer and closer to your objective.

Step IV, Transform, is where you sit with the change. You've achieved an objective or some major key results. Because you are not quite the same person who started your journey and if you don't take time to adjust to your new status or role, you may backslide. So here you reflect on your accomplishment and decide what you learned and would do differently next time. Because . . . there will be a next time. Right now, in fact. While you want to arrive in the feeling of triumph, you never want to feel like you are done growing and learning. You have a growth mindset.

So you will end where you began, by deciding where you will set your sights next, from your new vantage point of success.

It's complex to be Black or a POC. To be female. To be a Black female or female of color today—female and color do not exist independently of each other, but often inform each other, creating a complex convergence of oppression. But I found that while I may be looked at as an "other," by society or corporate America, my EDIT approach to driving my career and achievement is very much "mainstream," proven, and effective. To further help the Black women, or women of color, more specifically, I have written a chapter dedicated to the women of color to help deal with the nuances of our corporate experiences. That is Chapter 13.

To win means to be victorious or successful in a contest, conflict, or endeavor.

It will be important that you define what winning means to you. Early in this book, you will be tasked with envisioning a winning future for yourself—one that you have always wanted, or one that you feel is perfect for you in your current stage of life.

When you achieve that future, you will have the confidence to try again, and win again, even as roadblocks try to get in your way. I wrote this book to show you the right mindset and toolsets that you will use to always find a way to win. However you define winning and success for yourself, remember that you will truly be successful when you become a contributor in helping other people win.

WHO ARE "THEY"?

My book title says there's a "they" out there who doesn't want you to win. There is an often quoted saying about the opposition that goes this way: "First they ignore you, then they laugh at you, then they fight you, then you win." Who are "they"?

- They are people in your family who laugh at your dream and say you can't do it.

- They are people who are in your circle, but when you need them, they may not be in your corner because they don't really believe in you.

- They are the white supremacists dressed as company senior leaders or your non-POC neighbors who are agitated that you can afford to live next to them.

- They are the other women or other men you may work with who view *you* as the enemy, and not the external competition or the other threats in your business.

- They are the boss who just inherited you, who believes you are a falling star, even though the boss who originally hired you knew you were a shooting star.

- They are your college professors who grade your paper more harshly than they grade the paper of someone in the majority for no obvious reason, except because you are a minority.

- They are the people who focused more on unclear or racist criteria—and less on true capability—in confirming the first African American female Supreme Court justice.

- They are we who believe the negative and hurtful things that are said about women of color, or single mothers, or grand-mothers raising their grandchildren, and all of us who wonder if we really are impostors.

They are everywhere and can be anybody. We need to be aware that they exist around us, but rather than us listening to them, their skepticism and lack of support should catalyze us to win. We will hear what they say and do, but we will not listen to them, unless it is meaningful, helpful, and inspiring.

We are at a moment in history when the disparities in hiring and compensation for people of color have been laid bare. According to one Citigroup study, the US economy has lost $16 trillion over the past 20 years due to race-based inequality. And according to a recent study by McKinsey, Black women are less likely than men or women of any other race to feel supported by their manager. You may have found yourself stymied and stuck below your potential, and you want a blueprint for rising if you don't have anyone to lift you up. You need that now.

You will learn how to believe in yourself. You will be able to say, "I've been in a tough situation before, and look how I got out of it. I have won before, and I can do it again." You will have a blueprint that will give you outcomes you never thought were possible. This book will coach you and show you how to tackle problems and teach you how to persevere. You will read stories about very accomplished women who have dealt with setbacks through their life or career. You will read about how they thought and won in their lives.

As a woman who climbed all the way to the C-suite and worked at several global conglomerates, I have a view to share that will exponentially benefit readers who want to know how to rise in white- and male-dominated fields. This book will give you a strategy you can use to tackle any obstacle in your lives.

As my own journey demonstrates, this approach can create an ever-rising spiral of success—even for a poor Black girl from a tiny Midwest town. Even for someone who has been told—by teachers, by leaders, and by example—that she can never win.

I'm here to tell women of all races, you absolutely can—and if you have enough courage to grab your journal and flip to the next page, I will show you how.

ENVISION

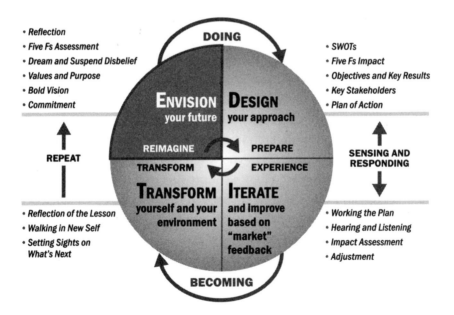

- Reflection
- Five Fs Assessment
- Dream and Suspend Disbelief
- Values and Purpose
- Bold Vision
- Commitment

DOING

- SWOTs
- Five Fs Impact
- Objectives and Key Results
- Key Stakeholders
- Plan of Action

ENVISION your future   DESIGN your approach

REIMAGINE   PREPARE

TRANSFORM   EXPERIENCE

REPEAT

SENSING AND RESPONDING

TRANSFORM yourself and your environment   ITERATE and improve based on "market" feedback

- Reflection of the Lesson
- Walking in New Self
- Setting Sights on What's Next

- Working the Plan
- Hearing and Listening
- Impact Assessment
- Adjustment

BECOMING

The first step in the EDIT process is Envision, and it begins with looking back at where you have been and assessing where you are in your journey now. This step gives you a realistic context to begin creating your unique vision. It also helps you consider and answer questions such as these:

- What brought you here?

- Who helped you arrive at this point?

- Were you just lucky, or did you have specific skills that helped you push forward?

Before you dream, apply critical thinking to what is or isn't working in your career so you can be strategic about your objective. Critical thinking includes conceptualizing, analyzing, synthesizing, and/or evaluating information you gathered from observation, experience, reflecting, reading. That evaluation serves then as a guide to what you believe and what you will do. In Chapter 1, I challenge you to embark boldly on your journey as a winner—because that's exactly what you are. You have superpowers that others don't have. You have connections that others don't have. You are unique in how you think, how you relate to others, and in how you will win. I mentioned in the Introduction that most products and services continually improve in order to remain viable and relevant. Continuous improvement is how companies win, and that's how you will win. In companies all around the world, the leaders who look at improving and ensuring relevance of products and services that are used in the market are called product managers. They understand the strengths and weaknesses of the product as it is perceived or used by the customers. They look to ensure customers have a great customer experience with that product or service. They know how other similar competitive products are advancing in the market or are gaining the most market share and price. They know when their product is becoming obsolete, and they work with stakeholders, such as R&D and operations, to design and manufacture new versions of the product or even a brand-new product that leapfrogs other competitive products.

With EDIT, you will look at yourself as a product of sorts—a product that has features as well as strengths and weaknesses, that has value in the market, that has "coopetition" (those peers that *cooperate* with you to help the company win, but may also be your *competition* for a promotion), and that has a set of customers who have come to rely on you. You are a product that has a market that is continually experiencing you—whether that market is your boss, your team, your business partners, or your family.

What is experiencing you like? You know how much your compensation is, or your market value, and if you don't stay relevant and continue to reinvent yourself, you as a product could become obsolete and discontinued and your value diminished, as a product would. To help ensure you remain relevant as a product, you will engage in this EDIT as a product manager to define who you will be as a new version of your product. I'll call you product manager from time to time, starting in Chapter 1. As product manager, you will not only manage the strategy or vision of your personal transformation; you will also manage it as an EDIT project that you will execute and own—you will be creating plans, calling the plays on your new product transformation project, setting due dates, gathering resources, measuring the status of your plans, and iterating on them. You will not be a bystander but rather an active participant and manager. You are and will always be empowered to drive outcomes that will get you closer to your purpose and your objectives.

In Chapter 2, you will learn how to use a metric I call the Five Fs—faith, family, fitness, finances, and furthering career—to ensure that you have thought through the impact of your objective on your key areas of life. This way, you will not make the mistake of attaining an objective that fulfills one area but undermines the others.

Finally, in Chapter 3, I'll show you how to commit to yourself to meet your newly identified objective, even if or when it gets challenging. You may have been stopped by other people's limitations or viewpoints, but this chapter will inspire and equip you to create and stand in new possibilities of your own.

YOUR VISION

WINNING HAPPENS AT THE BEGINNING, NOT JUST THE END

To the children, regardless of your gender,
our country has sent you a clear message:
Dream with ambition, lead with conviction,
and see yourself in a way that others might not see you,
simply because they've never seen it before.

—VICE PRESIDENT KAMALA HARRIS

Many thought leaders tell us to "dream big," just like the technology visionaries who have changed our world. But if you only dream big without a solid strategy for the foundation to achieve those dreams, that big dream can be more daunting than inspiring. And it will remain a dream.

This daunting feeling can ring especially true if you're seeking to be the first woman or person of color in a role. You may feel you cannot afford to get discouraged—because then you will also be distracted on what you are not and what you cannot do. And when you are distracted, you don't focus well, and you don't end up where you want to be. For those of us who are the first or second generation of women of color in business, it may seem that our families, our race, *and* our gender are depending on our success. Various companies hire us and seem to "give us a chance," and we can't blow it, lest we hurt the chances of those that come after us. We tend to feel that the entire burden is on our shoulders to win.

Your work here in the Envision step of the EDIT process is to set your objectives and get ready to take those steps that launch your journey to win when others say you won't. Otherwise, you're no better than the CEO who sets some arbitrary new go-to-market strategy without mapping out the tactics and metrics to achieve it.

In this chapter, I challenge you to jump in with both feet and give yourself permission to examine yourself, permission to dream, and permission to prosper. Remember you are already a winner, and you are simply looking to win again, win bigger, win stronger! As you begin the Envision step, you will begin to see yourself in that new role I mentioned earlier—as the "product manager" of your life. Throughout this chapter, you will examine and assess your life or career and assess what went well—and what didn't. As a product manager, you have the responsibility to choose how you will move, with whom, and when. I define "responsibility" as your ability to choose your response to where you are now and to what you envision so you can move to where you want to be. Regardless of what others say, you own this; you've got this; and as a product manager, you can direct and call the plays that you see on the field, so you can win.

Since this book is in your hands, most likely you are at a turning point in your life. You may have already considered sticking your head in the sand or pretending that this gnawing for change that you are feeling in your mind, body, and soul will simply go away. But I know that if you are willing to go on this journey with me, you will be able to use the energy of whatever challenge, setback, or exciting new opportunity you are facing and catapult your vision and your dreams into a new place with new information, behaviors, and outcomes.

YOUR NEW VISION BEGINS WITH REFLECTING ON YOUR JOURNEY

Envisioning begins with an assessment of where you are in your journey and where you have been. The good book says that without a vision, people perish. That means that your journey needs to have a destination—a reason—and that reason should be fulfilled. If not, you will go in circles, which means you won't really make much progress, and you will likely stagnate. And stagnation doesn't usually lead to victory. When you define winning, it is personal and specific to you. Reflecting on where you've been will help you put your life in context.

Imagine your life's journey as a rearview mirror. Rearview mirrors are small, but they still allow you to see where you were, what pothole you just ran over, or the street sign you might have missed. The reflection matters, because you will recall from the mirror those things that you encountered once that may also be ahead and could slow you down or distract you from getting efficiently to your destination. Your journey to your win will begin with your vision, but to know your vision, you have to step back a moment and see where you are, what you've done, how well you've done it, and what you should do using your powers that may be underutilized today.

My uncle Henry, who lived in the country of Jamaica, always said I would make a great lawyer. Why? Because I loved to talk. Well, actually, I loved to argue! What I didn't know was that using my voice to give compelling arguments, influencing others, and speaking in front of large or small groups of people is what I would do one day. On the regular. When I joined IBM years later, I had to do demonstrations of technology to customers, again using my voice. I did talks and sat on panels providing insight and inspiration to many. My voice was my gift, and although I was doing a good job at IBM, I realized that I wanted to be that person who used her gifts to ignite, excite, and empower others.

Although you too want to go forward, you won't effectively win unless you first evaluate your life and career on metrics such as your performance, your values, and your purpose. This evaluation takes the emotion out of why and where you may be stymied. You can start to apply critical thinking to navigate through the next step of your career. A thoughtful self-assessment will help you put your life in context.

Much of who we are today is based on where we've been and the choices we've made. For example, think how athletes in the WNBA, or tennis players, or figure skaters look at tapes of their recent performances on the court or the ice; they do that to better understand how they performed, so when the next match or game comes around, they know what they did prior and will have corrected their moves where necessary so they can win. Although we won't do this here, the athletes also see and reflect on how the competition moved during the game or match, to understand what the competition did that was effective/ineffective so they can understand the various things the competition may use to thwart their own tactics. So it is with the Envision step that you will do the same thing, using the following four activities (discussed in the next sections of this chapter):

- Reflect on your past performances.

- Connect with your values (how you decide and feel about things).

- Understand your purpose (why you exist).

- Set your vision for the future you (where you're headed).

The title of this chapter is "Your Vision: Winning Happens at the Beginning, Not Just the End." Yes, you win at the end, when you get the promotion or the championship ring. However, winning is conceived in the beginning, in your mind, with your vision. How you see the challenge and your future will set you up for the win, or it won't. So it happens at the beginning. Your path to winning will ultimately not be based on what others say or do, but rather on what *you* think, what *you* say, and what *you* do about your future. *Your* vision will set the ground rules; you will own and call the plays, even if someone else has called some first. Your vision will inform you on how you will respond to life's challenges and opportunities.

Your Past Performances Help Crystalize Your New Vision

Your past performances will help you begin to see the patterns of your actions in various situations. You get to know more about yourself as you see how you show up in both good and challenging situations. I found that I could learn a lot more if I would just pause for a moment, taking time during my Sunday afternoon, to think about how I showed up in various moments during the past week.

For example, later in my career, one of my bosses decided to defund some of my organization's budget to the point where I had no money left for innovation and experimentation. In tough financial times, you expect that to happen, but what tempted me to blow up was that he chose not to tell me in advance, showing the entire organization the pluses and minuses of the new SVP budgets—my team and I could see that he was actually deprioritizing our organization and elevating another one.

I was flaming mad, but I had to tell myself to look at the situation from an external vantage point—rather than being in the moment and simply reacting to the information that was coming my way. When I looked at things differently, I kept the attitude of continuous improvement in my mind and was able to look at the reduction, not as a loss, but rather as a lesson. I had to embrace my vision for the organization and use this revelation as information from which to formulate a winning business strategy, not an emotional outburst. I knew I had to take the long view about how I was going to win and find another way to achieve my organization's goal of driving new capability since my current approach wasn't working. I had to find another way to win.

I knew I had superpowers (after all, I had been promoted and sought after because of my skills), so I realized that I could use those superpowers to help create a more positive and sustainable capability in my team. Was it easy? Absolutely not. It became clear that this boss was not in my corner, so the catalyst

*of him taking funding came from a lack of support of my team.
Still I had to keep reminding myself that winning a battle was
not as great as winning the war. I had to EDIT my thinking and
view it as a lesson on how to win and use that information to
plan my strategy. I went to my business partners and was able
to gain their support to fund some of the initiatives—because it
would give them the value they needed to win. Thinking of it in
an emotional manner would have likely led me to not win my
goal for my organization.*

That is one of many examples that happened throughout my career
and personal life. You may have a story similar to mine, or you may
have one that is so much worse. In this "game called life," when you are
facing challenges or conflict, you will see that there are two sides—
yours and your boss's, or yours and your customer's, or yours and your
family's. The competition or challengers should not be your main
focus, just as I couldn't let this boss's actions be mine. The competition
does things that are temporary distractions, and if you let someone's
actions dictate how you respond instead of accepting your own ability
to choose your response (your responsibility), then the other person
will win, not you. I know you are committed to winning when others
say you won't, so it is time you reflect and look deeper at your disap-
pointments, setbacks, failures, and even your victories in your journey
and view them as information to pour into the context of your *new
vision* for your life.

1. Reflect on a Great Performance to Gauge Your Winning Formula

To help you see your own patterns of performance and reveal what
makes you successful, think about the outcome of your top three
career initiatives that went really well. You may judge your top three
based on size and budget, importance to the organization, degree of
difficulty, etc. You can use the questions in the sidebar to help you
begin thinking through this process.

QUESTIONS TO REFLECT ON A PAST GREAT PERFORMANCE

- What was the setting? Where were you? What was the opportunity?

- Who was involved?

- What happened?

- What actions did you take? What was your role?

- What mindset did you have that allowed you to handle the project or opportunity effectively? A *mindset* is a mental attitude or disposition that predetermines a person's typical responses to and interpretation of situations.* When people are successful in their work, I have seen that certain mindsets are more evident or in use than others. People don't have only one mindset forever, and once they know there are different mindsets, they can seek to apply the mindset that works best for the situation. That takes awareness of the mindset, and it takes agility to apply what will work best. See and then circle which of the following mindsets† most sound like you in your successful situations:

  o **Growth mindset.** Continually improving; seeking to be better today than yesterday

  o **Business mindset.** Helping others; solving problems; being entrepreneurial

  o **Dreamer mindset.** Creating vision for the future; thinking big, that anything is possible

  o **Gratitude mindset.** Feeling of thankfulness and not taking your team, your job, or your project for granted

---

* Dictionary.com
† Wealthy Gorilla

23

- ○ **Confident mindset.** Believing in yourself—that you are more than enough and you can get things done

- ○ **Creative mindset.** Coming up with unique ideas to old problems; seeing things through a new lens

- ○ **Productive mindset.** Making the most of your time; not being wasteful or distracted

- **Which of your competencies were most on display?** I've listed a set of competencies here. A skill and a competency often get interchanged, so here's how I look at those two words: A *skill* is something you learned in order to get something done—like learning how to cook or how to code. Meanwhile, a *competency* may include a skill, but it is mostly a behavior or attitude needed to utilize the skill. So knowing how to cook is a skill, but having the competencies of being customer-oriented, innovative, and goal-oriented will help you become a head chef in a restaurant.

  Circle each competency in the following table that tended to show up for you when you were successful in your times of great accomplishment and success. Note that these competencies tend to fall into one of four "SHIP" categories:

1. **S** = strategic

2. **H** = hands-on executor

3. **I** = influencer/leader

4. **P** = people/relationship builder

Use the letters to characterize the competencies. See if you notice a pattern—which letters do you see more often than others as you look at your performance?

24

Analytical—S	Attention to detail—H	Influential—I
Conceptual thinking—S	Consistent—H	Leadership of others—I
Continuous improvement—S	Creativity—H	Listening—I
Cool under stress—S	Disciplined—H	Manage expectations—I
Decision-making—S	Focused—H	Maximizer—I
Futuristic—S	Frugal/practical—H	Motivate/mentor/ teach—I
Integrity and ethics—S	Get it done/achiever—H	Personal accountability—I
Intellectual curiosity—S	Goal-oriented—H	Persuading others—I
Objective listening—S	Honor commitments—H	Self-confidence—I
Proactive—S	Organized—H	Caring and empathy—P
Problem or situational analysis—S	Persistence and perseverance—H	Connectedness—P
Regulatory—S	Problem management—H	Customer-oriented—P
Risk taking/ experiment—S	Reliability—H	Developing others—P
Strategic, long view—S	Responsibility—H	Positivity—P
Agile/versatile/ adaptive—H	Sense of urgency—H	Relating to others—P
Analytical—H	Emotional intelligence, self-aware/control—I	

- Who was on your team that most helped you win? What was the person's role—e.g., coach, supporter, mentor, role model, employee, boss, peer, sponsor?

- How did you know you won? What was the measure of success?

- How did you feel when you came through the other side with success?

One of my best performances happened when I was a CIO and brought my global team together for strategic planning. We knew what the business partners needed to drive their business in the next year, and we had to plan our technology portfolio—including what we would prioritize over other initiatives and how we would categorize it, fund it, and ensure business support. The session took place over three days, each day with a different purpose. We kept it moving, bringing in guest speakers to talk about the future of our industry and give eye-opening pitches on innovations and new technologies. It was a combination of strategic and tactical planning. We had to see far out, and then we used our far-out vision to determine what we had to do over the next year.

My top regional leaders and their top two staff members were there. Once in a while, we invited a junior leader as recognition of how positive we felt about that person's future role in the organization. We included our business partners, both those that supported us (finance, HR) and those we supported (manufacturing, R&D, others). We had games, ice breakers, and individual pitches of projects to business partners weighing in on the projects; it was very collaborative and inspirational. Each person there was assigned a different color "hat" so we could each look at the same idea or opportunity or challenge with different perspectives. This way we were able to look at ideas from a 360-degree vantage point, not miss anything, and ensure there was little bias, because we could all hear each other's vantage point. The best points usually won that argument.

I showed up with both a business mindset and growth mindset. I knew we could do more and better than the previous year, and my head was all around helping our business partners solve problems. I was the CEO of my team (at least, that is how I behaved). My competencies were mainly strategic and influential (specifically, futuristic, risk taking, and listening).

We ended the meeting having succeeded in our objectives—we did an anonymous survey that showed that people felt

*listened to and challenged with respect and that we had a plan
that everyone understood and would support.*

*As I reflected on this day, it showed me under which circum-
stances I'm at my best: growth, business, strategic, and influential. Knowing that helped me parlay that into my vision.*

2. Reflect on a Performance You Were Not So Proud Of

Remember your most recent and challenging experience at work,
which you don't feel you handled well. To help you look at what you
are good at, and what doesn't align well with you, ask yourself the
questions in the sidebar.

QUESTIONS TO REFLECT ON A NOT-SO-GREAT PAST PERFORMANCE

- What happened—e.g., did you miss an objective, get demoted, lose a customer, miss your sales objectives, lose a valuable employee, violate compliance guidelines?

- What was the setting? Where were you? Who was involved?

- What was your role?

- What actions did you take?

- Was there one action or event that turned the situation upside down?

- What mindset was more on display than others that should not have been?

- What SHIP competencies were you missing that could have improved the outcome? Were there skills that were not fully developed that would have been helpful? Which ones?

- If you had to do it again to get a better outcome, what would you change?

- Did you demonstrate that you had the right skills and experience to do the job?

As you reflect on both the great and not-so-great performances as a leader, do you see a pattern? There should be themes that emerge of your mindset and your competencies. You should be able to identify under what circumstances you shine versus when you don't seem to shine, or perhaps you can determine where your mindset or competency gap may be so you can turn challenging situations into winning outcomes even if they seem to be headed in a bad direction. I'm sure you've seen situations in which a sports team appears to be losing, or a student appears to be failing a class, or someone seems to be suffering a career setback, that made you think the characters were going to lose, only for the losing team to rally back in the fourth quarter to win the game by one point or by twenty points, or for the student to graduate magna cum laude, or for the person to achieve career highs.

At one point during his high school years, my son, Jared, wasn't doing so well, and it didn't look like he was going to be even considered by a college, or possibly even graduate from high school. With constant urging by my husband and me, he began to apply himself in high school, albeit late, and even got accepted into several colleges and universities. He went to Morehouse College, graduated, and then joined an architectural firm due to his love of drawing and art. He reflected on where he was at his best, and he realized that his lack of college architectural study and lack of excitement for math put him at a disadvantage with the other new college grad employees at the firm.

He could have stayed with the architectural firm, but he would have been miserable and would likely have failed. Architecture required different skills and competencies than he

28

had. As he explored other companies, like Apple and Airbnb, he found the circumstances under which he could excel: doing project management, designing user experience, having accountability for outcomes. He now has his own company, making more money than he did working for the architectural firm. He is using his capabilities to excel and not remain stuck where he would not win.

So even if a situation seems bad or even hopeless, you can use your mindset and competencies to turn the situation around so you can win. Remember, reflecting on your past performances is just the beginning of defining who you are and how you are being when you are at your best. The key is to be aware of what competencies (or skills) showed up for you, and which ones did not, in your winning or learning moments. That is a reflection of who you are and where you shine best.

How Do You Make Decisions?
According to Your Values

When have you last thought about what you value? Your values are the foundation for *how* you think; values help you decide *how* you feel or *how* you will respond about a certain subject. The way you feel and think will ultimately guide how you will respond and act in various situations, and how you act will result in consequences—good, bad, or neutral. Living through your values allows you to live your life more by choice versus chance. I was once told that "when we are born, we look like our parents, but when we die, we look like the consequences of our decisions." If the job you are doing or the person you are working for doesn't align with your true inner self or your values, you will have a shaky foundation and will be at war with yourself, and your lived life will look pretty miserable.

If my values are what is guiding me, and they are healthy, life-creating, or sustaining values, I will be less likely to engage in destructive or non-value-creating behavior, because I know where I'm going and what values and behaviors I'll align with to get there (and I don't want to ruin where I am with destructive behaviors). I'll be able to endure and persevere during setbacks or barriers that may arise. I'll have more confidence and focus. I'll know who my true friends are because their values will align with mine. And their values will show in how they respond to circumstances.

What are your values? Integrity? Empathy for others? Outcomes at all costs? Loyalty? Intelligence? Family? Authenticity? Next are some values, but not every value under the sun, and you will think of more; still these should give you some idea of how to look at what matters to you. In the following table, circle those that match you the most.

Achievement	Innovation	Safety
Analyzing/analytics	Integrity	Spirituality
Authenticity	Love	Success
Caring	Loyalty	Teamwork
Courage	Outcomes	Thankfulness
Creativity	Personal	Trusting your gut
Curiosity	development	Wealth
Family/friendships	Power	Winning
Forgiveness	Quality	Wisdom
Fun	Reciprocity	World peace
Growth	Religion/faith	Zen
Health	Resilience	
Humanity	Respect	

For everything you seek to achieve, your values will be those guard-rails that define how you will travel so you don't go out of bounds, or head away from those things that really matter to you. When you align with your values, you will be able to tolerate challenges better and have greater resilience. Who are people you admire and are role models for you? What values do they have? Do theirs match what you see or want to see in yourself? See if the values shown define you, and identify which ones you believe you are weak in. Which have you been told is a weak area for you, and if not improved may curtail your success in your organization? What actions and activities that you do reflect these values?

For example, those of us who want to win need to have intellectual curiosity. If you don't wonder about why, how, who, when, or where on key subjects in your business, you will not be able to advance very far. Appreciating innovation and valuing how things work and how they can work better are examples of values that will be important for winning. New ways of working are continually being discovered, increasing amounts of data are available daily, and we need to be curious and always seek to learn, because when you're done learning, you're done!

For me, while I value winning, creating outcomes for my company, and being curious so I can learn more and contribute more, I believe that not much is more important than family.

When I was at the peak of my senior analyst role at IBM, I had just moved from Peoria, Illinois, to Houston, Texas, when in the middle of my day at the office, I answered my phone and heard my mother's frantic voice on the other end.

"Daph, honey?" she said, her voice breaking.

"Yes, Mommy, it's me. What's wrong?"

"I just got out of surgery, and the doctor said I have only nine months to live!"

"What?!!!??" I screamed into the phone. "What is wrong?"

She went on to tell me she had stomach cancer. It had been there for a while and therefore had metastasized to her liver.

The next day I got on a plane and went to the hospital. I spoke with the doctor, and all I can remember is my screaming in the hallway with anguish, pain, and disbelief at the confirmation of her pending death. I valued my mother and family more than anything in the world. This woman who sacrificed everything for her children so we could win when she didn't think she herself could. How could I lose her? That value cut deeply, and I realized that my career at IBM was no longer as important as I thought it was the day before. If I had to quit my job or take a sabbatical, I would do that. I met with my husband, my dad, and my siblings, and I decided that she and Dad would come to Texas and live with us, which they did a few weeks after my mom's surgery.

I met with my boss to let him know what was happening, and I took several days off a week to take care of my mom and dad. I took my mom to her chemo treatments to try and shrink the tumor. She succumbed to the cancer less than nine months later, but I would sacrifice the momentum in my career again because a career is not much fun if your family is suffering. I came to realize that my career is not the only thing I valued in my climb up the corporate ladder, and at any point, multiple values are at play, but some may be more important than the others. It was because of this experience that I learned to think about life in more than a single dimension of only career. I need to take multiple dimensions into account anytime I'm making my decisions about my future. We will discuss those dimensions, what I refer to as the "5Fs" in the next chapter.

Understanding Your Purpose to Fuel Your Why

In my experience, I've come to know that purpose is the combination of one's passion and capability. Purpose is basically the reason you exist. The simple way I define a person's purpose is by understanding what that person loves and has a natural inclination or capability to do. If you have a passion for a certain vocation, but you don't have the natural instinct or capability to learn and do it well, that is not your purpose. If you have a capability but you aren't interested in exploiting or using it to a meaningful end, that is not your purpose. Only when those two aspects exist at the same time does your purpose get rendered.

Look at what gives you passion in your career or your venture by answering the questions in the sidebar. Your answers will help you understand even more about who you are and why you are the way you are. It is in having a purpose that keeps you moving forward and winning.

QUESTIONS TO HELP YOU REFLECT ON YOUR PURPOSE

- What is the reason you believe you exist?

- What achievements are you most proud of? Why?

- What do you love to do?

- What is the one unifying theme across your life that consistently brings you joy or makes you feel most valuable in your life? Analyzing and solving problems? Coaching? Creating? Taking risks?

- Is what you're currently doing in line with your passion and your capabilities?

- What do you believe your purpose in this world is, knowing that whatever it is, you know you will not fail?

- Is your current role in or out of alignment with what you really want to do, or want to be?

- Do you believe your career is headed to your achieving your purpose? Where is it heading? Where do you want it to be headed?

Now that you've answered the purpose-seeking questions, take a stab at outlining your purpose. Your purpose is what your life's work will be about. Why were you created? What were you born to be? Bear in mind: purpose = passion + capability. You may already be doing your life's work and want to expand it, or you may not be doing your purpose and want to begin now.

Look again at the SHIP categories shown earlier in the chapter and at the competencies that represent who you are. Look at the situations where you thrived and what mindset was activated, and look at the situations where you didn't thrive. Look for patterns. Look at your values. If you think carefully, you can put all those together and write a rudimentary purpose. Unless you've already defined what your purpose is, you will need a moment or two to do this. Take some time over the weekend or next week and reflect on:

1. Which competencies and mindsets are your strength and which are not?

2. Which top three or four values represent you the most?

3. What do you believe your purpose is that allows all those to exist together in you?

As you think about why you exist, are you existing in your purpose? If you are, that is wonderful. Many people are not, and that's where what they are "doing" is at odds with what they would like to "be." They are letting what they do define who it is they want to become. They are at war with themselves and others on the inside and outside. We are human *beings*, not human *doings*, so the way to win is by moving to what it is you would and should be. What you should *be* will help define what it is you should *be doing*, not necessarily the other way around

Planning Your Vision for the Future You

Now that you have reflected on what you have done well and not so well, what you value, and what your purpose is likely to be, let's define what you want to achieve, where you are headed, and what you will become over the next few years. That will be your *vision*!

Your vision is an image in your mind that reflects where you want to be. It reflects what you want to achieve and will be in support of your purpose. It will serve as a guidepost or reference point for the decisions you make in your life. It is somewhat high level and is usually several years away, but it is likely closer to today than your purpose is. But you decide how far off the vision is—it can be two or three years, or it can be ten years.

To help you get started creating your vision, ask yourself the questions in the sidebar about how you see yourself going forward, so you can define your vision and look forward to the objectives you want to focus on in your EDIT throughout this book.

QUESTIONS TO HELP YOU DEFINE YOUR VISION FOR THE FUTURE YOU

- If you could fast-forward five to ten years from now, what will you want to be?

- What will winning look like in your life?

- If you knew you wouldn't fail, what would you do?

- What changes would you like to make now and see the results of?

- How will you measure your success? How will you know you've "arrived"?

- Which of your superpowers or competencies will be most used in your future self?

- How will your vision for the next five to ten years align with your purpose?

- Do you believe you are well on your way to achieving your vision?

- What do you believe would accelerate it?

- What, if anything, is holding you back?

I had only been at Johnson & Johnson for two years, and I was providing support as a director of IT to the HR, finance, engineering, and architecture corporate organizations in J&J. My boss, Rich Wasilius, SVP and CIO at J&J, was a wonderful guy. He brought me into the company and nurtured me. When I saw his role, how he cared for people as he cared for the technology we delivered, my vision became "to develop and use my technology and leadership platform to inspire leaders and deliver value for companies around the world." In short, I wanted to be like him. I wanted his job, because that's what I felt he did. I was clearly a long way from being the CIO of J&J Corporate, but if you don't jump, you'll never reach.

For me, an early win occurred when I became the CIO or VP of IT at one of the J&J companies. As I looked at myself as critically as I could, I knew I had superpowers: I was an achiever; I honored commitments; I was a problem solver; I was organized and analytical. However, one of my weaknesses in my competencies was "empathy." That translated into my emotional intelligence. I was so transaction-oriented that I didn't always consider the people side of things. Rich was very empathetic, so I knew at some point I would need to embrace empathy a lot more than I did if I wanted to become a great leader like him. My vision remained the same, but having empathy and a "servant leadership mindset" became an improvement area that remains with me to this day.

After you've thought about the questions in the sidebar, aimed at helping you define your vision for the future you, write out a vision statement for yourself that embodies your answers. Your vision supports your purpose, so give it a go. Here are a few examples—can you tell what each person's purpose likely is?

1. "To be a teacher and inspire my students to achieve more than they thought they could."

2. "To be an executive coach for women and empower them to set and achieve their objectives."

3. "To be the CEO of a multinational company that focuses on improving nutrition and healthy living."

4. "To be a physician who helps improve the standard of care for disenfranchised, discriminated, or less fortunate citizens in the United States."

Your reflection of past performance, your values, your purpose, and your vision will work together to help you set your objectives and key results for going forward.

One of the people I met with closely to help her understand her vision was my colleague Kristen. As peers in the same company, Kristen and I met on various occasions, and she was a top VP of HR at a major healthcare company, and HR star. But she began to have many life disruptions, and so she decided to leave her large, visible, and difficult role. She relocated, she went through a divorce, she had knee surgery, and she lost her mom and dad within just a few years of each other. She had to decide what was next for her.

I shared with her how to look at her purpose and vision specifically in a different way to help guide her future. She knew she wasn't finished with her career, and she realized her passion and skill was to help others who have trouble helping themselves. After discussions and reflections, her purpose and vision emerged from the work. Her vision is "to give voice to the voiceless"—and that has guided her to win, to this day. She uses her vision to prioritize what she will work on, and she spends her time and money helping give voice.

Don't look now, but you have thought about a lot since the beginning of the chapter, and we are just getting started. You recognize the value of having your vision. But to know where you are going, you need to know where you've been. You have combined your past performances, identified your top values, stated your purpose and why you exist, and taken a stab at where you are headed via your vision statement. Your vision statement reflects your purpose, which reflects what your competencies and interests are. Now let's put those in context to determine at what stage of life you are.

ARE YOU LEARNING, EARNING, OR RETURNING?

Part of winning includes understanding where you are in your life. I've identified three stages, and the higher the stage, the more experience, money, and responsibilities you have. If you pondered the earlier question of "What would you do if you knew you would not fail?" you will think about where you are in life, so when you go further, you will be able to prioritize where and how you will spend your time to achieve your win. When you understand what life phase you are in, you will take into account what is at stake as you go to the next step in your journey. For example:

- Are you stepping into your first job and navigating your first city away from home? That is a different scenario than the next one . . .

- Are you in a mid-career or transitional phase where you are evaluating your career with your family and your future role? That has a different context than the next one . . .

- Are you closing out a successful corporate career and considering how to approach the second or third act of your life?

Depending on where you are along this pendulum scale in your life, you are in the process of *learning, earning, or returning.*

■ Phase I: Learning

You are in the spring of your life and are careful about what you choose to spend your time learning about, as that will likely set your career journey for life. Whatever you are planting in your spring phase, you will harvest in your fall phase. You may have financial challenges such as loans you are taking (or have taken) and need to pay back. You have an idea of what your career will be, but you are still open to the directions it may take. You may have gone after a trade or an advanced degree such as an MBA or another master's degree. You're building capital—intellectual capital that you will trade one day.

In your learning phase, you have a trade or a degree or experience in something that you believe will guide your ability to earn a living. You are hungry and ready to grab opportunities that will help place you in a trajectory that will take you up. What matters to you most? Ensuring you have a home? Satisfying any debts you have? Getting in on the ground floor with a great company or learning how to start your own business? Maybe starting a personal relationship with a great person?

You may be making 5 to 15 percent of what you will be making when you are solidly in the earning phase.

When I joined IBM, I was making $19,200 per year. Yes, I remember it down to the dollar because every penny was important. I had a used 1977 Cutlass Supreme that cost about $4,000. That seemed like a lot of money at the time, and it was. When I made it solidly into the earning phase, I was about 40 years old and was earning about $300,000 a year.

Although I now know that my purpose is to "teach wisdom to the world" based on my experiences, successes, failures, and learnings, I certainly wasn't thinking that I was wise enough or experienced enough to teach wisdom when I was in my twenties. I was in more "learning" mode then. I was just coming out of the traumatic situation of letting someone define my own vision and narrative. I had been told I wouldn't be anything but a secretary and should not go to college: "Black girls don't really go to college, and if they do, they don't graduate." Or so I was told.

Not only did I graduate with an MBA after only four total years in college, I interviewed with IBM and got into what we now know is the STEM (science, technology, engineering, and mathematics) field. Many years ago, finding women in this field was rare. Finding Black women in this field was impossible. I was learning, a sponge, embracing information, but still too intimidated to open my mouth, lest someone find out that I was not really a STEM person, I was just a secretary in a pinstriped suit, pretending to be a STEM person.

I think about Roscoe, the branch manager who hired me into IBM (and the only Black branch manager in the building), who helped me learn company values and culture—how to set goals and focus on outcomes, how to listen actively, and so much more. I got smarter, I understood more, and I began to apply what I learned, albeit with baby steps to the point where I got my own new account after being at IBM for 18 months. I was soaking in information all the time and hoped that one day I would be able to use that knowledge and grow my career in the company. I went from knowing very little to knowing more—the more I knew, the more I was able to contribute. My sphere of vision, and therefore my sphere of influence, widened.

With your vision firmly in place and the right tools to continually develop that vision, your sphere of vision of who you were in your twenties versus your forties, fifties, or beyond will widen and expand.

Although we all continue to learn, we have to get ready to do more earning to sustain our goals.

■ Phase II: Earning

After you have gathered desired learnings from your education and your life experiences, the next phase of your life will be focused on earning or building financial capital. You will take the intellectual capital you earned in your learning phase and "trade" it for financial capital. What you have learned before, you get compensated for now. Now don't get me wrong; as long as we are alive, we should always be learning something. Your focus, though, during the earning phase is about earning and building financial capital to sustain yourself and your family so that you can maintain or grow your lifestyle that is aligned with your values and vision.

When you make that shift into earning versus learning, you are looking at the financial rewards you are earning. You also begin to focus on nonfinancial rewards. You get to determine and evaluate your quality of life. You are earning, and what you are earning you are spending (while also saving!) on family vacations, houses, gym memberships, or whatever your heart desires and what you can afford.

You are in the summer of your life. You are active; you have a plan and a career you are nurturing. You see what you have planted starting to grow tall. You may have started your own business with or without a partner, or you have received promotions at the company you joined some years ago. You are more set on your trajectory than you were in the learning phase, as you have invested time and effort into where you are. You won't be easily swayed away from what your job is. You will be able to do many things with your money, but you will likely choose to focus your spending on taking family vacations, upgrading your house, paying for college for your nieces or your son, or saving for a rainy day—whether that is illness or other catastrophes.

With your greater responsibilities in this phase, you focus on more than your career. Your influence continues to widen, as does your vision of what's important to you. Other things outside of your career matter more than they ever did before. You got in on the ground floor of an organization, or you may have made lateral moves at higher levels. You are earning a salary but are also likely getting your velvet handcuffs (of stock and options) placed on your wrists each year, so your company makes it harder for you to leave without your leaving money and the intergenerational wealth on the table.

You are encountering and are more aware of politics in your organization and your team. Sometimes company politics work to your advantage, and sometimes they don't. You may notice folks at your level leave for other opportunities or may get promoted internally, and you begin to wonder if you should be doing more to ensure you are continually promoted at the pace you expected.

What you care about is advancement in your career; what you want is a sense of accomplishment and the trappings of a successful person, a winner. You occasionally wonder what your "retirement number" is, to know if you could actually retire early. At some point, you earn enough to not have financial achievement as your main focus.

> *In my earning phase, when I was about 35 years old, I had already begun moving around the country with IBM—from Peoria to Houston, Dallas, DC, and Atlanta. I figured I'd made it. But I remember being so focused on not being "sent back to being a secretary," and I gave those imaginary senders so much power in my mind, that I began to focus more on my career and neglected my husband and our marriage. I gave birth to my beautiful son, but I got divorced a few years later. Within my earning phase, things were more complicated than in my learning phase, and each decision seemed to have multiple consequences—good and bad. At the height of my earning phase, I began to realize that money wasn't everything.*

▪ Phase III: Returning

In the returning phase, you are usually in the fall of your life, unless you are in a position with your time or money to "return" earlier in your life. You may be at that point where you want to give back to society some of the intellectual and/or financial capital that you accumulated. Or you may instead want to give that time back to yourself or your family.

You have financial capital that you can spend on travel, cars, a vacation home, WNBA season tickets, or angel investing to help others. You are ready to give back some of your time to not-for-profit boards or coaching or advisory roles in your field of expertise. You care about leaving a legacy as a businessperson, a community leader, or a family member.

So as you sit, take a moment to reflect on the following:

- What phase are you mostly in? Learning? Earning? Returning?

- What matters most to you in this phase?

- What are you willing to sacrifice? What will you not put at risk?

- Are you where you thought you would be at this phase?

In whatever phase you see yourself, make sure you understand what that means. You need to understand how or when you will make the leap to the next phase, and what is required. That's especially important as you go from earning to returning. Make sure you know what it will take to go into returning (or retirement) phase and that you are working up to have the necessary resources to thrive there. You need to know what is important to you in this phase of your life, because it will shape and reshape your vision and your objectives going forward. No matter where you are, your vision will have the capability to unfold and reveal discoveries about you along the way.

In order to *Win When They Say You Won't*: Don't let other people define your narrative or your purpose; you must define your own. When you walk with another person's vision for yourself, you are not walking in your purpose; you are walking in that person's vision. Reflect on where you've been, and know that there's a purpose that wears your name.

Next, Chapter 2 describes how to go after your purpose and embrace the Five Fs that will show what's most important to you.

CHAPTER 2

YOU ARE NOT ALONE; YOU HAVE YOUR FIVE Fs

FAITH, FAMILY, FITNESS, FINANCES, AND FURTHERING CAREER

We must believe that we are gifted for something, and
that this thing, at whatever cost, must be attained.

—MARIE CURIE

Have you ever stopped to think about what keeps you going every day? Could it possibly be only our career and our purpose? There is much more to who we are than just what we do and what we are reaching for in our careers! There are multiple things that work together to keep us whole and intact as we encounter life day after day—a foundation of sorts that undergirds us. Let's discover more about that now. In this chapter, you will begin to understand the foundational pillars of your life—the Five Fs: *faith, family, fitness, finances, and furthering career.*

Uncovering your specific Five Fs is an important aspect of the Envision step of the EDIT process to help you evaluate your priorities, your passions, and your areas for growth. Once you have evaluated and/or defined your performance, purpose, and vision and are clear about which stage of life you're in, you can't leave the Five Fs hanging. They need to be recognized, defined, and assessed to see what shape they're in, and then you will prioritize which of them are most important and which one you will protect and nurture for the length of your EDIT project. As you dig into your Five Fs throughout this chapter, you will discover how each of these areas will further fuel your winning formula and allow you to ensure your win is not a one-dimensional win but is richer because you took more into account than meets the eye.

FOCUSING YOUR NEW VISION ON THE FIVE Fs

As a senior leader in corporate America, I have served as a coach to people at various levels, and I spent the early part of my retirement as an executive coach, where I used EDIT to help leaders aspire to and achieve more in their career than they already had. Muriel was one of my first coaching clients. I coached her on her desire to stay at her level but improve her brand from being an OK leader to being a great one, so she could get promoted in the future. She continually spoke to me about the job, her team, and the customer as if they were everything. She reminded me of myself when I was at her level: the job came first, and nothing else mattered. But something was going on: she missed meetings occasionally, with little prenotice; she also didn't seem to understand the gist of some strategic discussions, and she knew she could do better. As an expert in women's health products, she was a fountain of knowledge. But she wasn't hitting 100 percent.

I knew her current career vision and decided to do a quick intervention. I showed her a rough diagram of the Five Fs wheel (see Figure 2.1) and asked her about each one.

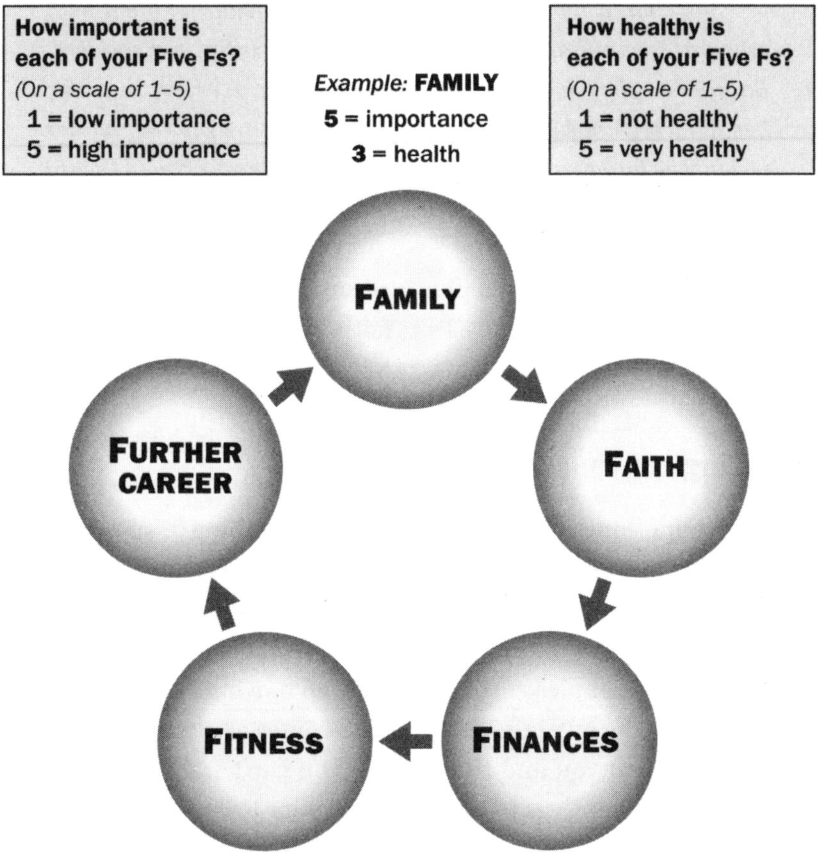

| How important is each of your Five Fs? (On a scale of 1–5) 1 = low importance 5 = high importance | Example: **FAMILY** 5 = importance 3 = health | How healthy is each of your Five Fs? (On a scale of 1–5) 1 = not healthy 5 = very healthy |

FIGURE 2.1   The Five Fs wheel: family, faith, finances, fitness, and furthering career

Then I asked her two questions:

- *On a scale of 1–5, what is the health of each one right now?*

- *Which are the top three of the Five Fs whose health is most important to you as you move forward to achieve your "right-now" vision?*

She shared her first thought about the health of them with me, and I saw that three of the five were healthy, not too bad. But the two she felt were most important to achieve her vision for her job were not healthy. Before she could start working on her vision, she had to include action steps to get those critical Fs into better shape.

We all have foundational pillars or support or influences that further define us. I define the Five Fs as faith, family, finances, fitness, and furthering career. Let's take a closer look at each one.

Focusing on Your *Faith*

Faith is having complete and total trust in something or someone—in many cases, without proof or validation. Often it is about God, but it doesn't have to be. It often has spiritual and religious associations.

Faith in the case of the Five Fs is that invisible cane (or extra leg) that often helps people keep going and keep moving regardless of how things look on the outside. But the value comes as a result of the relationship between you and the "cane"—you can't walk with only the cane; you need your legs to contribute to your journey. It is faith (the cane) that gives you the extra support you need so you can go further toward your vision than you might have been able to if you only had your legs to depend on. You have to believe and trust that the cane will help you get to where you are going.

This is an area that is historically a very strong focus for the African American community. Many African Americans have been brought up in church, or at least brought up to fear God. For many boomer parents and earlier, the main thing was to focus on the "cane" (faith), and the rest would take care of itself. But as in the preceding discussion about the cane, it's the cane *and* our legs together that move things forward.

Having faith without doing something to achieve your goal is not going to be fruitful. But regardless of how it is defined by others, what matters is what faith means to you. Do you believe in a power greater than yourself? Do you pray to something or someone daily, often, or never? As we connect with our bodies, or the heavens, or even nature, our faith can help us stay centered, thankful, and dedicated to be of service to others to help improve and sustain the spirit of others.

Susan, one of the presidents of a division of my former company, was about to make a radical set of changes. Her division was going to change out or discontinue some products and brands because the company had grown so much by acquisition and had all these different brand names that were never consolidated. Her group sold thousands of products—some that created loss and others that generated profit—and Susan had to get rid of some of those loss-leading products. But she knew customer reaction wasn't going to be always wonderful, because somebody was buying those loss-leading products. She also had to reorganize her team, some of whom would be consolidated under others, and she risked losing some great leaders.

We spoke about the decisions she was making, and she said she had been praying that she had the strength and wisdom to guide her because of the risk of business loss. She told me she was continually listening for God's voice to lead her through this, and then she asked me if my husband (who is a pastor) would pray for her. I told her absolutely he would. And he called her, and they prayed on the phone. She was using her two legs to walk through her decision, but she also relied on her cane (her faith) to lean on for support and confidence. She did it, walking by faith and not only by sight, which enabled her to feel supported, leading her to win.

Did she keep every customer? No. Did she lose some employees as a result of her restructuring? Yes. But her profit margins improved, customers were less confused, and she won. The vision can be more important than the pain it takes to achieve it.

Focusing on your faith can include developing a consistent devotional practice in the morning or making an intentional focus to be a greater asset to your spiritual community. Faith can be a strong force and is often used to help people believe there is a power that gives life more hope and meaning, and that it is something that is more than what we see. Faith doesn't work alone; it works in tandem with the other Fs to help us achieve our vision, especially on those days when it seems like the vision may slip out of our hands. We go back to faith, and that faith gives hope. When we have hope, we don't stop until we win.

The internal unshakable belief that the world can be better, that each of us individually and together can be better, is impetus for winning when people say you won't. If I believe I can, then I will. If I don't believe I can, then I won't. They say I won't win, but I have faith, so I will.

Focusing on Your *Family*

Focusing on your family F is not limited to your actual DNA-connected family; it's related to those you care for, love, nurture, or protect. Include your neighbors, your pets, your spouse, your siblings, or your Aunt Grace, who is not your aunt but is someone who is always around your family. This F is not about every single family member you have; it is about those people we most love, help, and care for, but also who we know will try to help and care for us in the way they can. They may provide an encouraging word or may be that needed audience when we want to practice our pitch before the big meeting. They may give us a loan or boast proudly about us to their friends. It is that group of people who love you almost unconditionally and are there for you and understand you when it seems no one else does.

The people in your family are the ones who benefit when you can maintain a regular schedule or can flex it, or when you continually increase your earning power; or they may get distraught when a decision is made about your career that may disrupt their lives. Sometimes new opportunities to increase the F for finances means the steady, reliable schedule for the F for family becomes unstable for a while or forever. The trade-offs are real. Having a healthy F for family can be something that is achieved daily, or often. You have to understand what your family members need in order for them to be whole, safe, and healthy. At the same time, you have to understand what it is that *you* need to be whole and able to focus on your career.

Our families are often the foundation of what motivates us to get out of bed every morning: they give us strength, are our biggest cheerleaders, and help us make it through bad times. When they suffer, we suffer; when they are OK, we can do well. Sometimes, though, there are family members who are not good to us or for us. You have to find the answer inside yourself to determine how much influence and contact those family members with unhealthy values or behaviors will be allowed to have on you. But at the end of the day, family will always be with us: we may not always have a job, but we will always have a family!

When I think about my F for family, my son Jared comes to mind. When he was a teenager, I was offered an incredible opportunity, promotion, and raise to become VP of IT, which required me to move to another division during my time at Johnson & Johnson. However, that move would have required my entire family to relocate across the country while my son was still deciding on his future college choice. I turned the position down.

At that time, I knew my family was at the top of my Five Fs, because Jared's college-selection season was right around the corner. Whereas my husband might have been able to endure the inconvenience of a cross-country move (from New Jersey to California), I knew such a move would have been harder for Jared to handle at that age. My focus then was to ensure that Jared had time to visit potential colleges and to prepare for and excel on his SATs and other precollege activities. When I chose not to accept the offer, it wasn't about the finances or furthering career that was most important; it was about my family, and I have never regretted making that choice for Jared.

Focusing on Your *Finances*

Where would we be if we didn't have money? Finances not only help us create and maintain a lifestyle that provides the basics of food, water, and shelter, but also enable us to be philanthropic and benevolent givers. Most of us (but not all of us) work to receive financial rewards. Our finances allow us to generate, preserve, grow, or trade—or squander! When we spend more than we make, we are on a trajectory toward bankruptcy or toward having an impact on our other Fs.

Taking the "long game" is the strategy for the Envision step. As you defined your purpose and your vision, you defined what you were here for. The ability to achieve your purpose and vision is done over time, sometimes a long time! Developing your finances necessitates taking the long view to build wealth, allowing you to live as you'd like, and return what you'd like when you are in the "return-all-you-can" season of your life. Part of your thinking as you envision your future should include how you will:

1. Make your money—i.e., generate it.

2. Save and grow it—i.e., preserve and maintain it.

3. Buy what you want—i.e., trade it.

A winner who has financial aspirations will seek to do more of #1 and #2, and less of #3, in a relative sense.

Healthy finances mean you are concerned about intergenerational wealth: you have an idea and have communicated how your wealth will be distributed upon your death. You may provide money to your children each year to help them build wealth while you are alive.

F for finances doesn't work alone, but in fact has a major interaction with your other Fs. Rarely will you not consider your finances in decisions you make on nearly everything. Even in faith, you may decide to tithe 10 percent of your earnings or help promote an organization's building fund.

There are extremes. I remember visiting a church that needed (wanted?) to raise money to buy another property. The church leaders actually asked the members to take the jewelry off their fingers, wrists, and necks and put the pieces in the offering basket—in addition to the cash that members had already placed in the baskets—to help the church afford to buy the new property. Not only did I find that horrifying; I never went back to that church!

But there are examples where, if you let it, even your faith may cause you to justify spending large amounts of money or giving away your gold! Your finances are a key part of everything you do, and how you take charge of your financial health can have long-term consequences. Your F for family will usually be a consideration for what and how you handle your F for finances.

There was a point during my career that my second husband, Max, was in the hospital for eight days, with several issues. I was living in Illinois, while he was living in New Jersey. We saw each other monthly, but I came home to be with him for those eight days in the hospital. He asked me to consider leaving Illinois and coming back permanently to be with him—which I did (after a lot of envisioning and designing).

Several months later, after he had completely recovered from his health scare and was back on his feet, I was offered another great opportunity in Milwaukee with GE that I just couldn't turn down. Although my husband (F for family) was extremely important, this opportunity was a chance to make a lot of money (F for finances), which I would bring home to him. (As a pastor, he couldn't go with me; his church was in New Jersey.) I talked with him and prayed with him about this decision, and he gave me his blessings. He said, "Daphne, promise me this will be your last position, and then you will come home for good." When I said yes to my husband, I had his blessing to again prioritize my finances over family so that I could ensure greater financial security for both of us in the future.

Focusing on Your *Fitness*

It is said if you don't have your health, you don't have much. With poor health, you are limited in how much you can work, entertain, travel, have healthy relationships, serve others, work out, live a long life, or do anything else you may want to do. Your F for fitness is about being healthy, where all parts function as they should. That includes your body and all its systems.

Your health is not only about physical fitness; it should also include emotional and mental fitness. Emotional fitness doesn't mean you are always happy, but it does mean you are able to control how you think, feel, and cope with your life events or those of others. It encompasses how you take in and respond to feedback. The term "emotional intelligence" is the ability to be aware of and in control of our emotions and handle relationships empathetically. It is the key to personal and professional success. Just as when we are physically unfit or sick, we go to the doctor or whatever we do to heal physically, the same is appropriate if we are emotionally unwell.

Dr. Hal Baumchen* indicates a few things we should do to be in good emotional health:

Stay honest with yourself and others	Stay peaceful—be a peacemaker and overlook offenses
Stay grateful—remain humble; say thank you	Stay intentional—don't engage in any more random living; be deliberate
Stay positive—be upbeat; smile; laugh	Stay balanced—keep work/love/people/ projects in balance
Stay determined—own your purpose and vision	Stay hopeful—know that the future is filled with good things

When there are external forces that distract you or pummel you on a regular basis, the way to fitness may include incorporating more meditation into your life, joining professional or casual networking groups, working consistently with a physical trainer, or making strides

---

* Dr. Hal Baumchen, author of *Destinations*, psychologist, and speaker on mental health and recovery.

to consume a healthier diet. While we recognize that fitness plays a role in one's ability to win, it often takes a back seat to the other Fs. It shouldn't! But many people (mostly women) default to taking care of themselves last (even though airplanes instruct us to put the mask on ourselves first, so we can then help others).

Focusing on fitness for you or your family can prevent work downtime and absences. A fitness regime needs to be built into your schedule, and if you do it with a friend or family member, you can integrate fitness with your family goal; or if you work out with colleagues at your job, you can integrate fitness with your furthering career goal. Prevention is better than correction, and early detection of any fitness challenge (whether it be mental, physical, or emotional) beats late detection.

My protégé Kim was a very successful leader and had been for some time. She wanted me to serve as a sounding board for her—as a married friend, not as an official executive coach— and I agreed. She had been working as a director of enterprise risk management, and she lived with her loving husband and two kids. She didn't feel she was winning, because she was spending a lot of time working and her husband was growing emotionally closer to the kids; his schedule and job allowed him to be there more for them than Kim, while she was growing farther away from them. Although she was happy that her husband could do that, she was not happy that she could not. In addition, her fitness was waning: she was gaining weight by eating fast food, and to add insult to injury, she became prediabetic.

We discussed what really mattered in her life now. She said she was ready to stop devoting all her time to work, because she saw how other people seemed able to balance their lives better than she was doing. She needed to reset her Five Fs priorities and realized if she could go home earlier at least two days a week, she could enjoy time with her children, eat better food at home, and work out, accomplishing all of it in the same amount of time as when she worked late. She wasn't shifting away from furthering her career, but she created a better balance for shifting care to her family, while enabling focus on her fitness.

Since Covid-19, she has even integrated fitness into her meetings. For example, during Zoom meetings when she is not presenting, she walks on the treadmill. Fitness doesn't have to be an either-or with the rest of your Fs to win; it just needs to be there.

Focusing on *Furthering Career*

Furthering your career is about being intentional, thoughtful, and strategic on how you will continue to grow in the vocation you choose or how you may enter into a new one that fits your vision and purpose. Often it is this F that causes a response to or reevaluation of the other Fs. Sometimes it is the reverse—that is, your family requirements to live near an aging parent may impact your furthering career choices. The point here is that once again, these Fs all work together, and you will rely on knowing the health and priority individually and collectively of each of the pillars in your life these Fs represent as you move forward to furthering your career.

Your vision is your key, but knowing the position of your surrounding Fs is key to the win. You may be on the off-ramp, heading to take a sabbatical, but you will get back on the on-ramp someday. You may be seeking to be an entrepreneur for the first time, you may want to get a promotion, or you may just get a new job. Whatever it is, being clear about and aspirational of your objective is critical to moving forward.

Furthering your career isn't the only thing that contributes to your life, and if you focus only on that F, you could very well be a public success and a private failure. The other Fs are mainly private pillars that hold you up or support you. If those Fs are not healthy, and only your career is, eventually they will crumble. Your relationships may fail; your health will deteriorate; you will have no accounting for your money. In other words, you may have a partial win, but it will not be a total victory.

During the last few years of my corporate career in Milwaukee, I was armed with more information about my worth and value than I had ever been, and my focus was on generating more income (F for finance). In addition, I was able to negotiate a travel allowance for my husband to visit me monthly. I knew from his previous health scare that I did not want to be away from him for more than a few weeks at a time. I could not let my F-for-family ball drop.

We created an arrangement where we saw each other once or twice a month or we met in other countries. This wasn't always easy, as my husband had to manage his career as a pastor while being vigilant about staying healthy. But we discovered how to make it work; we enjoyed adventures in India, France, Spain, Belgium, and other countries, and whenever my husband visited me in Milwaukee, we loved doing treks on the lakefront and spending precious time together.

DETERMINE WHAT'S MOST IMPORTANT TO *YOU*

I developed these Five Fs based on my quest for furthering my career, while also taking care of the other dimensions that, if the wrong one or two Fs were negatively impacted, might have resulted in an overall negative impact on my career. There are so many dimensions to who we are. There will be times where you are focused on the immediate objective of widening your circle of influence so you can advance within your current company to move to a larger corporation. There are times where you will need to be dormant and patient as you move into becoming a new parent or altering your career timetable to make time to take care of an elderly parent. There are still other seasons in your life where your health may take top priority and everything else must come second, like mine did recently. You are not just your bank account, your home, and your accomplishments.

When you embark on a new part of your career project, you need to know which of your Five Fs will be most stable and which pillars can be temporarily deprioritized or otherwise impacted. For you, it could be that you can scale back from jogging every day, because you are running for local political office, which requires more of your daily time-off hours. Or maybe your children need more academic support during Covid-19. Your Five Fs are key pillars within your life that you may try to ignore, but you can't ignore them for long.

As you reflected earlier on your performance, your purpose, and your values in Chapter 1, you now need to assess where you believe each of the Five Fs stands right now and how important each is in your current stage of life. When you have a greater understanding of where you stand with your Five Fs, you will have a fairly good picture of the major attributes that brought you to where you are and what you will need to consider as you go forward. The status of any or all of these will influence where and how you will proceed.

Take another look at Figure 2.1, shown at the beginning of this chapter, and define and determine (1) how healthy your Five Fs are and (2) how important each will be for you going forward. You don't have to only use Five F categories; you can add more. Tailor this tool to fit your personal situation. *Do the wheel now.*

IDENTIFY YOUR SOURCES OF SATISFACTION AND DISSATISFACTION

People usually want to feel energized by the thought of doing something meaningful each day that enables well-placed use of their skills, talents, expertise, and experience. But when a career or profession fails to provide that level of fulfillment, the result is naturally disillusionment and dissatisfaction. To envision a future that is different from your past or current state, it helps to identify what you are dissatisfied with today and what must happen for you to be satisfied in a future version of you or your circumstances.

The sidebar that follows is a SAT (satisfied)/DSAT (dissatisfied) survey for you to take that will give you a baseline on your level of satisfaction—or dissatisfaction—in your career life. When you are done answering the questions in this survey, check to see if your list of dissatisfiers is longer or stronger than your list of satisfiers. It is important that you note but not focus on what is *not appealing* to you; rather, focus on what you *want*. I have coached leaders that they should not focus on running *from* "doing" something, but instead focus on running *to* "become" something new. So try to define as much as you can the things that would satisfy you versus the things that would dissatisfy you.

Do the SAT/DSAT survey now.

THE SAT/DSAT SURVEY: ASSESSING HOW SATISFIED OR DISSATISFIED YOU ARE WITH YOUR LIFE

Your Dissatisfaction

Answer the following questions:

- What aspects of your current position are neither gratifying nor fulfilling, and are even perhaps highly dissatisfying?

- Describe what you wish you had more of:

  o Money?

  o A supportive boss?

  o Better work-life integration?

  o A more meaningful role?

  o Greater autonomy?

  o More responsibility?

  o A less stressed-out life partner?

  o A healthy lifestyle?

  o Something else?

- What aspects of your current position lead you to feel unappreciated? What leads you to feel underutilized?

- What leads you to feel underchallenged and, as a result, unable to grow professionally?

- What other aspects of your current position are less than optimal for you?

- Which of your Five Fs are suffering as a result of your current situation?

- What is your reaction to being dissatisfied?

  - Procrastination?

  - Irritability?

  - Inability to focus on your job and/or your family?

  - Not doing your best?

  - Something else?

Your Satisfaction

Now answer these questions:

- What sort of position would be more gratifying, fulfilling, and highly satisfying to you?

- What type of role would you appreciate because it more aptly utilizes your skills and competencies?

- Which of your skills, competencies, talents, expertise, or experience would you like your next position to use more of?

- What is an example of the type of contribution you would like to make to your company, community, employees, or another group that is in line with your purpose (passion and capability)?

- What sort of position would enable you to feel challenged and, as a result, able to grow professionally in a supportive and empowering environment?

- How and which of your Five Fs would be favorably affected by a position that offered you better opportunities?

- Which of your Five Fs would you need to fortify or focus on to ensure they thrived as your career does?

One of my protégés, Roman, was not happy with his current role at his company. He felt underappreciated and undervalued; he wasn't getting the assignments—or the financial recognition and promotions—that he wanted. Roman was considered a high performer but just wasn't advancing as quickly up the corporate ladder as his white peers were. He was the go-to person when projects needed rescuing or heavy lifting, and he was getting tired of being called in to fix problems but not get the status he felt he deserved.

As my protégé, he and I often spoke. One day he told me he was leaving the company. He had found another job, but he hadn't submitted his resignation yet. I asked him if he was excited about the new job, and he admitted he wasn't. When I heard this, I told him, "Roman, don't take that job."

As I mentioned earlier, you should never run away from a job you have unless you are running to a job you truly want. Think about what or where you want to be in the next five years; then assess whether a new job will get you to that goal. In this case Roman told me he didn't know if it would, but he thought it probably would not. I suggested he wait before he resigned and find the job that he wants to run to, that will help him achieve his vision. After all, he had a great reputation at the company and was in no danger of being let go. He just needed to be patient.

Fortunately, Roman took my advice and did exactly that. He's been gone about four years; he was promoted twice at his new company, and he recently accepted a higher-level position as a VP at a different company. He won and is still winning!

DREAMING, IMAGINING, AND SUSPENDING DISBELIEF

In Chapter 1, you reflected as though you were looking through a rearview mirror at where you've been. Now you have the opportunity to ask, "If that is where I was, where can I now go?" You can dream of possibilities of who or what you want to be, and that will be like looking through the windshield. The windshield is bigger than the rearview mirror, because your future is bigger and is right in front of you. Depending on the weather conditions on your road, the visibility of your future may be miles out and is yours when you are willing to dream and suspend disbelief. Suspending disbelief involves giving ourselves permission to envision a new venture or capability without being locked into a habit of telling ourselves, "No, we can't do that." It gives us permission to know that we can prosper, and when we know we can prosper, we will prosper. It requires us to change how we think, how we feel, or how we dare when we suspend disbelief. We can virtually put any disbelief high up on a shelf and throw away the ladder so we can never reach it again. You engage your head, heart, and guts as you are dreaming and suspending disbelief:

- Your *head* (how you think) probably wants more certainty and results and is accustomed to setting priorities and thinking about things in a strategic manner. Logic prevails!

- Your *heart* (how you feel) may continue to think of other people's needs before it lets you dream about your own vision. After all, we are nothing without our people, or without our family. We know that "teamwork makes the dream work." Women tend to care for others before we care for ourselves.

- Meanwhile, your *guts* (how you dare) have longed for your boldness to step out and innovate within your own life and take risks, as long as they are fairly intelligent risks.

All aspects of head, heart, and guts come together and help you dream and take a moment to reimagine what is possible. Reimagine a new role, a new business, a healthier body, a new product that may seem impossible to create. Some of the most successful people I know have aspired to be more than what the naysayers would have said was possible. "Impossible" is true until someone gets the impossible done, which then makes "the Impossible" become "the Inevitable."

My friend Sherry Taylor was an SVP at a large Fortune 100 technology company, reporting to the CEO. When her loving sister died of breast cancer, she reevaluated her life and career, and determined that she needed to focus more on her family and fitness. She decided to further her career in a different way. She wanted to pivot from working at the company to instead helping the healthcare industry with better technology. She wondered, "How can we help hospitals make people better and not have to come back for the same illness? A good hospital is basically an 'empty' hospital."

She decided to start a company that would provide the technology brains to the hospitals to help them track their patient outcomes, patient readmissions, patient days of stay, and other Medicare metrics. She is one of the most successful people I know, but when she shared that idea with others, they told her it was a pipe dream—that it was impossible for a Black woman to raise capital and start up and run a business in such a complicated industry as healthcare.

In fact, she had a hard time raising capital to start her business—at first. But when she looked at her finances, she realized she had enough to at least get started. She finally decided to leave her job and redefine what a new career would look like—as the CEO of a health-focused data analytics venture. She systematically put her vision out there, realized what success looked like, and suspended disbelief. She aspired to be more than what her naysayers said was possible, and she won.

She used her logic, analytical thinking, and expert experience in technology (head). She focused on the memory of her sister, and her desire to help patients be better and live longer through her quest of improving healthcare efficacy (heart). She took risks in communicating her vision, selling some of her investments to fund the business, hiring talent, listening to various advisors who helped her set up, and going to friends and family to raise initial money (guts). She swallowed her fear of failure because her desire to help improve healthcare access and outcomes to help patients be healthier and live longer was bigger than her fears.

Now she has a business with a valuation of more than $50 million (and my husband and I recently invested in her business). Impossible? No. Inevitable? Yes. She won when they said she wouldn't. It was just a matter of time.

In order to *Win When They Say You Won't*: Establish a baseline of where your faith, family, fitness, finances, and furthering career pillars stand right now. When you know that, you can suspend any disbelief you have in yourself, so you can aim for an even higher vision than you ever thought you could.

Now get ready to aim higher and bolder in Chapter 3.

CHAPTER 3

COMMIT TO THE FUTURE YOU

The secret to change is by us not spending
all our energy on fighting things of old,
but rather by building things anew.

—SOCRATES

Now that you have clarified your purpose (in Chapter 1) and your Five Fs priorities (in Chapter 2), it's time to commit to a bold vision, which we'll do in this chapter. It's here that you are leaping outside your lived experience of what is possible. This step in the EDIT process calls on you to be a visionary and reimagine nearly anything—a new role, a new business, a healthier body, a new product, or more. This chapter challenges you not only to think outside the box but to throw the whole box away and create a new vision beyond your wildest dreams. You don't want a box to be your frame of reference. This chapter should inspire and equip you to create your own possibilities and frame of reference.

In this chapter, you will go after a vision or aspiration bigger or more impactful than the vision you set in Chapter 1. Your Chapter 1 vision may have been based on something you believe is easier to reach. But I encourage you to aim for something bigger. If you aim to hit something that is already within your reach, you're not reaching very high. That's the low-hanging fruit. When you finish picking that fruit, you'll starve if you don't go higher and grab for the fruit that's higher up. And, if you only lay out an easy aspiration, you might hit it, and then what—are you done? In contrast, when you have a 3x or 6x or 10x aspiration, not only will you likely hit your "nearby" objective, but you will exceed it and be closer to your far-out aspiration than if you just solely aimed for your nearby one.

> *I recently talked to my dear friend Shellye Archambeau after the wonderful launch of her book* Unapologetically Ambitious. *Shellye mentioned how so much of her life was built around going after three goals: when she only 16 years old, she declared she wanted to be a CEO, have a supportive life partner, and have children. No one told her she couldn't get married or have kids, but people showed her—through body language, certain questions they asked, and her job assignments—that going after the CEO role was too ambitious. She was too young, too female, too Black. What was she thinking? She was told she couldn't win.*
>
> *Well, fast-forward to present day. She retired a few years ago from being CEO of MetricStream, a risk management and governance solutions company, where she was one of Silicon Valley's first African American female CEOs. MetricStream is valued at nearly half a billion dollars. She is now on the boards of Nordstrom and Verizon.*
>
> *Shellye had ambition. She aimed high. She remained committed to her vision. And she won when they said she wouldn't.*

BUILDING AN EFFECTIVE AND POWERFUL COMMITMENT STATEMENT

In this chapter, you will create your commitment statement. It is a promise to yourself and your family, and it will be a beacon of hope for those who have yet to experience your greatness in a way that only you can share. It is something you will commit to and work on every day. Yes, there will be moments during your journey when your commitment may be delayed or altered, but continuing to focus on creating and *editing* a *new version* of yourself as a product is a key activity needed for you to win.

Why is this important?

I've seen many people who have been very successful in their careers only to reach a point where they become discouraged, or disenfranchised, or distracted from reaching a higher, more fulfilling objective. There are a multitude of reasons why people stop reaching for the moonshot. But then again, they can redefine their moonshot and go for it anyway.

A former COO at a Fortune 500 company left suddenly, after a stellar career. She got tired of the CEO revolving door, where she reported to a new CEO every two years, and she began to realize she had different values and approaches than the latest CEO expected. She didn't have the patience, nor the political strength, to stay and fight. So she left: she packed up her home, and she and her husband moved out west to Montana. She told me the pace is slower there, and less political, and she can be a better servant leader in her new role as COO at another company than she was able to do in her prior job. Same role, different environment. She redefined her moonshot and hit it.

Here's another example: A dynamic VP of procurement (purchasing) at one of my former companies was a sharp and energetic leader. She drove down materials costs and supply chain costs, and she focused on reducing the risk of having single- or sole-source suppliers. But she got tired of working so hard with no evidence that she would ever crack the concrete ceiling, and although she was good at what she did, she had no joy. The company didn't encourage her enough, and she wearied of going for the prize that seemed to keep moving away from her. In her spare time, she enjoyed and was successful at buying, renovating, and selling condos and homes. She reflected on what she really wanted to do and the industry she wanted to be in and not stay stuck in a job that didn't give her joy. She now sells real estate in the hot market in Florida. New role, new environment. She created a new version of herself.

You need to commit to your vision, or an objective, and stick to it. But there are times along the way, as you look at your Five Fs, you may realize you need to make a change in your commitment. That's OK. Winning is in the eyes of you, not someone else. If you need to change, then change. But your purpose, and the corresponding vision, is not something that changes often. Envision what you want to be and go for it. The two leaders I just described changed their life based on their work environment and their change of passion, but they recommitted and followed through on a new aspect of their life. I believe that most people who envision their win will stay connected to it, because they explored their purpose and know that their purpose/vision is worth the struggle. Else it could be the wrong vision. It is said that *to be a success you must achieve a goal. But to be successful, to be "full of success," you need to continually achieve goals.* Going for the win should not be a one-time event. And I have found that winners commit to making it through—and to winning.

> *I am friends with a four-time Ironman competitor. The Ironman Triathlon requires participants to swim 2.4 miles, ride a bike for 112 miles, and then run a 26.22-mile marathon. People compete against others of their gender, and they seek to beat everyone else's time; however, many people compete in an Ironman simply to perform at their own personal best. That was my friend's goal, too: he wanted to beat his time from the previous Ironman he had competed in.*
>
> *When I asked him if he ever got to a point where he felt he couldn't go on, he answered emphatically, "No!" I expected him to say, "Of course, Daphne, but I keep pushing through." For him, quitting is not even an option.*

When you continue to think about going after the purpose and vision that you reflected on in Chapter 1, you may think it is not possible to achieve the goals you envision. You may no longer believe you can. After all, you've been at this for years, and you haven't achieved them yet. You may be skeptical.

I know I was skeptical when I went after breaking the concrete ceiling during my time at one company. No woman and no person of color had ever reported to the CEO of this company. It hadn't been done yet, so what made me think I could do it? I was that girl that was supposed to be a secretary, not a concrete ceiling breaker! Nevertheless, I suspended my disbelief and did what I needed to prepare for the interview. I went after the job—and I got it.

Of course, there were also times I did not get the job I went after. I wanted to be the CIO of Avon Products, Inc., but I didn't have the right approach when I went after the role. When I don't get what I go after, as long as it fits my vision, I don't let it erase my vision; I just go after another opportunity later or try a different way. I find another way to win.

You also have probably experienced disruptive things that will crop up when you're on your way to achieving your vision or objective.

One of my coaching clients was a divisional CIO at a large insurance company. She reported to the enterprise CIO, and I was working with her to help her get ready to step into his shoes, because she was told he would be retiring soon. In the early stages of our working together on her vision and plan design, her company was acquired by a larger insurance company. Not only was she not going to get the CIO position; she realized she would have to find a new job somewhere else, as she was likely going to be made redundant with the larger company tech leader taking over her role.

At times, we have self-doubts, self-loathing, or fear of failure, or (like me) we can be stuck and focused on recent or past failures.

When I was downsized at IBM in 1990 due to cost-cutting measures, I looked at myself as the ultimate failure. I had just moved to Atlanta at my first husband's request. I was new, was not given a manager's job when I arrived there, didn't have influential sponsors or mentors to call on in Atlanta, and didn't know the IBM team there very well. I had not built up credibility, results, or relationships there. As a result, it was easier for the folks in charge to put me on the "downsize" list. Failing to stay at IBM— the company where I had started my postcollege career—was a devastating prospect. I mourned and felt really sorry for myself for a while. I received the "you're downsized" letter and was told I had 30 days.

But as those 30 days ticked by, I spoke to one of my mentors, who coached me out of that funk by helping me see that it would be even more devastating if I let that development cause me to become stuck and not seek to move on. As a result, I put a plan together to get back on my feet, because finding a way to win wasn't only about me; I also had a six-year-old child that I had to nurture and protect. I didn't know it at the time, but that was the beginning of my creating the EDIT process. It wasn't as developed as it is now, but I knew that I first had to have a vision of what I wanted. Where to live? What type of job? Did I want to stay married? Big questions. After creating a vision of my future, I had to design my plan of attack. And after working through my EDIT, I ended up in New Jersey as a director of IT.

When your disbelief has free rein in your life, it becomes a barrier in your mind that translates into things you do. The way you think will affect your actions. We can be naturally logical and think critically in our day-to-day work. So if your mind remains logical, systematic, and critical when it comes to dreaming, your mind will say you cannot attain what you are imagining. You will disbelieve that your aspiration is possible. And those actions you take based on your disbelieving mindset will affect your results. What's in our mind controls our actions. Where your mind goes, energy follows.

Therefore, if you want to ensure more positive results, you need to change how you think. Suspend your disbelief. Your mind needs to say, "Those obstacles are not going to stop me; they are only going to test me." If those obstacles are there, they need to become less relevant so you can get going on your way to achieving your vision. Sometimes we are the very people who talk ourselves down from the summits we seek.

YOUR WINNING PATH IS IMPOSSIBLE UNTIL IT ISN'T

The word "impossible" is not a fact; it's merely someone's opinion at some point in time. Something is impossible . . . until somebody does it. We witness impossible things all the time. We've seen people of color become CEOs and board chair. We've seen a woman become CEO of GM, the largest US automaker. We've seen disabled people win Olympic gold medals. We've seen the first Black and South Asian woman become vice president of the United States. And we've seen the first Black woman become a Supreme Court justice.

My friend Barbara Bowles is a retired board member of Wisconsin Energies and has spent much of her career working in Fortune 500 companies in finance.

When she was working just outside of Chicago, as the VP of Investor Relationships at Kraft, Inc, she became one of two Black women allowed to join the University Club in Chicago. It was very much a "boy's club" and women were not initially allowed to join, and certainly not Black women. She asked her company to boycott the organization because it wouldn't let her in. Her company did that, and because of the widespread support she had of many women, the club opened up membership.

As mentioned before, how you think will affect what you do, which will affect your outcomes. If you want to change your outcomes, then you need to change how you think. Since the plan is to win when others say you won't, having the right mindset is critical.

There are various philosophies about mindsets and how they impact success, but the one I ascribe to is simple in its description. There's a *growth mindset* and a *fixed mindset.*

People with a *growth mindset* believe they can continuously improve their intelligence: they exercise their minds, they achieve new skills by training well, and they don't really believe in giving up and are more likely to achieve what they set out to do, or more. Learning doesn't stop the minute you leave school or university. With a growth mindset, you're always learning and growing even as you're earning and returning (remember learn, earn, and return?). Just because you failed at something in the past doesn't mean that you are a failure. It means that you are learning how not to do that, or how to think differently about your approach. That failed attempt was just a lesson, an event, or a data point—not a life sentence. It's not win or lose—it's win or learn!

The opposite is the *fixed mindset*—where people believe they have all they are going to get, and they currently know all they are ever going to know. If you're not good at something, you won't ever be. People with this mindset believe that the resources in the world are limited and fixed, and that if they fail at something once, they will always fail at it. Or they try to cover up their failure so people won't know they did not succeed at something. They believe in documenting their capabilities instead of developing them further. They often give up.

Which mindset are you? You can be both—sometimes having a fixed mindset can save your life. But a growth mindset allows you to go further. Which mindset do you think you need to have to win when others say you won't? I have an opinion.

A growth mindset helps you play the long game. The reason we discuss purpose and vision in the beginning of this process (and this book) is because they keep your mind focused more on the long term. Visions and purpose are not usually achieved in a week, a month, or even a year sometimes. They happen in the future. When a challenge occurs during your journey to your moonshot, remember that you are going for the long journey; and when you keep that in mind, you will likely persevere, and you will look at the challenge as something to learn from, instead of something to give up on.

One of my girlfriends, Vaunetta Clark, who used to work with me at IBM, switched her career to work in financial services in New York City. As a woman in her mid-forties, she still had some runway to go before she would retire, when she was passed over for a promotion. After years of glowing performance reviews and profitable growth as a result of her work, she was given no reasonable explanation of what happened—or why the higher-level position was given to someone else.

She was going to quit, but then she decided to hold her peace and assess what happened with the job she knew should be hers. She adjusted her approach to her peers, her boss, and her clients. She waited about a year and a half, and then she received the promotion she wanted.

She took a long view, even though that was hard. However, the key to her success was to not be emotional or bitter, but to look as objectively as possible at the situation and have a growth mindset to treat the disappointment as a learning opportunity: What skills or emotional intelligence did the person who won the position exhibit that she didn't? What extra value did the person deliver to the organization that she didn't? She learned, and then she decided to leave the company for another, bigger role—one that she interviewed for and got before she quit the financial services company. She got what she wanted. She played the long game—she didn't react emotionally and quit, but instead used a growth mindset, learned from the experience, and won.

You need to have a long game about the multiple aspects of the journey you're on. You will not get permanently discouraged by setbacks. That doesn't mean growth-mindset people are never discouraged. But you will learn that disappointment doesn't last forever. Our commitment to ourselves should be done with the long view. You have to be bold enough to disrupt the status quo. But if you are riddled with self-doubt and feelings of being a fraud, you will be too afraid to fail, and your talents will be hidden under a blanket of fear. You will be afraid to move, and when you don't make a move, your commitment to yourself is at risk. When you don't appear, you will disappear. When you hide your light and talents, not only will you suboptimize your own achievements, making it difficult for you to be authentic and win, but dimming your light will suboptimize the impact you could have on your company, your family, and your community.

When I was at Johnson & Johnson, there was a woman colleague named Catherine, who was a senior executive in our Consumer Products division. The company wanted to send a representative to Germany for an expat assignment that was scheduled to last about two years. The management team was all set to send one of the men on its team (I'll call him "Bob"). Catherine also wanted the opportunity to go, but she was initially denied because she didn't speak German. She confidently (but respectfully) stood up for herself and said to the company group chairman: "Well, [Bob] doesn't speak German either. I have continually delivered on my annual targets of revenue, profitable growth, and EBITDA, so we both should have the same opportunity to compete for this expat assignment."

Catherine eventually won the opportunity to go abroad based on her business history and results. She set a new, bold standard for calling out the micro-inequities that were occurring in our workplace. She eventually became the company group chairperson for the consumer division. You can see that she did what it took to commit to her future, taking a risk by challenging the company. But she knew that if she didn't stand up for furthering her career, no one else would do it for her. The company's knee-jerk reaction of "sending the man" was cut short, and Catherine probably taught people a thing or two about bias in the workplace.

WHEN YOU CHANGE YOUR VISION, YOU CAN CHANGE YOUR LIFE!

During my senior year of high school, my guidance counselor made it clear that, as a Black girl, I had two career choices in life: I could become a teacher or a secretary. He told me if I tried to go to college, I wouldn't get in. If I were "lucky" enough to get in, I wouldn't graduate; I'd flunk out. If I were "lucky" enough to graduate, I wouldn't find a job: the business world wouldn't accept me. In the 1970s, the bar for my future had been set, as there were no other career opportunities presented to me as a young Black woman. I was given limits and labels at the same time! Because shorthand and typing were offered in high school, my guidance counselor had knowingly made sure that those classes were on my schedule. I excelled in both skills and received a scholarship to attend Moser Secretarial College in Chicago. For me, Moser was more like a two-week secretarial finishing and placement school. I knew how to take shorthand and type, but Moser taught me how to make coffee and how to behave in an office setting.

After graduating from Moser, I interviewed for a secretarial position for the assistant editor of Woman's Day *magazine, and I received an offer. At 17, this was my first real job. It was in downtown Chicago. I thought that my career was set in stone and that I had it going on! Taking the train from my hometown to Chicago was exciting. I didn't think about what a career trajectory might be for a successful secretary. Would I become senior secretary? And then what? I didn't even know enough to think about things like "career planning." And I was OK with that, for a moment.*

During my brief tenure there, I learned through rookie mistakes, through condescending treatment by the white men who worked there, and from their casual in-office chats that I listened to—what they talked about sounded like something I could do if only I could go to college to learn that. One moment led to another, and something woke up inside me. "I shouldn't be a secretary," I said to myself, "I should have one." The counselor was wrong! I knew I had to transform what seemed like my destiny, switch my life around, and strive for more.

This was my first inkling of envisioning something better for my future. It was as though I could see myself in a better career, and because I was in a business office for the first time in my life, my ambition rose. It felt weird, scary, and exciting at the same time. I didn't have role models to help me, but members of my 1974 graduating class were in various colleges and could help me quickly figure out where to go. Even though I was a teenager and inexperienced in the workforce, I realized I had the power to lead my life, instead of merely being led.

When I began to envision myself into a new frame, without the limits and labels that my counselor put on me, that's when my actions became more purposeful and my vision for my life began to change. I had to understand what satisfied and dissatisfied me about my current situation. I realized that I had to take control of my personal narrative and that I, and not the high school counselor, was the owner of my future.

Over the course of 30 days, I committed to going to college and graduating and finding my purpose at Illinois State University. Although I couldn't get into the university for the fall semester, I made it in the winter. I envisioned I would make a difference and help change the world. I didn't know then how I was going to do it. But first I had to change my life, and college seemed like a good start.

You will now explore in your mind and identify those things that you believe *you* were meant to be and really want to do. You may not believe you can achieve those things. Your past experiences might make you gun-shy. Then again, you may be ready to go, excited to keep going, and happy to start moving through the EDIT process to the Transform step. As you go through this first step, Envision, the goal is for you to move from dreaming about it, to suspending disbelief about it, to actually defining your *bold vision*! You want to make your dream so enticing that any doubts you have will not matter as much.

You need to think about and answer the following in line with your purpose/vision/values and SAT/DSAT:

1. What problem did your vision in Chapter 1 focus on? Is it still what you want to focus on? Was it one of your Five Fs: Furthering career? Family? Fitness? Finances? Faith?

2. If this is about your dreaming for a new career, what would you do for free if all your other living needs were met? If you knew you would not fail? Same question for you to ponder for any of the other Fs, or anything else.

3. What has been taking up space in your mind as unfinished business that you really want to do? Is it the same as in question 1? If it's not the same as in question 1, identify what would take you closer to achieving the purpose you defined in Chapter 1.

As you answer these questions, look at your vision ideas from Chapter 1 and see if you can make them bolder. If you wanted to get a promotion, can you go for a higher or more global promotion? If you wanted to learn how to swim, can you think about becoming a swimming teacher? Or a scuba diver?

Now answer the following questions:

- How can you take your vision and make it bigger?

- How would you modify your vision to take it up a notch to be bolder?

Your former vision from Chapter 1 will become an even bolder vision. Swing for the fences! Aim for the moon!

THERE'S VALUE IN YOUR VISION: HOLD ONTO IT!

Having a solid vision is the first requirement to drive your EDIT project and enable the next version of yourself. If I didn't set a new vision for my own life, I likely would not have gone to college, and I don't know where I'd be now. Your vision serves as your destination on your career's compass, aka your "true north," and serves as the guardrails on your journey along with your Five Fs. Focusing on your vision will help you know which behaviors, thoughts, strategies, ideas, and projects you should embrace because they align with your vision, and they will help you reject those things that do *not* align with your vision. As the product manager of your life, you will be besieged with people coming at you, some who mean to be helpful, but some who may intentionally or unintentionally force you off the track you've set for yourself. Remember, there are haters out there who don't believe you will win, and they might just be on a mission to help you fail. Your vision is where you turn back to remind yourself of your direction and what you were meant to be.

When you have a vision, you go from just doing to being. I believe that many people spend time "doing"; but with EDIT, I hope you will transform into who you are meant to be. I said it before, and I'll say it again: we are human "beings," not human "doings."

As a human, what are you meant to be? You become something intentional. You may not get it all with your first transformation project. Even when you achieve your purpose, you will continuously improve and expand into a greater purpose you may not have even originally envisioned.

The purpose of developing a vision is to be able to move from just doing your life to *being* in the fullness of your life each day. You behave in a way that is aligned with your vision. When you have a vision, you're choosing to not just operate only by chance, but also operate by choice.

A vision will not eliminate the inevitable scrapes and bruises that you will experience along the way. However, you are unique, and your vision will allow you to focus on your purpose and tune out the noise and get to the finish line. You can't control everything that happens to you, but if you have a vision for your life, you can control and manage how you respond to those challenges. It is your responsibility to respond in the way that is most helpful for you. Responsibility, to me, and as a concept in this book, means you have the "ability" to choose your "response" to life's stimuli or challenges. Each situation you find yourself in, especially if it is negative or challenging, should receive an intentional and thoughtful reaction—not based on emotion, but based on data, and on how to ensure you can win. When your vision is in place, if a new opportunity comes along, you can see how close that opportunity will take you toward your vision, and then you can act on it or reject it. *It's your choice!* You have the ability to choose how you respond to life's stimuli. Choose right.

Every person who is up to something big and courageous in his or her life will need a vision, a purpose, and an approach in order to win, but if you have *only* a purpose or a vision, it's just a dream.

WRITE YOUR VISION AND MAKE IT PLAIN

While the world is spinning around, it threatens to take you round and round with it. Your vision is what you will stand on or hold onto—and it will be your guide to help you navigate through decisions in your life or your stage of life.

As you identified what phase of life you are in (in Chapter 1— learning, earning, or returning), having a clear true north vision will help you say yes to those things that enable you to stay focused on the phase that you want to live in. Or you will say no to those things that take you away from where you are headed. When something comes into your frame to respond to (and something will always come up), your clear vision will help you see the opportunity or obstacle as it presents itself. You will decide how you respond to it because you will assess whether it is in support of or against your vision. Having a vision that is "plain" is important because it will be a clear path to what winning looks like for you. Not only will it help you know where you are headed, what you will be, or why it matters to you at this point in time, but it will help you start thinking about the steps to take to get you there. When you have clarity, lightbulbs go off in your head and at your feet, and you can see more clearly where you're stepping.

Use the sidebar to get clarity on your vision by answering the following questions:

1. **Clearly define what you want.** Take this time to clearly state the vision you have for yourself with *bold* statements such as, "I will seek to become a CEO at a small-cap company," or "I will start my own cosmetics company for women of color," or "I will explore building a new family with my partner." This can be a three- to five-year vision and you should suspend disbelief in order to achieve it.

2. **Understand why you have decided on this particular vision for yourself.** What will it do for you, your family, your finances, your faith, or all the Five Fs that apply? What values does your vision help you bring to life? Does the vision for yourself help you in the stage of life you're in? Will it help you learn, or earn, or return? Will it help you achieve your purpose?

3. **Envision yourself in that role.** Do you see a corner office? Do you see yourself with a new degree? What are you doing with it? Can you see more details? What do you want your MBA to specialize in? What size are you going to be when you lose weight? How will your health change? Does your vision feel right to you? Is it exciting for you to think about it? When you can see your vision in more detail than just an idea on a piece of paper, you are gaining clarity. We will build on that. We will also use your vision to shape your future objectives. *Do the following exercise now.*

DEVELOP YOUR BOLD VISION STATEMENT: GO BOLD OR GO HOME!

Look at your vision statement from Chapter 1. Can it be bolder? Answer the following questions to see if you can make your vision bolder.

- Clearly define what you want:
  - Restate your vision.

- o What did you want to be or change that compelled you to read this book?

- o Based on that answer, what would you do for free if all your other needs were met?

- o Or what would you do in your life if you knew you would not fail?

- o What has been taking up space in your mind as unfinished business? Untended-to business?

- Understand why you decided on this direction for yourself:

  - o Remind yourself what problem you are looking to solve: Is it career? Family? Health? Financial?

  - o What values will your vision bring to life?

  - o Will your vision help you learn, earn, or return?

  - o Will your vision help you achieve your purpose?

- Envision yourself in the role and make it bold:

  - o Can you see yourself in that new place/space? Describe it to yourself.

  - o Can you suspend disbelief and defy your logic to make a more impactful vision statement?

  - o Can you make it bigger, higher, stronger, faster?

DON'T RUN FROM YOUR VISION—COMMIT TO IT!

If there was ever a time for you to make a promise or commitment to yourself, it is now. A way to seriously demonstrate commitment to your new venture or vision is to write a commitment statement to yourself. You have envisioned a new version of yourself with a broadly stated vision, so let's go. This commitment statement is a statement about you, from you, to you. It resembles a deal you are making with yourself, but you can also share it with your supporters, stakeholders, or others so they know what you are planning to be. They can use it to provide support or track you to help you be accountable.

My vision for the next five or ten years is to speak truth to power and empower leaders who are underserved, overlooked, and undervalued. How did I get to that vision? I serve on boards and work with board members and C-suite leaders. Using my experience in various areas, I help the board explore governance topics such corporate risk, diversity, inclusion, equity, cybersecurity, and digital (that's speaking truth to power). That is my strategic and influential side. But I also value growth and development, am a maximizer, and have a passion for women from whom life or society doesn't expect much. So I coach, give motivational speeches, and I have written this book to empower, ignite, instruct, and excite those who are not where they want to be, who may not feel they are enough, or who feel they are voiceless.

I recently decided to make my vision bolder, which became "to use my platform to create a global power 'movement' that is inspirational, instructional, and empowering for women to win when others say they won't." This includes "win when they say you won't" T-shirts, mugs, and hats; blogs; talk shows; social media; and "the win of the week." It also includes connecting with other female-empowering organizations.

However, at my current age, as a Black woman, I began to doubt whether I could ever achieve a bold vision. Yes, even I have to push myself to be bolder! But I'm the person who believes that the video should always match the audio. I needed to practice what I'm writing in this book. So I'm committing to and jumping into this bolder vision headfirst, suspending disbelief, because I will not fail. And I have just added to this vision and will now additionally help women become prepared for serving on boards of directors.

You need to be able to make a commitment to yourself that you will honor and carry through. This commitment to yourself is one that shouldn't come lightly. It doesn't assume that you know and have thought of everything. It doesn't assume you know exactly how you will become what you have envisioned. But it says you are serious about it, and you are going to do something about your vision. This is, after all, *your* dream, *your* purpose, *your* vision. If you don't commit now, when will you? When you are ready, we will continue to walk with you through your next steps, and help you win when others say you won't.

You're committing to your future, your family, your health, your company, your growth and development, or whatever it is you have chosen to be. Your vision statement should be no more than 200 to 250 words, but it should clearly state what you'd like to be and that you will do what is required to get there. These brief but comprehensive paragraphs will act as an inspiring reminder of what you want to achieve as you undertake the journey of creating a new version of yourself.

Use the word "commit" in your statements to make it an affirmation that connects with your spirit. Give yourself ample time to write and gradually refine your commitment statement. Write a first draft, wait a few days, and rewrite your first version several times, in order to arrive at the best description of your ideal work-life. To help you get started with creating your own *commitment statement*, use the following sidebar as an example. Fill in the blanks and add/delete what you need to so this can be *your commitment*, and date it.

YOUR COMMITMENT STATEMENT

In support of my purpose and my vision, I commit to doing

_____

that will allow me or _____

to _____.

My new position or capability will reward me with

_____. I will feel fulfilled because I will

have _____ and pushed

through to a greater _____

as a result of my commitment. In my new position, I will be able

to help drive _____ and become a

better _____ .

Signed _____

Dated _____

When you've arrived at the final version of your commitment statement, keep it visible on your phone, refrigerator, or tablet to reread often. Allow it to become a source of inspiration and motivation on your more satisfying work-life journey. Share it with others—your family or coach or boss—so they can help you with your growth, and maybe they can be a spotter for you as you manage this EDIT project of your life.

In order to *Win When They Say You Won't*: It's time to commit to going forward. Commit to not letting go of the vision, future, and purpose that is wearing your name. When you commit to your bold aspiration—what it means to you and how it will serve others—you will be able to take that next step toward Transform. You will be able to design your approach that will drive you toward your vision. Coming up is Step II, the Design step of the EDIT process, which will allow you to do just that.

DESIGN

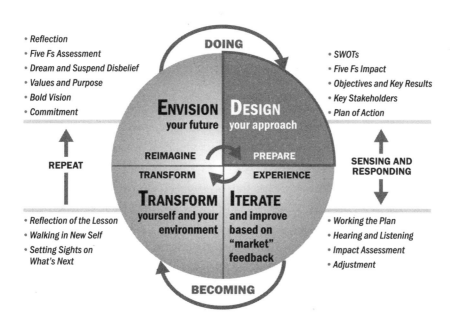

- Reflection
- Five Fs Assessment
- Dream and Suspend Disbelief
- Values and Purpose
- Bold Vision
- Commitment

DOING

- SWOTs
- Five Fs Impact
- Objectives and Key Results
- Key Stakeholders
- Plan of Action

ENVISION your future

DESIGN your approach

REIMAGINE

PREPARE

REPEAT

TRANSFORM

EXPERIENCE

SENSING AND RESPONDING

TRANSFORM yourself and your environment

ITERATE and improve based on "market" feedback

- Reflection of the Lesson
- Walking in New Self
- Setting Sights on What's Next

- Working the Plan
- Hearing and Listening
- Impact Assessment
- Adjustment

BECOMING

Now that you have carefully constructed your commitment to win when others say you won't, Step II shows you how as a product manager you can begin applying what's known as "design thinking" to your career and life project. Design thinking, which is used in technology development teams, helps you look at and define approaches to problems in a new way, a nonlinear way. The way the real world works. Design thinking helps you ensure focus on stakeholders and assumptions, and builds your project up to be able to iterate between your design plan and reality—fixing what didn't work and doubling down on what does. You identified a bold business or life opportunity to go after in Step I; now you will make the solid blueprint, or what we will call a "plan of action," that will help you work effectively toward your vision. The Design step of EDIT requires you to focus on *how, when, and with whom* you will accomplish the vision and commitment you defined from your Envision step planning. Whether you're contemplating a career change or launching a new product or service, the Design step is necessary to create the change you are seeking. This step will take you closer to your win.

In the Design step, you look more closely at your vision, break it down into objectives, prioritize them, and then learn more about them—i.e., understand what it will take to achieve them, recognize the risks and opportunities you need to consider and mitigate, and identify the resources and stakeholders you need to successfully move forward. The successful end of the Design step results in a risk-adjusted product plan with activities, dates, and resources all put together serving as a guide or recipe for you to begin to test your prototype or your assumptions in the Iterate phase. In Step II, you will design your objectives and assemble your plan correctly and realistically, so you'll be ready for Step III, where we "go live," aka iterate.

Chapter 4 describes a Design toolbox to help you break your vision into objectives, with metrics that will let you know if the results you expect along your way to achieving your vision are actually happening! You may be familiar with some of the tools in this toolbox; others maybe not. First, you'll break down your vision into objectives and key results (OKRs), which will enable your vision to become SMART:

specific, measurable, achievable, relevant, and time-bound. You will then prioritize your objectives so you can focus on the ones most likely to help you win. Following that, you will start making some assumptions of the good stuff and not-so-good stuff that may occur on your journey to your win. We call those SWOTs—strengths, weaknesses, opportunities, and threats. Any of them may occur during the course of your project. You will have put together a basic plan based on your most important objectives.

Chapter 5 is where we will look at your headwinds and tailwinds to identify the most likely opportunities and threats so you can create a risk-adjusted plan. Having a plan is good, but having one that recognizes the things that could most likely go wrong is better and improves the likelihood for you to have a winning outcome. It's better to prepare for something that could go wrong but doesn't, than to not prepare for an issue and it does occur.

Chapter 6 reviews your stakeholders: Who is your tribe? We are not here by ourselves, nor are we here only for ourselves, nor do we always move and act in isolation. We need to learn everything we can, from everyone we can. Stakeholders are part of our lives. In Step I, you identified your family as one of the Five Fs, but there are more people who are around you, working with you, for you, and on your behalf, that you will find important to put in your Design step: mentors, role models, sponsors, and coaches. You will identify yours and ensure you know where they will be relative to your plan.

The Design step can be thought of as the "prepare-to-execute step." So let's get ready to prepare!

DESIGNING YOUR FUTURE LIFE ON PURPOSE

If you can tune into your purpose and really align with it,
setting objectives so that your vision is an expression of
that purpose, then life flows much more easily.

—JACK CANFIELD

FIVE KEY TOOLS IN THE DESIGN TOOLBOX

As we begin the Design step of the EDIT process in this chapter, you will bring forward your *bold vision* (your "10x" high-level mental image of what you want to be that will help you achieve your purpose) and your *commitment statement* from the Envision step. With your vision and commitment statement, you will use other tools in your Design toolbox to get more specific and action-oriented about your vision, so it can become a plan. There are five tools you will use in the EDIT Design step:

1. Vision.

2. OKRs—objectives and key results.

3. BOs, MOs, and NOs—*bodacious* objectives, *moderate* objectives, and *nonessential* objectives.

4. SWOTs—*strengths, weaknesses, opportunities,* and *threats*—which, when all used together, will help generate your plan of action.

5. POA, or plan of action. It is your POA that will guide you to your win. It is like a recipe that you will follow to create an amazing meal!

Before we go further, let's break down the key tools as you move into "your future life design." The first part of this chapter defines these terms; the second part of this chapter shows how you should use them to help you achieve your vision, which is all about winning when they say you won't. I will share with you some examples from my own experience and from the experiences of other people.

Vision

The first tool in your Design toolbox is your *vision* (which is what you defined for yourself in the Envision step of the EDIT process): it's a reflection of what you want to be or achieve in your time period, or in your lifetime. It aligns with your values, brings your purpose to life, and helps you set your future objectives. Your vision may be a bit general, not quantifiable per se, but it should be bold and inspirational enough for you to transform! A vision tends to be high level, such as these:

- "To show female corporate leaders how to think bigger and achieve senior leadership positions in their companies, by systematically using business strategies to break through personal and professional barriers."

- "To help children in a third-world nation have the same opportunities for education as children in developed countries."

- "To get to and remain at my ideal weight, improve my health to not require medicine, and become a fitness instructor who also will inspire my family to get and remain healthy."

Your vision will answer the question generically, simply, and futuristically of "What do you want to achieve?" that may directly or indirectly impact your purpose. From there, you will shape your objectives, described in the next section.

Objectives and Key Results

The second tool in your Design toolbox is OKRs—objectives and key results. (Feel free to Google them to learn more, but this section covers what you need to know for our purposes.) Objectives are measurable and specific versions of your vision that will set or disclose the parameters around what you want to accomplish. Your objectives will also allow you to "fill in the blanks" of your vision more specifically. Your objectives will answer such questions as:

- "Where are you specifically going, and what do you want to be?"

- "What job do you specifically want that will advance your career?"

- "How will you have a healthier body; how much weight do you want to lose, by when, and how can you role-model your behaviors?"

Your answers will be specific statements, such as these:

- "I want to be promoted to divisional VP in three years."

- "I want to lose 50 pounds in 18 months, improve my BP to 120/80, and share my results to help others."

Key results go right along with your objectives; key results represent (1) what you need to do to achieve your objective and (2) your measures of success that let you know you are on your way to achieving your objective. They are your key performance indicators and will answer the question, "How do you know you're getting there?" and they define leading milestones or accomplishments that you will reach to achieve your objectives. Key results help you assess what you did or did not achieve along the way. Using the key results outcomes, you either adjust your approach or keep it moving! They tend to be partners alongside the objectives, like these:

    a. Objective: "To be promoted to divisional VP in three years"

- **Key Result #1.** "Lead two visible, valuable, and difficult international initiatives in this calendar year for one large division or the global enterprise."

- **Key Result #2.** "Deliver project outcomes at least two months early; deliver project 3 percent underbudget and with favorable divisional business partner and team feedback."

- **Key Result #3.** "Get a 360-degree assessment and coaching, ensure my brand is that of an inspirational and strong leader, be considered a high potential, and develop stronger relationships with my superiors, peers, subordinates, and key clients."

For the preceding career objective, there are three sample key results. For each of your objectives, the norm is to have between two and five key results. They should be specific and measurable.

You can see the following fitness objective has four key results.

    b. Objective: "To lose 50 pounds in 18 months, improve my BP to 120/80, and share my results to help others"

- **Key Result #1.** "In the next 30 days, get a physical exam with my doctor to ensure I can start my weight-loss journey in 30 days."

- **Key Result #2.** "Change how I eat to include <1,300 calories of more plant-based meals and 70 ounces of water per day."

- **Key Result #3.** "Start a healthy lifestyle group within 60 days with women from my community or church so we can support each other."

- **Key Result #4.** "Work out four times a week for 60 minutes and take BP daily, aiming for 120/80, and measure weight weekly."

Your OKRs should be what we call "committed" OKRs (having little risk), or they can be "aspirational," aka a stretch target (higher risk) for you (or your family). For example, delivering project results two months early may be an aspirational target—but you wouldn't get "dinged" for not delivering early, so if you miss the two months early and deliver results on time, you're still OK. Delivering late? That's something else altogether. You don't want to do that! The committed OKRs are the ones you absolutely commit to and 100 percent will expect to achieve.

You wrote your commitment statement and vision in Step I, Envision, and the OKR you will write in Step II, Design, will be in line with your commitment statement and vision. You may not achieve your aspirational goals during this EDIT, but as you go through the EDIT and continue to work on it, the aspirational ones will remain on your set of OKRs. I would expect you would have at least one or two committed OKRs and one aspirational one. But it's your call based on your time and your priorities.

BOs, MOs, and NOs: A Different Way to View Your Objectives

BOs, MOs, and NOs are a way to prioritize your objectives into groups that consist of those that are most important above every other objective, and without which we won't achieve our vision, versus those that are less critical. Each objective is looked at relative to the others and to your vision and commitment. Some of the objectives that you are considering working on for your win seem urgent but may actually be less impactful or valuable. Sometimes you have to work on the less important objectives, but I want you to do so with your eyes open—knowing that you are working on objectives that are important, but also working on some that are not. Here's what these acronyms mean:

- **BO—bodacious objective.** This objective is most impactful on your vision and has high relative value to your commitment or your stakeholders. Nothing is more important than your BOs. And just in case you are curious about the term *bodacious*, it is derived from the words "bold" and "audacious."

- **MO—moderate objective.** This is also impactful on your vision and may have good relative value to your vision or your stakeholders, but less so than the bodacious objective.

- **NO—nonessential objective.** This is least impactful on your vision and has low relative value to you, your vision, or your stakeholders. Sometimes you have to do these, but be aware that you are working on an NO!

The BOs, MOs, and NOs are important at this Design step of EDIT, because identifying your BOs will help you create your objectives and key results; your BOs will help you focus more on and build your plan of action. Meanwhile, your MOs and NOs will be, respectively, in second and third place.

Business product managers have to exercise due diligence—i.e., do research ahead of time—to first understand the priorities of their business, and then they assess which initiatives or projects will most quickly and likely achieve those priorities. Because of limited resources, time, or money, they want to work on the initiatives in their portfolio of initiatives that will most likely render the biggest bang for the proverbial buck (or Bitcoin). That is what you will be doing—prioritizing your objectives as the product manager of your life.

My client Maryann was what I will call "interrupt-driven." She went from task to task, and she did not seem to know which of her actions would help her become known as a high-value add to the IBM technology team. Since she was a new hire from a giant competing company, she brought the fame of being from that other company, but she wanted to be seen as a great hire and a value-add contributor to IBM. She was female, she looked very young, and she was part of the LGBQT community. (It had been tough for me, as a Black female, to be in STEM; I can only imagine what it was like for her as female, young, and LGBQT.)

After we discussed her vision and her SAT/DSAT on what it was that would satisfy her, we also discussed her top objectives on our way to building her OKRs. Initially, because she was excited, anxious, and insecure, everything to her was a BO, which in my experience is a clear way to failure. If you have only one objective, then it can be a BO and you can win. But if you have five objectives and they are all BOs, then you will not likely win; something will suffer—one or more of your prioritized Five Fs (including furthering career) will take a hit.

I had her draw on the BO/MO/NO a 2x2 matrix where we mapped each of her objectives. We managed to squeeze two of her objectives into the BO, one into the MO, and two into the NO category, with the agreement that she would let someone on her team track the two NOs and bring to her attention on an exception basis if the NOs were in jeopardy.

Strengths, Weaknesses, Opportunities, and Threats

The fourth tool in your Design toolbox is a SWOT analysis, which helps you look at your life from four different angles—two that are good, two that are not so good. The SWOT helps you answer this question: "What can help you win, and what can hinder you?"

SWOTs will help you be forewarned about what could stand in your way and slow you down or thwart your efforts, and SWOTs can also help you see what could be an accelerator for you and propel you forward. Your objective is to understand all four of these areas so you can exploit your strengths, close your weakness gap, seize your opportunities, and mitigate your threats. Winning sometimes involves being in the right place at the right time or being lucky. But it's mainly about being prepared for the unexpected as we do what we do and being able to integrate the unexpected into our product plans. Louis Pasteur said that "chance [aka being lucky] favors the prepared mind." He meant that the more prepared you are, the luckier you will be! Later in this chapter, I'll show you how I used the SWOT method in my own career, and I'll describe in more detail how you can use SWOTs to reach your own goals.

PRIORITIZE YOUR OBJECTIVES WITH BO, MO, AND NO

You are now about to map your objectives onto the BO/MO/NO chart in Figure 4.1 so you can ensure you have the right prioritized objectives.

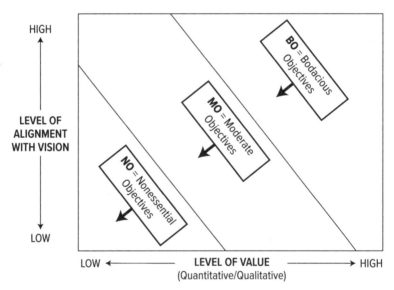

FIGURE 4.1 Prioritizing your objectives

Unless you have the time, resources, and capability to do all the objectives and key results that may be in your mind, without prioritizing, you could seriously dilute your impact and success (like Maryann was about to do). Your BO/MO/NO assessment ensures that you are clear on what your top OKRs will be. If you have too many bodacious objectives, you may spread yourself too thin. Likewise, if most of your objectives are NOs, you may be responding to things that are urgent but are not as important as your BOs.

If you have only one objective and you know it is a bodacious objective—and therefore wildly important, because the links to your vision and value contribution are both high—then you can write it in the upper right third of Figure 4.1. If you have several objectives—i.e., two or more, in your mind—take this moment now and write them down in your journal so you can capture them somewhere. We will prioritize them next. You may have ten objectives, or you may have three. No matter what number, we need to ensure they are the right ones that you believe have the greatest impact on your vision and that you will have time to achieve. You need to confirm how important they are for this stage in your life and to what extent they support your bold vision and purpose.

Once you have written all your objectives down, prioritize all your objectives and write them into the corresponding parts of Figure 4.1 Just write a short one-line objective, and don't worry about the key results yet. From this one-sentence statement, you will be able to determine your most important objectives that will most closely align with your vision and are worth spending the most time on. And from there, you can draft your key results.

Let's do your BO/MO/NO analysis now.

Your objectives will go in one of the three sections based on how you or your stakeholders value the objectives and how they fit with your purpose or vision. For example, somewhere on Figure 4.1, you would put the objectives (without the KRs) I described in the beginning of this chapter: (1) Advance career. (2) Lose weight and be healthier. They will be a BO, an MO, or an NO.

To help you decide where to place your objectives on Figure 4.1, answer the questions in the following sidebar.

QUESTIONS TO DETERMINE IF YOUR OBJECTIVE IS A BO, AN MO, OR AN NO

- Can you clearly define success for this objective?

- Is this objective more important than others at this point in your life?

- How much does this objective help you achieve your purpose and vision?

- Is this objective either *more* or *less* valuable than each other one? (Answer is *more* or is *less* versus each of the other objectives.)

- What will the level of value be when you achieve this objective? *High* or *low*? Can you quantify it?

- Who will benefit from you achieving this objective?

- Is this objective worth the price you will have to pay in your life?

- The price could be a sacrifice of any of your Five Fs. The more important the F, the potentially greater the sacrifice.

YOUR OBJECTIVES ARE SUPPORTED BY THEIR KEY RESULTS; CREATING YOUR POA

Once you know what your BOs are, you now should continue your due diligence as a product manager to work through a better and more specific definition of how you will go after your BO. Your key results will be action-oriented, specific, measurable, and time-bound, and they will help you know if you are on track. The key results should really be those results that if you achieve them, you will achieve the objective. They must be tightly related and create a cause-effect—an "if/then" type of relationship: "If I achieve these three key results, then I will achieve my objective." However, note that those three results are *necessary* to achieving your objectives, but they may not be *sufficient* to achieving them. In other words, you may need them to achieve your objective, but you may find out that you will need other key results along the way, as well, to achieve your objectives. That is part of project management and part of life. You anticipate as much as you can, but then you adjust your key results when you get new information.

Once you know your prioritized objectives, have written down your key results, and understand your SWOTs, the next step is creating the list of action steps you need to do to actually get those key results done! When you begin doing those steps, you will be creating your plan of action. A POA is just what the name implies. It's a document like a project plan that identifies the tasks that need to be accomplished to achieve an outcome. It outlines what you are looking to achieve, what the milestones are (key results), and what activities (action steps) are needed to bring those milestones to life. In this case, your vision led to objectives, and your objectives led to key results (aka milestones). Now the key results will require you to take some specific actions to achieve them. You would outline those actions to include when you need them done by and the resources you need to achieve those actions.

The wise saying that goes "When you fail to plan, you are planning to fail" is real! This POA is to help you plan to win, not plan to fail. Distractions can come and divert your attention from your objectives and your action steps. If you have a plan documented—much like an architectural drawing and plan for building a home—it keeps you on track to remember what it is you're trying to build and the key steps to get there. When you come back to your objectives, your plan is right there waiting for you.

Take a look at the preliminary POA template in Table 4.1.

Here's a guide to how to develop it into your POA:

TABLE 4.1　Plan of Action Template

ONE	TWO	THREE	FOUR	FIVE
FIVE Fs Which F will be involved in this objective? Impacts or is impacted?	**OBJECTIVE** What do I want to achieve? (SMART)	**KEY RESULTS (KR)** How will I know I'm on track to achieve my objective?	**KR BY WHEN?** When should this Key Result be done?	**ACTION STEPS** What needs to be done?

The Five Fs are Faith, Family, Finances, Fitness, and Furthering Career.

SIX	SEVEN	EIGHT	NINE	TEN
AS BY WHEN? **#1** When should this action step start and end by?	**HW or TW or FIVE F IMPACT?** What considerations matter most?	**AS BY WHEN?** **#2** Risk adjusted start/end date	**STAKEHOLDERS NEEDED?** Whose help do I need? When?	**STATUS?** Was this action step successful? What is status? Any new steps identified?

- Column 1 is the "Five Fs" column. Based on your objective, what Fs are potentially going to be involved (either impacting your objectives or being impacted by your objectives?)

- Column 2 is for naming the specific objective you are focused on, and making it as SMART as you can at this point.

- Column 3 is for the key results that you specifically need to achieve; otherwise you will not likely be on track to achieve your objective.

- Column 4—skip over this shaded column for now; we'll come back to it later.

- Column 5 is where you will put each appropriate set of actions for each of your key results, which match with that one objective.

Now, using Columns 1, 2, 3, and 5 in Table 4.1, jot down your Five Fs, your objectives and your key results, and your preliminary impression of all the action steps that need to be done to reach those key results, which then need to be completed to hit your objective time frame. OK? Remember, action steps help you reach your key results. Your key results help you achieve your objectives. You should have at least one or two committed OKRs and perhaps one stretch OKR.

Table 4.2 shows some sample OKRs. (*Note:* These are the same objectives listed earlier in the chapter in the description of key results.)

After you finish filling out Columns 1, 2, 3, and 5 in Table 4.1, take a moment and reflect on those key action steps you identified. If you can think of more, then capture them on the plan of action form. For example, you may have decided (in Chapter 2) that your family F is critical to your well-being, and you always have a monthly pizza night with your sister, or you check in with your elderly mom every Friday. In your plan of action, you want to add as a key result that your family maintains its level of happiness and support for what you are doing. An action step might include for family the reminder to have the date night, or counselor meeting, or whatever you believe is needed to keep

TABLE 4.2   Sample OKRs and Preliminary Plan of Action

ONE	TWO	THREE	FOUR	FIVE
Five Fs	Objective	Key Results (KR) Required	Key Results by When?	Action Steps for Each Key Result *(Action steps below are for KR #1 only)*
Furthering career	Promoted to Divisional VP in 3 years	1. Lead two visible, valuable, difficult projects 2. Deliver results 2 months early and 3% less cost. Improve GM by 200 basis points 3. Ensure my brand reflects strong and collaborative leadership		KR #1: • Review development plan with boss • Include project leadership as key • Review project portfolio with biz sponsor and ID project with best value • Incorporate into performance objective • ID internal resources and capital • Define project charter and project plan • Review integrator candidates • ID project admin • Launch project
Fitness	Be healthy, lose 50 pounds in 18 months and improve BP to 120/80	1. See doctor and begin research 2. Change eating 3. Start healthy lifestyle group 4. Work out 4x per week.		• Make appt with doctor • Begin reviewing healthy eating magazines, blogs, etc. • ID recipes for vegan lifestyle • Start shopping for organic foods • Decide on gym membership or home gym • Decide on trainer or self-taught • Etc.

the family F intact. The better and more specific the plan, the better you can get to your win.

In my example (in Table 4.2), for Key Result #1 for my promotion to VP objective, I believe I need to *lead two very significant projects* to show my leaders that I have the organizational strength, political savvy, and experience to motivate a team to deliver results. What are the action steps I needed to do to get *that* going? I jot those things down in Column 5 ("Action Steps") of Table 4.1; there will be multiple action steps for each key result. Sample answers are given in Table 4.2. If you need five action steps, then use five lines. If you need ten action steps, then use ten lines. Jot them down just as they come to mind. You are answering the question, "What would I need to do to get Key Result #1 going and completed?" What I do is simply write down all the actions that come into my head, or are suggested by the people I look to for guidance, that I believe will be important for me to achieve those key results.

Don't worry about the sequence of steps or how difficult they are; just write them down in the smallest increments. These might include:

- Identifying people for the project

- Hiring people

- Defining the project

- Acquiring a temporary office

- Acquiring capital

- Scheduling an appointment for your physical

- Researching the best plan to help with healthy eating

- Research if your church or neighborhood YMCA has a program already

- Finding research firms that could help with market research

Later on, you will sequence them into some type of order, but for now just jot them down. To move on through the EDIT process, you should jot down your objective and use an effective timekeeping method to keep you focused on reaching it.

My husband calls me "the list lady." I am always writing action steps down for some key result I'm looking to achieve. I do that because I believe it is not very easy to get something done without it being written down. Companies have mission statements, vision statements, strategic planning documents, annual revenue plans, etc., documented so that the ideas, expected outcomes, and required actions are memorialized, so folks are aware of the plan and can look to it for guidance. If the plan was created with good and clear thinking, it will more likely be executed.

The sample list of the action steps in Table 4.2 represents the beginning of a preliminary plan of action for Key Result #1 (KR1). If you have more than one key result for your first objective, then you would jot down those action steps required for the Key Result #2 (KR2). Give your first key result some room, and then start jotting down what action steps are needed to do KR2. As you think about KR2, it may cause you to think of another action step needed for KR1.

For each key result, there are more things to consider. For starters, dates/deadlines and resources need to be part of your action steps in addition to deciding what could go wrong and what could go right, and allowing for it in your plan of action. For now, this is a great start, and you should be able to see how your vision from Step I is beginning to turn into a plan of action. Yay!

Your prioritized objective (your destination) and your key results (to know what to do and to know if you are approaching your destination) are two of the most important things you can do as a product manager embarking on your EDIT journey. The objective is what you are stating as your intent or the inspirational outcome you are reaching for. You are welcome to use an Excel spreadsheet and simply re-create or modify Table 4.1 to suit your own style and level of detail. But you should always know what you are committing to, to keep track of where you are versus where you thought you would be, and to always monitor your actions against your plan.

TAKE STOCK OF YOUR SWOTs

Your SWOTs help you know what you have going for you, and what you may have going against you. When you identify these, you have a heads-up to help you be proactive or respond with agility. Strengths and weaknesses are *internal*, while opportunities and threats are *external:*

- *Strengths* are natural *internal* attributes or capabilities you personally have that can help you win. You want to exploit them to your advantage.

- *Weaknesses* are *internal* challenges or mistakes you may make that could slow you down or hinder your success. A weakness creates a gap of some sort that can hurt your ability to move rapidly or successfully. Some people will ignore a weakness if they believe it's not serious enough or can be outweighed by their strengths. Close the gap on a weakness if the weakness is serious enough.

- *Opportunities* are connections or circumstances that are *external* to you but may help you accelerate your progress. You can't really control opportunities, but you can leverage and seize them to your advantage.

- *Threats* are *external* things that *might* happen to you from external forces that might also slow you down or stop you in your tracks. You want to understand which threats are most likely or hurtful and mitigate them whenever you can with a "Plan B."

You may not know what things may rise up as a positive or negative surprise, but the objective is to be as prepared as possible. You want to know what is possible, what is probable, and not be blindsided. This is an important part of how project managers plan their projects with their teams, and they then allow for contingencies in extra time, money, and activities, just in case.

Here's an example from my career. I mentioned in Chapter 2 how my husband became seriously ill while he was living in New Jersey and I was living in Illinois, and I saw how my Five F priority needed to shift from furthering career to family. In reality, I realized that I had actually risen as far as I could go at my company, which was something I hadn't even considered possible before. I reported to the CEO, I was the highest-ranking female in the company, and I was the first African American female to report to the CEO and chairman. I could only go higher if I wanted to be CEO or COO—neither of which was in my purpose: I felt I didn't have the level of skill required to be CEO of a $4 billion company, at least not yet!

I concluded that not only did I want to move back East, but I wanted the growth opportunity of a bigger company so I could continue to learn, stretch, and grow professionally. So I first envisioned the type of role I wanted (SVP and CIO), the industry I was interested in (healthcare or manufacturing), the person I wanted to report to (must be CEO, or top CIO if a multidivisional conglomerate), and other factors.

Then I used SWOTs to understand my competencies and what I needed to focus on. In the following sections, we'll take a look a deeper look at each of the four areas of SWOT, and I'll describe how I thought about each area to help me decide my next career move at that point in my life.

When I evaluate a project or problem I'm looking to solve, I understand what is needed for me to win, I identify where I will apply my strengths, and then I identify people and stakeholders whose strengths are my weaknesses. *Together* we solve problems because we are using the best of what each brings to the table. We all have innate abilities that should be tapped into as often as possible. Our greatest potential for growth is in the area of our strengths. Our strengths match and correlate to our roles at work, at home, and in our communities. Using our strengths will ultimately help us be fulfilled because we are using our talents. What are your biggest strengths? How can you build on them for self-improvement?

Determine Your *Strengths*

Determine your *strengths* by addressing the following questions:

- What do you have going for you that can help you succeed? (You can review your SHIP competencies from Chapter 1.)

- What are your cultural, intellectual, and experiential advantages?

- How or why are you better than others who may be considered for this same objective?

- What resources do you possess or have access to that will help you win? People? Money? Tangible or intangible resources?

For me, at that time, here's what I listed for my strengths:

- *My years of experience*

- *My strategic, long view and decision-making orientation*

- *My skills in talent management and collaboration*

- *My reputation in my industry*

- *My networks of connections both inside and outside the tech sector*

- *My strong communication skills*

- *My executive presence*

Now let's turn our attention to the other three areas of SWOT.

Determine Your *Weaknesses*

Determine your *weaknesses* by addressing the following questions:

- What do you see as a gap within yourself that may be holding you back from achieving your objective?

- Where could you improve?

- What are you lacking in terms of resources? These factors could include time, talent, treasure, skills, and experiences.

- What weakness do you need to personally improve and that you should augment with someone else?

For me, at that time, here are what I saw as my weaknesses:

- *I had been in healthcare-oriented roles that I might be typecast as only a Healthcare CIO—would another industry be interested in me?*

- *Key people at my former company either had moved on, had retired, or were out of touch.*

- *I still had a full-time job in Chicago, which made it difficult to do an effective search and schedule in-person interviews in the New Jersey area.*

Identify Possible *Opportunities*

Identify possible *opportunities* by addressing the following questions:

- What is a trend or happening outside of your influence that may give you a "leg up" in your industry? (For example, if you want to pursue a career in brain imaging, it will be critical for you to understand that the field of brain imaging will be growing 14 percent in the next 10 years.)

- What environments will be more favorable to women?

- What environments will be more favorable to people of color?

- What outside factors could positively influence your sector? These factors could include government actions, technology innovation, competition, and social, cultural, ethnic, gender, and socioeconomic changes.

For me at that point in my career, I believed my opportunities included:

- *The fact that CIOs were in demand nationwide.*

- *The rise of digital was on a favorable and steep upward trajectory.*

- *Being both a racial minority and a woman was actually a benefit since companies were looking for a diverse hire for their senior leadership teams.*

Identify Possible *Threats*

Identify possible *threats* by addressing the following questions:

- What factors in your Five Fs could hurt your chances for achieving your objective?

- What outside factors could negatively influence your sector? These factors could include government actions, technology upgrades, competition, and social, cultural, ethnic, gender, and socioeconomic changes.

For me at that time, I saw these threats facing me:

- *An increasing number of mergers meant many companies were interested in CIOs with leadership experience at very large corporations, grossing $20 billion or more each year— yet my experience was with a $4 billion-a-year company.*

- *I had to consider the fact that my age could be a factor: companies looking for CIOs might prefer someone who offered my skills and experience but who was 10 years younger than I was.*

Table 4.3 is a blank SWOT analysis to help you answer these questions within the context of the BO and key result *you* are trying to achieve.

TABLE 4.3 List Your SWOTs in the Appropriate Column

Bodacious Objective: _____

Key Result: _____

STRENGTHS	WEAKNESSES	OPPORTUNITIES	THREATS

Complete your SWOT analysis related to your BO and key results now.

As you compile your answers to the SWOT questions, make sure your SWOTs are relevant to your BO and your key results.

For example, if your BO is to open up a restaurant and retire from corporate America in two years, you may have a weakness of not knowing how to swim. But that is not relevant to your opening up a restaurant (unless your desired restaurant location is on a pier jutting out into the ocean!), but if you have another weakness of not knowing the various roles in a restaurant's kitchen—then that is a relevant weakness for your SWOT.

It is also important for you to ensure you include feedback from relevant research for your respective field and from others who you believe are influential or experienced in what you are working on, or those who may know you well enough to speak about your strengths or weaknesses.

As I reviewed my SWOTs, I concluded that my leadership strengths and opportunities as a CIO outweighed both my actual and potential weaknesses and threats. But just to be sure, I enlisted the help of Kaye Foster, my dear friend and business partner, who led the global HR organization at a multinational pharmaceutical company. She and I discussed what I wanted to accomplish and reviewed the resources available to me, and she helped me clarify my thinking to improve a few elements of what I'd envisioned. After that, I was eager to be in the Design step of the EDIT process to design my plan.

My F was family.

My BO was to get home to my husband, Max, in 60 days.

Key results included:

1. *Ensure a smooth transfer of power to the new leader from the job I was leaving in Illinois.*

2. *Sell my Illinois condo.*

3. *Identify job opportunities in New Jersey.*

4. *Continually track and confirm Max's health was improving.*

I concentrated on designing the steps in my plan of action across each key result. For Key Result #3, for example, my plan of action included:

- *Study the current job market in my field.*

- *Select my top recruiters.*

- *Assemble a list of people who might know about job opportunities.*

- *Reconnect with all those who could provide strong references.*

- *Prepare for interviews by making a list of hypothetical questions that companies might ask—and then developing answers that I revised until I felt confident in my responses.*

- *Create a "persona"-based interview to be ready for job interviews assuming different personas would interview me and would be coming at me from different vantage points. For example, a CHRO would likely ask me different questions than a CEO. I had to anticipate the differences (and similarities) in their questions so I could nail the interview.*

Once I finished doing my SWOT analysis and preparing for a new job, I returned to New Jersey to be with my husband—which meant I achieved the first part of my Envision and Design steps. Less than a month after arriving in New Jersey, the rest of the plan started falling into place (or so I thought). I was offered a CIO position with a large medical device company in New Jersey; unfortunately, the role reported to the CFO, which didn't align with my expectations and experience from my prior company. I felt that reporting to the CFO would compromise the ability of the company to truly look at IT (and me) as anything but a cost to reduce, instead of viewing IT and me as an asset to exploit to drive great competitive advantage. At that point in my life, the Fs that were most important to me were family, furthering career, and finances. (Fitness and faith would be unaffected and were therefore OK.) It was the furthering career itself that was the gap due to the reporting arrangement. So I turned down that job offer. I stood on my principles and beliefs, and I kept looking.

As you work on your SWOT analysis, you should continue to identify the weaknesses or threats that can stop you cold, and what you can do/will do to mitigate these areas. You will include these actions in your risk-adjusted plan of action (which we will discuss further in Chapter 6). At the same time, take a deeper look at your strengths and opportunities to see how you can cultivate those qualities to be even bigger and better to help you win.

Being keenly aware of your strengths, weaknesses, opportunities, and threats early on is incredibly important, because knowing these internal qualities about yourself and the external opportunities and threats will help you be prepared in your planning—and winning is about preparation; remember what Louis Pasteur said, "chance favors the prepared mind," and I believe it. Companies that know the SWOTs in their respective industries can look at nearly any situation in an informed and objective manner so they not only can hope for the best, but can understand and prepare their plans of action for what the worst might be so they are not caught off guard. This can also work for you in your EDIT process.

In order to win *When They Say You Won't*: Just as pilots don't take off without a flight plan, neither should you. Create a flight plan for your journey that reflects where you're headed, what milestones you will reach, and how you will know you've arrived.

Chapter 5 picks up on this theme and describes the headwinds and tailwinds that come from your SWOT analysis as factors that may show up and help you accelerate toward your objective or may slow you down.

CHAPTER 5

YOUR HEADWINDS AND TAILWINDS AFFECT YOUR OUTCOMES

First comes thought; then organization of that thought,
into ideas and plans; then transformation
of those plans into reality . . .

—NAPOLEON HILL

In this chapter, you will look at the external forces that shape your journey to win: headwinds and tailwinds. In addition to your objectives and preliminary plan of action, you identified your SWOTs in Chapter 4. Now we will see if any of those are significant enough or serious enough that may make them a game-changing headwind or tailwind.

It is said that when we make plans, God laughs! And Mike Tyson said that everyone has a plan "'til they get punched in the mouth." This is why I seek to have a risk mitigation strategy or a Plan B for those projects that are most important to me. I ask myself, "Hmm, what could go really wrong?" *That risk mitigation gets incorporated into the plan of action, which will make the POA more robust and real.*

You never know when your plan will encounter a dose of unexpected reality. You need to objectively anticipate as many things that could (most likely) go wrong and bake them into the equation, so you will be as well prepared for a worst-case scenario as you would be for a best-case scenario.

INCORPORATING THE IMPACT OF HEADWINDS AND TAILWINDS INTO YOUR PLANS

We spend so much of our time planning and working that we don't always consider the fact that there are events, people, or assumptions about situations that can help us or can impact us in our tracks, like a deep pothole that slows us down or stops us altogether on our journey. I have friends and relatives who assure people that they will get something done, when they haven't factored in what could go wrong. They assume that whatever they speak, life will deliver just what they say as they say it. Then when life delivers a curve ball, there is shock and confusion.

A former client, Uma, is an Indian woman who lived in New Jersey and worked for a manufacturing company. Because of her strong performance in finance, Uma felt she was being groomed for the next position up in the organization. The CEO knew her name, and her CFO at times invited her to speak at board meetings as a way to develop her and give her exposure. He told her that she had a great future at the company and that he felt she was nearing readiness for movement. She knew she was going places. Our engagement was to help her get ready to plan how she would show up in the next 12 to 18 months to do the right things, and to do things right, as she got ready for her anticipated promotion.

As we looked at her POA (among other things), I noted that one goal was to ensure she had sponsors—those influential leaders in an organization who could speak on her behalf as a strong performer and VP candidate. She said, "Daphne, I believe I have two executive sponsors in the company—a woman and a man. The woman, Natalie, is very bright, is highly thought of, and has been an SVP at the company for about a year. She's powerful and delivers on major company commitments and seems to engage really well with me. The man, Eric, is an old soul, is the head of our industrial automation division, and has very high organizational respect, and I work with his team as its finance leader. He has the CEO's ear and will be very impactful to ensure the CEO sees me favorably."

I was comforted to know that she had two sponsors, but I didn't really know if what she was saying was actually so. What could go awry? That she was wrong about these people—and if these leaders were not willing to be her sponsors, she'd have to figure out something else or be doomed. She might need to have a Plan B. So I suggested she go to each of them and confirm they would:

- *Discuss her career aspirations with her*

- *Support her as a contender for this promotion*

- *Give her feedback on how she was doing whenever they see or hear about her performance*

- *Provide her with company insights to help her get ahead*

I also wanted her to get their assurance that they would proactively speak on her behalf during the next 12 to 18 months in her current position.

As part of good sponsor/protégé relations, she needed to ensure their top business needs were supported by her and her team. It is good when your potential sponsors can help you, but it is better when you can also help them in some way—perhaps by sending them an article about their industry or by informing them of something that may be of interest to their personal life, just to show that you care about them, too. Unfortunately, when Uma talked to Natalie and Eric, their time for her wasn't quite as open or flexible as they should have been as real sponsors. Sponsors are willing to spend their precious time with you—during the workday or after hours. They invest their time and their political capital on you. Uma could see that Natalie and Eric were being less open and supportive than she thought they would be.

As things turned out, sponsorship was a headwind for Uma. These leaders were not detractors per se, but they didn't seem to care about really spending their political capital on her. Their attitude was pretty nonchalant. She needed to activate other parts of her plan of action, including getting a 360, doing a DiSC profile (dominance, influence, steadiness, and conscientiousness) to understand her style versus theirs to ensure she was approaching them in a way that aligned with their style, and seeking additional insights from mentors in the organization. That would have taken time.

So instead, her Plan B became to leave the company: she accepted a lateral position somewhere else because she felt she didn't have a handle on her relationships. She simply didn't want to go through the effort to reposition herself, given she felt that 12 months or so was her time frame to get promoted. Natalie and Eric were the two most important people she thought were in her corner. She didn't seek to understand where they were coming from until she needed them, and we didn't get to do a 360, or DISC, or other interventions to see which way the wind was blowing. She felt her choices were to wait it out or to leave. She chose the latter.

When you look at headwinds and tailwinds in relation to a plane taking flight, tailwinds give you support and help you accelerate to get to your destination faster. Conversely, headwinds give you resistance, so it takes longer to reach your destination. Headwinds and tailwinds are a smaller but more concentrated version of SWOTs and represent the most major or likely strengths and opportunities and the most major or likely threats and weaknesses. The most-likely-to-occur positive ones (strengths and opportunities) are tailwinds, and the most-likely-to-occur major negative ones (weaknesses and threats) are headwinds. By focusing on what is likely to occur, you will have a more risk-adjusted plan. Remember from Chapter 4 that SWOTS are internal and external. We will collapse the four SWOTS now into two categories: one tailwind category (internal and external) and one headwind category (internal and external).

- **Headwind.** A headwind is unfavorable and will be internal to your journey (i.e., your personal weaknesses):

    - And/or will be externally oriented and represent your challenges (i.e., your external threats) and is more likely to occur.

    - For an airplane, a headwind traditionally is the wind/jet stream pushing against the nose of the plane, but for the purposes of illustration in this book, it could also be air traffic congestion, causing the plane to take a slower route; or it could be that the gate the plane is assigned is already occupied; or there is disruption on the plane that causes the pilot to have to deal with rude passengers, possibly delaying the on-time arrival of the flight, etc.

- **Tailwind.** A tailwind is favorable and will be internal to your journey (i.e., your strengths):

    - And/or will be externally oriented and represents good favor (i.e., your opportunities) and is more likely to happen.

    - For an airplane, a tailwind traditionally is the actual wind pushing the plane forward from the tail, but for the purposes of this book, it could also represent an experienced pilot who found a faster route, or a plane that arrives early, or an assigned gate that is ready for the plane's arrival, or light air traffic.

Your strengths and weaknesses represent what you have or may not have going for you, personally, that may help or hurt your product, whereas a threat or opportunity represents what might or might not happen externally that may hurt your product. Some of the headwinds and tailwinds are current, while others may be in the future.

"I wish I knew then what I know now" is something I often say when reflecting on mistakes I've made in my career and my personal or professional life. I didn't focus enough on my first marriage, I made mistakes in whom I hired, and I haven't always anticipated the things that could have gone wrong with a large project. My due diligence wasn't always 100 percent. I know that you, too, will make mistakes. Surprises will show up when you least expect them, and they won't always be good surprises. So first of all, identifying risks and mitigating them to the best of one's ability is natural and expected in business, and it should be a natural part of our lives.

Tailwinds and headwinds help you be prepared as you design and execute your objectives. Weaknesses and threats are not positive, and you need to know about both, because unless they are identified and mitigated, they will slow you down. You need to consider them before you embark on a journey, buy a house, say yes to someone who wants to marry you, or agree to a transfer to another division of your company. That advance thinking and plan is called your risk mitigation strategy. You can define it as "I hope all goes well, but just in case, I need to think of the things that could go wrong and bake them into the equation."

I recall getting ready for a compensation discussion with my boss. At the time, I knew my compensation was below market, and I was concerned that was going to continue and that I would get nothing but an excuse about why I had to be below market again, even though I was deemed a high-potential manager with a long career runway. That was a potential threat to my having gender pay equity with the men.

(Being underpaid as a female, as a minority, and as a female minority is another systemic inequity many of us are accustomed to. Women are usually paid 84 percent of what men receive for doing the same job. But the wage gap is narrowing for certain age brackets and demographics, so we are on a good path for the most part.)

My Plan A was to do nothing because my boss would recognize my worth and give me a great compensation improvement and I would accept it. My Plan B was to show my boss my business case and get into a debate with him! Not walk away. Not quit. Not sue for discrimination. I'm told that many men may just walk in with their contribution data and high expectations, so they may not need a Plan B. Most women take what is offered, so I was shaking in my boots when I countered him.

When my boss told me what my compensation was to be, I didn't get bent out of shape. Instead, I reviewed with him the amount of value my team and I had generated for the organization as a result of our solutions, to show my boss that the value we had generated far exceeded the total compensation we were receiving. When I spoke to him about this and shared the math from our great year, and also provided feedback from our business partners, he was speechless. He didn't expect this info. He told me to come back in a few days, and he would share my "new and improved" compensation.

My Plan B worked because I had anticipated a potential problem that is common to women and minorities, I had a Plan B, and that Plan B wasn't just words and emotions. I used the language of the business—money, value, margin, and profit. And it actually worked! (I guess you could say I won when I wasn't sure I would!)

If you are not aware of all the tailwinds that can propel you, you may miss something great around you that can help you achieve your target at a faster rate than would otherwise be possible. Likewise, the headwinds that can slow you down should be known to you as much as is possible so you can avoid them. When you design risks and take proactive steps to mitigate your risks, you will have a better outcome.

With your objectives, key results, and plan of action, you need to think ahead of time about what could help you and what could slow you down in your journey to win when others say you won't.

My niece Alexis has three children and a wonderful husband. But she has high aspirations to win when others say she won't. She and I have spent time together where I informally coach her or send people her way because they may have a skill that she needs. She graduated from nursing school and remembered times when white patients in the hospital in Indiana would say to her that they didn't want a Black nurse, and they rang the bell in their room to request a white nurse. So she's had experiences with those who didn't want her to do her job and clearly didn't want her to win, at least not while helping them heal.

Although her nursing job provided her with income, she wasn't feeling successful or desired or able to fully live her purpose, which was to help people in need while getting a larger home for her family. She had not anticipated that nursing headwind, and she stayed in her job, but she was not happy at all. However, she already had a Plan B that aligned with her purpose. She accelerated her Plan B, which was to become an entrepreneur running a nanny business, due to the lack of childcare in and around her zip code, including a lack of outside childcare for her own young children. Her tailwinds: She knew nurses who wanted to do childcare, and because of her familiarity with her neighborhood, she knew people who needed childcare. Her headwinds: She didn't know how to run a business and didn't know how to organize staffing. But she went after her new vision anyway.

A year after her business was off the ground, she had another objective—to use her science background and help Black women with hair-care products. Aligned with her purpose of helping Black women grow healthy hair, she founded Uniqurl (the product name), which took off like a rocket in the market—reaching $1 million+ in annual sales, even during Covid-19. She was beyond happy! Her nanny business and her hair business are doing well. She has also been able to maintain her Five Fs, and she is able to flex when headwinds come up between Plan A (travel nursing), Plan B (nanny care—which takes more planning to ramp up), and Plan C (producing her hair-care products).

In my own EDIT, one of the roles I played prior to becoming VP IT was as director of IT. I had responsibility for IT solutions for the internal supply chain for J&J consumer products. My main emphasis was in manufacturing, but I didn't know a lot about manufacturing and knew I had to learn on the job.

Part of my plans included the assumption of obvious headwinds; as a woman, a Black woman, and a Black IT woman who was not a manufacturing person on the shop floor, I knew I would find it tough to gain acceptance and trust. Manufacturing facilities are highly technical, engineering driven, tight relationship–oriented, and male dominated. It was rare to see many women on the shop floor, let alone as the director of IT. I recall the plant manager at our J&J liquids plant, James, who wanted to help me win. I wasn't sure why, because he didn't know me or owe me. He was just a good soul that wanted to optimize his plant's capabilities. In a meeting room, he assembled each of his manufacturing line/cell leaders, plus finance, supply chain, and QA, plus some folks who reported to these top leaders.

As James went around the room introducing each person, I walked up to each of them to give respect and shake their hand. Most of them obliged me, most of them looked at me with curiosity, and some even stood up to greet me. (After all, I was a woman in a man's shop! However, I found that even when they stood up, that didn't mean they were welcoming me or would work with me—they were, in some cases, just being polite.) Then one person, when I held out my hand to shake his, didn't shake my hand; he just nodded my way, which sent a negative charge through the room.

But I simply moved on to the next person, a female leader who was the head of plant HR.

I saw that I was facing a rough road, with suppressed hostility, rudeness, or lack of respect, or all three. But from that experience, I knew I had to include time and action steps in my plan of action to allow for the relationship headwinds I saw coming. I already had the headwind of not knowing the manufacturing process, and my POA already allowed for that. In addition, now I knew I would need to build a relationship with each person. That relationship building sought to find common ground and create victories together. It included the following:

1. *Understanding people's backgrounds—both the career and personality of each leader.*

2. *Being aware of their future career desires so I could understand motivations.*

3. *Learning their plant facility hot buttons, so I could approach the leaders from their vantage points and their interests.*

4. *Assigning one of my leaders to work with two leaders who were more clearly not aligned with my working with them. My leader's job would be to create a more impactful and trusting relationship with them, as well as create a joint project in IT that would measurably get at their hot buttons without killing my budget and without suboptimizing the larger plant issues.*

Looking at your headwinds and tailwinds is a critical part of your continued self-exploration EDIT journey. Keep honestly and openly looking at who you are and what is required to help you transform into the person you want to be. That anticipation and honest prethinking of the headwinds and tailwinds could be the difference in your achieving your destiny—or not.

DEVELOPING YOUR RISK-ADJUSTED PLAN OF ACTION

The Design step of EDIT requires you to focus on how you will accomplish the vision and commitment you defined from your Envision step planning. Whether you make a career change or launch a new product or new service, the Design step is necessary to create the change you are seeking. This is the step in the plan that will take you closer to EDIT greatness.

The plan of action represents the actions you will actually take to ensure you achieve your key results, which in turn helps you achieve your objectives. The POA answers this question:

What do you need to do to get there?

That's a big question. Although it is said that a journey begins with the first step, if you don't have an idea about your journey in more detail, then it will be difficult to take the "right" first step. Your objectives were specific, and your key results were more specific. Now your plan of action that you started in Chapter 4 needs even more specificity. The more specific the POA is, the better you can act on the action steps. The Design step is to help you better understand what is needed, so your plan can be built, will be effective, and will work.

You can start with your own mind to answer the question if you have any idea of what you might consider to be some action steps. These may not be perfect—plans rarely are—but try to think of what you believe is needed as much as you can. Do research if you need to about the subject matter—that can include talking to people who have been there and done that. It can also include getting a special coach, or looking at videos on YouTube, or Googling the subject matter to give you more insights. The goal is to identify those action steps (and further define the time frame, resources, money, etc., for those steps) needed to achieve your key results.

Now consider this question:

What could go wrong with your action steps or POA?

What steps do you need to take that will mitigate possible headwinds? You have your bodacious objective, you identified some key results, and you have started identifying the action steps needed to achieve those key results. What headwinds do you think are already there or could pop up in the middle of your executing? What assumptions are you making in your plan that could be a little off? A lot off?

When my team was working with the business on implementing a new IT software product, we put time in the plan for cleansing and transferring the data from the old system to a new one. Since certain business technologies should be about using great data to make great decisions, we knew we had to get the data transfer right. What headwinds did we assume about the data? Did we assume the existing data was accurate, uncorrupted, correctly formatted, without duplications? Or the opposite? The bigger the headwind, the bigger the negative impact. If the data was in great shape, we wouldn't need that much effort or money to cleanse or normalize the data. If it was in poor shape, we would need a lot of effort to greatly improve the data before it was transferred—otherwise we would have "garbage in/garbage out." How likely was it that the data was in great shape, or was middle of the road, or was in poor shape?

Based on the likelihood of any one of those—great shape, OK shape, or poor shape—there are assumptions of time, money, and resources that are on the line if our team is right or wrong about what it will take to extract, transform, and load the data into a data warehouse (where a lot of data sits that can be accessed and shared by multiple users). Normally, there is an issue with data during systems integrations, so we assumed there would be data headwinds and not tailwinds. We made as informed a decision as possible, being on the lookout for a clue that this might be a wild card, and we then allowed for extra time, money, and resources in our plan of action.

We also anticipated some tailwinds: for instance, we might need less time to do process reengineering, since the current "as-is" business process was similar to the "to-be" process; therefore, reconciling any differences might take less time than anticipated.

Either way, however, we needed to be prepared and have contingency plans in order to win.

In addition to what you know, there may be things required to achieve your objective that you don't know, don't have, or have never done. For example, when I was writing this book, I didn't yet know that I was sick—and that I had never before been sick like this. I sure didn't plan that into my writing or my precious plan of action timetable. I had to take time off and get healed so I could continue writing. Sometimes a headwind results in a real delay.

Part of the journey to the Transform step includes getting out of your comfort zone, building new muscles, meeting new people, experiencing new things, and achieving new results. This list you create is just a way to help organize your thinking and then organize your approach. Remember, you committed to your vision, and by extension, you've committed to your objectives, key results, and the POA you are building.

It will take thought and patience to create a fairly complete POA, because the POA you started in Chapter 4 was preliminary. You wrote out your objectives, made them SMART, identified your key results, and began to identify some action steps needed to achieve those key results. However, you didn't sequence them, nor did you risk-adjust them to allow for headwinds or tailwinds. Your POA is what will guide your steps when it is time for you to execute. So let's do that now. What sequence should they be done in? Can you do some of the tasks simultaneously? Etc.

Table 5.1 provides another POA template.

TABLE 5.1 Plan of Action Template

ONE	TWO	THREE	FOUR	FIVE
FIVE Fs Which F will be involved in this objective? Impacts or is impacted?	**OBJECTIVE** What do I want to achieve? (SMART)	**KEY RESULTS (KR)** How will I know I'm on track to achieve my objective?	**KR BY WHEN?** When should this KR be done?	**ACTION STEPS** What needs to be done?

The Five Fs are Faith, Family, Finances, Fitness, and Furthering Career.

SIX	SEVEN	EIGHT	NINE	TEN
AS BY WHEN? **#1** When should this action step start and end by?	**HW or TW or FIVE F IMPACT?** What considerations matter most?	**AS BY WHEN?** **#2** Risk adjusted start/end date	**STAKEHOLDERS NEEDED?** Whose help do I need? When?	**STATUS?** Was this action step successful? What is status? Any new steps identified?

As you look at Table 5.1, you'll see columns you are familiar with from Chapter 4:

- Column 1 is the "Five Fs" column. Based on an objective you have, what Fs are potentially going to be involved (either impacting your objectives or being impacted by your objectives)?

- Column 2 is for naming the specific objective you are focused on and the time frame associated with it.

- Column 3 is for the key results that you specifically need to achieve; otherwise you will not likely be on track to achieve your objective.

- Column 4 (which you didn't use in Chapter 4) is where you will define the date that you believe you must or will achieve that key result you captured in Column 3. Every key result needs to have a date that it should be done by. Make sure you don't write a date that you believe is unrealistic. If you don't know you can achieve it in that time frame, you will not have good outcomes. I recommend a conservative/later date over an aggressive/ sooner one.

- Column 5 is where you will put each appropriate action for each of your key results, which match with that one objective. Every key result needs one or more actions to be completed to achieve the key result in Column 3.

Table 5.1 also includes three new columns:

Column 6 is simply the time frame for which you will start and end each action step. If you have three action steps, for example for your key result, then each action step will have a target start date and target end date. If you achieve the action steps on time, logically you'll achieve the key results on time. When you complete Column 4 and then Column 6 (i.e., the two "start/end date" columns), you will need to look at your dates carefully. Make sure the dates are logical and doable between the key result date and the action step date(s). For example, if it will take five months from today to get all your key results done, but you needed your objective to be met in three months from today, then you have a problem. Likewise, if you won't get your action steps done until one year after the due date for your key results, then you will obviously miss your key results. And we know what will happen if you miss your key results. You will miss your objective. If that happens, after you get over the disappointment, you will need to identify a new date for your objectives and/or streamline your key results to get close to hitting your target date for your key results or your objectives. The idea is to not set dates that don't make sense.

Now you will play around with the timing, sequencing, and priorities. You will sequence your action steps to ensure you have them in priority order based on what must come before others. Look at the start/end date and know which action step has the longest lead time and see if that step can be started earlier than others. See if some things can happen simultaneously and whether they may require more resources to run parallel to another action item. At this point, start adding your dates for your key results (in Column 4) and dates for your action plan (in Column 6). Do that before you continue to the next step. *Do that now.*

Column 7 is next: when you have your dates and they make the best sense to you, Column 7 is where you think about and articulate risks—to help make this a true risk-adjusted plan. Ask yourself, "What could go wrong or right?" You now consider what are the potential headwinds and tailwinds, what is the impact any of your prioritized Five Fs may have on your action steps, and what is the impact your action steps may have on your Five Fs. Will you need to relocate? Work longer hours? Jot your answers down and decide what F they will impact and if you need to add another action step to mitigate that. For example, if it's a family risk, that may also include finances, but it may have a positive impact on furthering your career. Will there be any issues about your family-care situation that may cause your relocation to be delayed or even canceled? Are there any special certifications you will need to achieve your key results and action plans?

When you identify those headwinds that may impact you or your Five Fs, jot down what they are, and think about what you need to do (in terms of perhaps a new action step or date change, etc.) to mitigate that risk. Which of those risks are most likely to occur, and how bad of an impact might it be? Same for tailwinds—which tailwind is most likely to happen where you might catch a lucky break, and what will its impact be? (I tended not to count greatly on tailwinds in my projects—because I got more accustomed to negative surprises than positive ones.)

Column 8 comes next. In the Envision step (in Chapter 2), you assessed the importance and relative health of your Five Fs. Your OKRs are probably related to your Five Fs (e.g., furthering your career, or fitness to lose weight, etc.) and may also impact the other Fs as you seek to achieve your objectives. It's time to include the impact your OKR may have on any of the Five Fs you believe you want to keep healthy or get healthier.

Let's talk about Columns 6, 7, and 8 as a group and ensure you know how they work together.

In Table 5.1, we already know Column 6 is for you to put dates that correspond to the action steps you defined in Column 5. Right? You may have selected those dates without thinking much about the risks your project or your Five Fs may encounter that may cause a delay in reaching those dates. Column 7 is for you to describe "What could go wrong?" (aka headwind) or "How might my objective truly impact my Five Fs, or vice versa?" Once you've thought about the things that could be a headwind, then you use Column 8 to record a new date that reflects the risks you may have just thought about. Then you readjust any sequencing or assumptions that may change with the new dates.

If you have already thought about the risks, and the dates in column 6 are valid with any identified risks—then the dates you put in column 8 are the same as they are in Column 6.

At this point, you will have an even better sequenced and risk-adjusted plan. That will help lead you through your journey to achieving and being! This plan will still change as reality strikes, but it is *your* plan to manage, and you will win when people say you won't. The step to winning is by achieving one objective at a time. The more you can achieve your objectives and key results, the closer you will be to winning. Own it, use it, and change it, as circumstances require. Don't rush to get to Chapter 6. Do a great and complete job with Chapter 5 and Columns 4 through 8. You will focus on the final two columns in Chapter 6.

When you do that, you will have not only a plan of action, but a risk-adjusted plan of action. Remember, you won't be able to predict everything that may go wrong, but as a leader, your past experience probably will give you some idea of how the weak areas may generate a headwind. Plan on being ready to mitigate it if it should happen. Take a moment using your OKR and action plan from Chapter 4 (Table 4.2) and your SWOT from Chapter 4 (Table 4.3) to see which of the SWOTs rise to the level of being a headwind or tailwind and which of your Five Fs' impacts you need to allow for in your plan.

For me, the headwind I had to anticipate from time to time as a project manager and as a CIO was the possibility that the project capital or expense dollars allotted to my project might be at risk to be significantly reduced and reallocated to another project outside of my control. This could happen before the capital was deployed to my project, resulting in the risk that the project would be delayed or canceled. This could happen due to the portfolio management process we used, where money went to the projects that would deliver the best ROIC (return on invested capital). Companies want to allocate money to those projects that will deliver the best return or for those that are required by law or to meet regulatory requirements, especially in health-related organizations like mine.

The required projects were "safe and not likely to be canceled," "discretionary" projects could be canceled. So although the team would have a project plan, we had to look at that headwind and make sure we had done all we needed with our business partners, the CFO, and anyone else who could have a say, to ensure that they deemed that IT project as critical and necessary to help make their numbers. Sometimes there are projects that all seem to deliver great value: the decision to proceed then comes down to the voice of the users and their level of influence to decide which (if any, including mine) would be cut. Our action steps would include reaffirming and redefining the value of the project, as well as scheduling any sidebars/premeetings needed with the leaders of the portfolio management process to ensure our project was in the bag.

As an example of how we had to think about risk adjusting our plan to handle the risk of our project being canceled—consider the following. My digital team wanted to help the R&D organization do drug discovery around the clock—in a handoff-type fashion with the various R&D sites around the world. The benefit was the drug would come to market sooner, and the company would reduce "mean time to revenue" than if they did R&D work only in the United States for 12 hours a day.

- **Key result.** *Deliver on project to enable R&D to do global 24x7 drug development. Proof of concept due by xx/yy.*

- **Action step.** *Drive approval process to ensure capital and resources are secure.*

- **Headwind.** *This is a tight year in the company; certain projects will likely get cut. No impact on Five Fs.*

- **New action steps added.**

  - *Even though it passed the first portfolio management approval process, we will reaffirm value, need, and business support above others.*

  - *Ensure business leader has support and influence to keep project allocation intact.*

We made sure that of all the projects that could be cut, that that one would not be. Having a proactive plan and stakeholder commitment and involvement (and maybe promising doughnuts every Friday) was key to mitigating the chance of a project cut.

This list of action steps and new action steps and new dates will continue to evolve as you know more about your objective. Don't worry; being a winner can be messy, but you just need to make sure you are focusing on your OKRs and not let anything take your eye off them!

Know that how you think impacts what you do. And what you do impacts the outcomes you get. Therefore, to successfully transform to achieve the objective that you defined in Step I's Envision, you need to proactively think about (and capture in your Plan of Action template) those things that need to happen in order for you to achieve your objective as a product manager would. You are driving changes to your product, which is you! How you change your product with your OKRs is up to you, and you will reveal a new version of your product as you go through the steps of EDIT. When you go through the Design step, you are doing your due diligence. For me, due diligence requires four things:

1. **Thoughtfulness.** Think about your prioritized objective(s), what it means to you, and what it will take to win and achieve it. You are thoughtfully using similar tools used in business, i.e., project planning, SWOT, OKRs, etc., but you are using those to get your own personal win when they said you wouldn't.

2. **Resourcefulness.** You may need friends, coaches, experts, business leaders, books, blogs, and podcasts to understand more fully what it will take to win.

3. **Reflection time.** You will need time to research and envision yourself in the situation and spend time on achieving it. Give yourself the time you need to invest in you!

4. **Organization.** You will need time to be able to prioritize the many things that may come at you, seeming to be urgent, but may be less important than your objective. Use your BO/MO/NO approach and see if new objectives that want your time are new bodacious, moderate, or nonessential objectives.

In order to *Win When They Say You Won't*: Understand your headwinds and tailwinds. Forces will help propel you forward, but other forces can push you back. Identify what positive and negative forces may help or hinder you, and create a risk-adjusted plan of action so you are ready. It's the surprise of the sudden negative development that throws others off. But it won't throw you off. Ensure you know who is in your circle and in your corner, as you will need stakeholders to help you win. We will cover that in Chapter 6.

CHAPTER 6

LEARN ALL YOU CAN FROM EVERYONE YOU CAN

If you want to go fast, go alone;
but if you want to go far, go together.

—AFRICAN PROVERB

N one of us can transform by ourselves. And as the product manager of your personal transformation, an essential component of the Design step is to map who your key stakeholders are. In this chapter, we explore how having the right tribe has the potential to propel your goals even further. Throughout this chapter, I describe how to create a *stakeholder map, and I will guide you through the process of designing to have the right people in your life. You will also learn how to identify, assess, and prioritize your stakeholders and plan for how you will engage with them, adding all this into your plan of action.*

When I was younger, I didn't know the value of role models, mentors, coaches, accountability buddies, and sponsors. I didn't know there was a thing called "networking," and I certainly didn't think there were folks who would want to help me win, so I didn't go after them. But the millennial professionals today are some of the most connected and stakeholder-oriented people I have seen. However, even these well-connected millennials will still need to ensure they are connecting with the right people. There will be people who may not be interested in you but will still influence the outcomes of your project, your career, and even your compensation. Still, you are the product manager of your personal transformation, and as we know, products have:

- A market of customers—those who buy/rent and consume what the product offers

- Supporters

- Detractors

- Competitors

As a product going into the market as a new and improved version, you will encounter people who want what you have to offer, who may not want what you have to offer, and those who don't care. And they will all have varying degrees of power and influence over how successful your product will be in the market. Let's see how having a map of stakeholders is critical to your being able to win when they say you won't.

STAKEHOLDERS ARE CRUCIAL TO YOUR SUCCESS

Who are the people who have an interest in your growth and development, and/or may be able to influence your success? It could be your boss, your bank, your fellow employees, your mentor, your former college professor, or your spiritual advisor, for example. Stakeholders include anyone who will speak on your behalf; will pour wisdom, guidance, and support into your life's bucket; has an interest in or is impacted by you as product, or your plan; and/or can influence your journey in any way. Determining as much as possible who these people are and how they feel about you and your project will help you decide how much and what kind of attention you should pay to each of them in order to keep your plan on track. This is sometimes a difficult thing to embrace—that you cannot "go it alone" or that you are not "self-made" and don't need anyone. Yet as we listen to winners we know—most people who win talk about those who helped them along the way.

My sixth-grade teacher, Mrs. Long, introduced me to the "time out" if I played during class or caused other mischief. I learned about consequences of my decisions from her. Mrs. Buckner (the mother of former NBA star Quinn Buckner) was a teacher at my grade school and taught me the importance of understanding history, which I value to this day. Those two teachers were just the first of many people who helped me win, in some way.

There are internal stakeholders, such as a spouse, a partner, a child, work colleagues on your team, a close family member, or a best buddy, who will be affected if you take a larger new job or move to a new city. If the context is strictly your job, then your team, your boss, your peers, your mentor, your sponsor, your CEO, and perhaps the board of directors would be internal stakeholders.

You will also have external stakeholders who may be less affected and may impact your life objective or project less than the internal stakeholders, but they could still be important. You may not know them well but may still need to get their support. These could include suppliers, end users, customers, the community, and professional organizations that are a little further away from your initiative than the internal ones. Their low influence could easily change into high influence—for example, with an acquisition, a new role, or someone whispering in their ear—so their status as an influencer may be fluid.

Here's an example of how I really got the point of the value of stakeholders and how they can affect not only a project but an entire career. When I was making my high-power move across the J&J enterprise (albeit slower than I wanted), I was on my way to J&J's Medical Device & Diagnostic Division, and Connie S. was the president of OCD—Ortho Clinical Diagnostics, one of the companies in MD&D. During my onboarding orientation, Connie told me she was leaving. "Leaving to go to which other J&J company?" I asked.

I was disappointed that she was leaving OCD, but I assumed she was going to be around J&J, which I was glad about. I'd never worked for a female president, and I had accepted the move to this company because I wanted to work for a female president.

She told me she was leaving J&J. "Why?" I asked. She then sat me down and told me about the facts of sponsorship. She hadn't met her revenue quota for a second consecutive year, and she didn't have anyone who would spend influential capital on her to help her get a third chance to hit her targets in the upcoming year. In other words, she didn't have a stakeholder who could be her sponsor and support her.

Sometimes it is an effective strategy to rely only on yourself to drive your own performance. But I believe we should not move alone or in isolation. We can be leading the pack, or we can be part of the pack, but we can't go everywhere alone. It's far better to have other people in your back pocket or on hand to come in on your behalf in case you eventually encounter a tough situation, like Connie encountered. You may at some point need someone to speak on your behalf. Connie didn't have that network of support, so her warning for me— especially as a relative newcomer to J&J—was that I needed to establish my network of contacts and stakeholders early and "keep them warm" so they would always be ready to go to bat for me.

That made me think, "Who were the people in my corner?" After this experience with Connie, I thought about my stakeholders, and as I identified them in my mind—both inside and outside J&J—I realized that some stakeholders I was thinking about would have an interest in me and others would care less. Not all stakeholders who were in my circle would be in my corner.

Also, some stakeholders will have high influence in certain circles about my career, and others will have low influence. I had to make sure I knew who had high influence over my career and what was important to them. For me, those stakeholders were IT people, executives in the J&J ivory tower, and the business leaders I worked closely with. On the outskirts were any non-J&J people who may have been there for me, like my IBM branch manager, Tony Waiken or my desk mates and friends, Maggy and Pat, in Houston. I needed to understand who my stakeholders were and why they were influential. Then I had to ensure they would have a positive influence on my career. The best way for me to do that was to ensure that where appropriate, I had a positive influence on their objectives!

RECOGNIZE THE IMPORTANCE OF PERFORMANCE, IMAGE, AND EXPOSURE

Around the same time that Connie told me about the value of stakeholders, I also learned about *performance, image,* and *exposure* (PIE). Sadly, as an African American young woman, some of the most basic things in business were not shared with me. Many of us who grew up in Black families were not afforded to have executive mothers or fathers who understood what it really takes to win in corporate America. Mom and Dad were more about us being obedient and following guidelines than understanding relationships, politics, or brands. Although many people in the majority may have not had exposure to executive parents, I came to find out that they were given mentors and sponsors to help close the gap faster and more readily than what came to people like me.

At J&J, I was cochair of the African American Leadership Council (AALC)—a Black affinity group that focused on driving more insights, information, and promotions into leadership within the Black professional community at J&J; AALC also helped those majority (white) leaders work closely with us to enable executive sponsorship for Blacks into positions of increasingly higher leadership. One of those things we learned was "It's not only about performance [to our collective surprise], but also about exposure and image."

As we talked about it, it became clear that that's why deals are made on the golf course: those folks playing golf together have a relationship, and exposure to one another, that goes beyond nine to five. They sit together at lunch, or their kids go to the same school: they have things in common. The Black employees were pretty much left out of that—until we realized we needed to focus on more than performance and had to forge a way to understand, improve, or maintain our image, and to establish more meaningful relationships to drive greater exposure.

When you are at a higher level in your career and in your community, excellent performance is assumed. Your performance must have been great all along, or you wouldn't have gotten to a senior-level position. You are likely on par with or maybe a little better than someone at the same level, so it is mostly your brand/image and your exposure to influential leaders that will actually be what differentiates you from others (in other words, that's your competitive advantage, or for many people of color or women, that is our cultural advantage/culture add). It is the combination of your brand (image) and the people who know you and will speak for you (exposure) that will likely determine if or how quickly you go to the next level.

In his book *Empowering Yourself: The Organizational Game Revealed*, Harvey Coleman describes his concept of PIE. I highly recommend his book. Here's my brief synopsis of PIE:

- **Performance ideally** means you do your job very well. You and your boss likely discussed and agreed on performance criteria. Where possible, you deliver earlier than expected, at lower costs than budgeted, and with greater impacts than planned. You don't only meet objectives; you exceed them. You understand the business drivers and are a value-added contributor.

- **Image** is your brand. How do people describe you—in terms of how curious or innovative you are, how you dress, how well you work with others? Are you a servant leader? Do you have empathy for others, and are you a silo buster? Are you always late? Are you confrontational? Do you have integrity? When people find out you will be attending a meeting with them, are they glad, concerned, or indifferent? As a product, your brand is in your "market." And markets will always have a point of view of a product or service they consume or encounter. TV shows get renewed or canceled each year, products get taken off the shelf or placed higher/lower on the shelf, products get repackaged or redesigned, or have a new recipe as a new version of themselves. Products that are very popular may have their price rise because the market values them more than others. So it is the same with our image and our brand. Our image needs to remain high.

- **Exposure** is about whom you know and who knows you. Exposure is the most important element of driving your career forward. You can't get promoted without your boss agreeing. You won't get mentors without them knowing who you are. Who will speak on your behalf when you are not in the room, or not on Zoom, with the others? Performance is table stakes, but exposure is the lifeline that keeps you floating and rising. Exposure can be a two-edged sword: beware! Usually women and minorities tend to be underexposed; and if you are under-exposed, you risk not being known or recommended for an opportunity, because folks have simply never heard of you. On the other hand, if every time someone participates in an extracurricular event or looks at an internal magazine and continually sees you or your name or picture, you risk being overexposed. You may be doing your job very well, but at some point someone will wonder if you are selling yourself too much and not doing your job enough. Exposure is key, but it's the right level of exposure that works.

My former colleague and still friend Connie may have known the principles of PIE, but she sure didn't seem to apply them. I can only imagine that as one of the very few female CEOs at J&J, and the only one in MD&D, she may have felt alone, didn't feel exposure mattered, or maybe was uncertain about how to drive relationships with the men.

There are cases where women help other women—I was also a member of WLI (Women's Leadership Initiative), led by Joanne Gordon. Joanne was a great financial leader and became the CIO of J&J while I was there. Similar to the AALC, WLI helped improve women's leadership and awareness to enable them to get into and stay in leadership positions. Why didn't Connie benefit? I don't recall Connie coming to many of the WLI events, which may be the reason she didn't reap much. She didn't sow much into the value of WLI.

Identify Possible Stakeholders

Table 6.1 is a stakeholder list spreadsheet to help you identify your stakeholders.

The first thing you should do is list every key or influential person by name (in Column 1) and add what role(s) they do or did play in your business or personal life (in Column 2). These influencers can be customers, your boss, and/or your top team leader who served as your go-to in times of challenge or who might have become your successor. It is anyone you assert is key and influential in your life.

In Column 3, assign whether or not you have a real and current relationship: you can assign none (N), low (L), medium (M), or high (H). For example, you might put "none" if that person is a role model you haven't met—yet. Or a neighbor you don't know at all, but you may know about the neighbor and could use her help.

In Column 4, assign the likely "influence" that person may have on your Plan of Action—again, low (L), medium (M), or high (H). Will the person have a high level of influence over resources, money, or the outcomes of your objective? For example, if your boss's name is in Column 1, then I would suspect he would be a high. Your CEO's influence may be high or low, depending on your level in the organization.

In Column 5, assign the level of likely "interest" each person may have in your Plan of Action, again using low, medium, and high. Will the person be highly interested in what you are looking to do? Or just moderately? As you fill in Column 5, keep these questions in mind:

- If you indicated someone will be interested, why will that person be interested in your objectives and key results?

- Will that person be positively or negatively impacted?

TABLE 6.1 Current Relationships				
NAME Influential people in your life	**ROLE** What role do/did they play?	**CURRENT RELATIONSHIP?** How current, productive, and real is the relationship? N/L/M/H	**POTENTIAL INFLUENCE?** Level of influence on your project: L/M/H	**POTENTIAL INTEREST?** Level of interest they will have on your project: L/M/H

- How would you like that person to contribute to the project? (What do you think you may need from that person?) It will be difficult to get a stakeholder to support your objectives if he or she will be highly negatively impacted by the project. But that person still may be interested. You need to know if each person will be interested or not—because that will affect your plan of action. For example:

  ○ Do you need money/capital to start your own business?

  ○ Do you need that person to coach you?

  ○ Do you need that person to support you by picking up your child after school for six months while you complete your degree?

- If you don't have a current and real relationship with the stakeholder, do you need to build one?

Do this stakeholder exercise now. Free form is fine—just make sure you can read your writing!

Bear in mind that the purpose of identifying the individual stakeholders is so you know who they are and can pay attention to them at the right moment so their impact is minimized or maximized depending on their negative or positive influence on your objective. First, you will see if any of them are in your corner (promoters), are not in your corner (detractors), or don't have a point of view (neutral). You will eventually map them into one of the four boxes in Table 6.1, and you will see what category they fall in. Don't do the mapping now. You will do that later in the chapter.

UNDERSTAND THE POWER OF SPONSORS, MENTORS, COACHES, AND ROLE MODELS

As you read about the need for performance and image, remember that the third word in PIE—"exposure"—is important because it is through your exposure to your stakeholders that you win. Stakeholders can be anyone who will invest time, money, wisdom, faith, experience, influence, connections, and other factors to help you win. Let me briefly review the different types of stakeholders, including one type that may not even know he or she is your stakeholder.

Sponsors

Sponsors are people such as CEOs, other C-suite leaders, and high-level community, political, or religious leaders who may (should) know you. They vouch for your character and your performance as you are progressing through your professional career or through different aspirations that you have in your personal life, your community, and educational settings. These sponsors have a high degree of influential capital. Their influence is likely reserved for the most promising of leaders, and they usually reserve their capital for leaders at a higher level whose performance and brand they get to observe. You can trust them to speak on your behalf and suggest your name when you aren't in the room or on Zoom.

When I wanted to join a board, I needed to reach out to my former SVP peer (who was a white male chief human resource officer) to speak on my behalf as a reference. He had high influence on my soon-to-be chairman—they had gone to Harvard together—and he was ready to support my joining a board. He spoke on my behalf to the board chairman.

Even after I achieved the objective of getting on the board, I continue to connect with him on LinkedIn. I call him occasionally to check in, and I send him quick messages congratulating him on his latest achievements. I want him to know that our connection extends beyond what could benefit me at a specific time and I am grateful he served as my sponsor to join a board.

Mentors

Mentors can also be C-suite leaders, board members, other colleagues, community leaders, revered elders in your community, and other stakeholders in your life who will be available to you for regular feedback on a monthly or quarterly basis. You will have fairly easy and regular access to them via periodic in-person meetings or phone or video communication.

When I was in Texas around 1987, ten years after joining IBM, I had a branch manager who was intent on helping me succeed. His name was Tony Waiken (I briefly mentioned him earlier in the chapter). He was a highly successful and older white man who took an interest in my career and wanted to help me win. He saw when I worked well, and he saw my mistakes, but he also saw my love for our customers and my desire to solve problems to uphold IBM's values. He gave me feedback to help me serve our customers even better. When he promoted me, he gave me some advice, the kind of advice a mentor would give you, and I viewed him not only as my mentor, but as a sponsor as well. After all, he spoke on my behalf to his constituents, and he promoted me to a position in Dallas where I had responsibility for teaching new systems engineers how to manage large systems. In the way he spoke to me and the advice he gave to me, he seemed like my dad sending me off to college. He gave me great life management advice, including this:

1. **Know whose career is primary between you and your husband (or partner).** *Whoever has the primary job may have a larger say in when or where you could relocate for a new job. (I never would have thought of that on my own.) He was talking about the Five Fs, and I didn't know it. The family may be impacted by a relocation that comes as a result of furthering your career. In your POA, you would have put your family as an area to focus on to ensure your POA is "risk adjusted." This is a consideration*

he was giving me. "Who's going to decide whether your family should move? Daphne, right now, it's you."

2. **Understand how many nos you're worth.** *There are only so many times you can reject a company's job offers. Tony told me I would be offered many jobs and relocations and I would find something wrong with each one; they wouldn't all be perfect. But he advised me that I could not say no indefinitely—at some point, companies would stop offering. This made perfect sense—it was like me trying to find the perfect spouse who had perfect hair, clothes, finances, fitness, faith, and a private jet lifestyle. At some point, I needed to know what part within an offer was a dealbreaker for me, and what was not, and just say yes.*

3. **Be aware of the differences among role models, mentors, coaches, and sponsors: they are not the same, so be clear on when you need which one.** *If you don't know, then ask one of your stakeholders who has career experience in whatever objectives and key results you're going after and who will look out for your best interests. Identify who is in your life as a role model, a mentor, a coach, or a sponsor. Engage people before you need them, and certainly engage them when you do need them; don't go it alone.*

4. **If you want to win, watch and see which people have the power and winning actions in your organization or team.** *(In the EDIT vernacular, these are role models.) Watch and learn how, why, and when they move. See the patterns and learn from them. Then you will be able to predict how they will move—and then use applied learning to then move better than they might have when you find yourself in a situation that is similar.*

5. **Be ready to play the game, and score points.** *Either you will watch—and earn no points on the board—or you*

will play and get the chance to put points on the board. Know when to move, and when to watch, and know which moves will or will not score you points. (Scoring points is when you achieve a win—could be successfully completing a tough project, landing a big client, beating a competitor, integrating your ERP, launching a new business services function offshore, or leading the pack with revenue, share, margin, customer satisfaction, etc.)

Mentors will shine a light for you on the virtual ground so you know where to step, where the potholes are, and what the culture of the organization or team is, and more. What time does the 8 a.m. meeting really start? Probably at 7:45 a.m., your mentor will inform you. In contrast, a sponsor shines a light on you in a differentiating way so other influential leaders can see you more than they see your peers. The sponsor will use his or her positional capital to go on the record advocating for you, the protégé.

A mentoring or sponsor relationship could last a lifetime. The mentor or sponsor could be inside the company or may be a professional with a similar background who is outside the company. Your mentor or sponsor could also be a person within any profession who understands how to handle the challenges you may be facing.

As a high-potential performer at J&J and the head of the African-American Women's Leadership Council's Affinity Group, I could, with other members of the council, connect with the highest-ranking leaders of J&J. (Note: This group was similar to the AALC I mentioned earlier, but the members were all Black women. We decided that the AAWLC was redundant to the AALC [which had men and women] and combined it with the AALC. We chaired the new combined group with one female cochair [me] and a male cochair [Zack]). Even in 2004, we discussed and sought to influence such issues as Black lives matter; and the high percentage of Black turnover in lower management. We were asked to help change the number of Blacks that made it into senior management and we set targets against a baseline. In support of driving more Blacks into senior management, J&J asked me to help the company create a mentoring program where high-potential senior African Americans would be assigned to high-ranking white leaders who would serve as mentors and sponsors. The relationship was more formal and would sometimes include reverse mentoring, which allowed Black protégés to give back and coach the white mentor or sponsor on business, cultural, or technology topics.

Coaches

Coaches are the people in your life who will be in the trenches with you to help you improve your professional performance at work. For example, you could be assigned to a voice coach to help you with your vocal delivery and presentation style. Another example—we had acting coaches from Second City (where many *Saturday Night Live* actors come from) who would help us know how to "act and look comfortable" on stage when doing a presentation, and how to ad lib when thrown a tough question from the audience we are presenting to. You could also work with a life coach in your personal life to help you develop confidence, or hone conflict management skills, or improve your parenting skills. Coaches will give you one-on-one support to help you improve in areas where you are weak or help you refine your strengths.

You should not mistake the need for training with coaching or mentoring. If you have never managed a team before, you need to go to a management development class. Your mentor or coach will not teach you all you need to know about managing a team. Your coach will help guide or offer advice on the foundation you already have as someone who has gone through management development.

Role Models

Role models are those aspirational "targets" of your attention, whom you look up to and may not ever meet. They may not be influenced by your project, and they may not care. They may have little direct impact on your project, but they may indirectly impact it because you may be encouraged and inspired by their ability to win, their approach to challenges, their level of capability, or any number of other things. As you think about them, you wonder how they might handle your situation, and as a result how you think may reflect a higher or more tactical or more holistic way of thinking, and you may begin to channel them in some ways. Some of my role models include Oprah Winfrey (entrepreneur, ability to scale, give the people what they want), Elon Musk (intellect, risk taking, innovation) and Harriet Tubman (courage and reaching back to pull others forward). I respect the leadership and innovative qualities that I believe each of them brings (or brought) to the table, and I aspire to incorporate their best leadership qualities into my own life.

FIND THE "RIGHT" MENTORS WHO GIVE AUTHENTIC FEEDBACK

I've been asked if mentors should be the same race as the protégé—in my case, as a Black woman, should I have a Black mentor or a mentor of color? Most of my mentors have been either white men and women or Black women. I've been fortunate to also have a few Black men as mentors, but the availability of Black men was lower in my various corporations. Either their levels were not as high as mine (which doesn't mean they could not have been my mentor on a particular issue), or those who were organizationally higher than I seemed either less "available" or less secure. In white corporate America, I've seen Black men be hired to impressive roles, only to find that they just couldn't assimilate or fit in with the culture. Their fault or the company's fault? Each case was different—far too often, they were the ones who were called on the carpet when things got challenging (not the company). Often, Black men are waging their own battles of being the "only" or the "first" Black in their senior leader role, and they were doing what was needed to jump the glass cliff or stay focused on winning at their level. So I found more Black women and white leaders to support me.

I do believe, however, that cross-gender and cross-race mentoring taught me nuances about how to move up in organizations, given that as we go up, we will tend to be surrounded by mostly white men anyway. I've had mentors I selected and some who selected me. I've participated in formal mentoring programs (i.e., J&J) and natural selection mentoring. It can work in multiple ways, but at the end of the day, you want to be a good protégé.

And in regard to mentoring, this is a question I get asked a lot: "How do you ask someone to be your mentor?"

Personally, I found people who I believed were good or great role models, who had values that aligned with mine, and who were in positions at a level that was close to or at the level of responsibility I felt I could eventually achieve. All my mentors were highly regarded and respected leaders, and all were successful.

As a member of WLI and the AALC (and the former AAWLC), I was able to be in the company of senior business leaders. For example, WLI included presidents, senior female officers, and VPs. One of the women at WLI, Karen, was the company group chairman of another part of J&J. She and I connected and worked together on a WLI survey aimed at all J&J women directors and above, to understand their challenges with rising to the next level. She invited me into her office, or we met for lunch.

As we worked on aspects of WLI, I also gave her an idea about how to drive not only gender diversity but also race diversity into leadership ranks. She was intrigued. I shared with her my ideas, and she liked them. At the same time, she asked me how things were going and what my career goals were. Without complaining or disparaging—it's important to never bad-mouth anyone, because you never know whom the people you're speaking to know or in what high places their friends are—I spoke of how I wanted to do something significant for OCD. She told me to find a problem that OCD had, a problem that was big, impossible, valuable, and visible. If I could solve that, my name would be virtually "carved in stone" (not a headstone!).

I took her advice and asked her if I could meet with her again on this specific topic of my career, and she was very open to that. I met with Karen continually, not only about my career, but about other issues as well, because I had free access to her. I found the project I wanted to do; I just had to gather up the courage to do it. To this day, I would still call Karen a mentor.

This isn't how every mentoring situation starts, but if you can find something of interest to both parties (you and your mentor) to serve as an icebreaker, then you can drive a relationship with the benefits of mentorship.

It also works if you share with someone you've seen at a distance something complimentary—perhaps that you admired the speech the person gave, or that you liked an article you read about the person, or that you thought the business results in Q2, for which the person was responsible, were outstanding. Let the person know you would love to pick his or her brain on a certain topic: that is flattering to the leader, and most leaders want to give back to employees or the community, even if they may not already be doing it.

You set up a meeting with them, and then you can spend time listening to their story and their approach to whatever the subject was. Then you seek to get some small advice on the opportunity you are facing. Start small—don't unload everything at the first meeting. Afterward, make sure you reflect on these three questions:

1. "Did I appreciate their time, and did I send them a quick email (not too long) thanking them and specifying what my take-aways were?"

2. "Was I open to trying their suggestions?"

3. "Am I willing to follow up with them in two to four months?"

The answer to all three questions should be yes!

After repeating that cycle and meeting them again (and again) to give them a recap on how their advice helped you, as I did with Karen, they will become a de facto mentor.

Some companies have formal, arranged mentoring opportunities. Talk to HR and find out if your company has that. Sometimes it is for those deemed as high potential. If you are high potential, you will get the tap on the shoulder. I have been asked to coach a high-potential leader in one of my board companies to help prepare her for public board service. The coaching/mentoring opportunity is coming to her.

Other people can simply ask someone to be their mentor, but I've found more times than I can count that the leader in question believes he or she is too busy to be a mentor for yet another person. The way I suggested earlier achieves the same thing, without the formal label of "mentor." Over time, it will be a label you can use for that relationship, but not in the beginning.

However, no matter how you find your mentor or how your mentor finds you, it's very important that whenever your mentor suggests you do something, *do it.* No one wants to advise someone who will not listen and not follow through. That is an easy way to never get on the mentor's calendar again. Even if you had to alter the mentor's suggestion to fit your situation, that's OK. Mentors want to know you are a good protégé.

My dear friend Monica Bertran (a digital leader and former TV broadcaster at Bloomberg) and I were sharing stories about protégés who don't listen. Monica was working for Bloomberg in London when a woman came from Spain to work on the London project management team. This woman was smart, proactive, and eager to learn, and she did well while in London, but then her boss left, and a new boss came in. (As I mentioned earlier in the book, sometimes the person who hired you leaves, and then you have a new boss who "inherited" you, and the new relationship doesn't always work.)

This woman was not ready for the shift and didn't adapt well, because of many factors: the Covid-19 lockdown, her isolation from her family back in Spain, her new boss doling out some of her responsibilities to others, their poor relationship, her getting Covid-19, and more. As a result of all this, she was miserable. The nature of her work was changing, and she didn't know what to do.

Monica stepped in to coach her and talked through a plan with these steps:

1. *Write down her satisfiers/dissatisfiers.*

2. *Define the dream job so they could see the gaps.*

3. *Discuss which of her skills were transferable into other roles.*

4. *Identify who might be willing to sponsor her.*

5. *Speak to her manager about goals and ask for help.*

Monica encouraged her to do some self-reflection and praying, plus she needed to focus on herself more, and not on the negative aspects of her manager.

Monica's protégé seemed eager to move with this plan, but when Monica didn't hear back from her for four months, she figured something was going on. It turned out that she didn't use the tools or the approach they had discussed, and she was now contemplating running away. But she didn't have a plan she was executing or a job to go to.

Remember, we shouldn't run from something, but rather run to something. This woman was about to do the wrong thing. She was still focused on her negative relationship with her boss and not focused on how she could learn from her situation or highlight and showcase her great skills.

The end result? Monica did not see a way forward with a protégé who wouldn't listen to her advice and try to help herself. She is no longer her mentor.

BUILD YOUR STAKEHOLDER MAP

Now that you know the difference between sponsors, mentors, coaches, and role models—and how each type might help you win when others say you won't—let's take another look at the stakeholder assessment introduced in Table 6.1. Let's identify what you will need to do with the various levels of influence or impact your stakeholders have, by building your stakeholder map—see Figure 6.1. Remember you identified in the stakeholder assessment spreadsheet to what degree you believe your stakeholders have influence on your project (L/M/H) and the degree to which they are interested in your project (L/M/H).

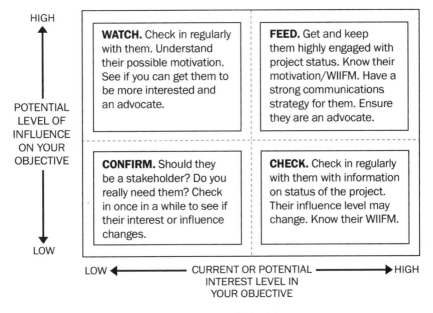

FIGURE 6.1 Your stakeholder map

You will be placing your key influencer's name in the appropriate quadrant based on what you believe the person's level of influence and level of interest will have be. You will use your work in Columns 3 and 4 in the stakeholder assessment to determine where to put the stakeholder on the chart.

Figure 6.1 shows which category people will fall in to help you know how and when to get them engaged: *watch* them, *confirm* them, *check* in with them, or *feed* them.

Instructions for Filling Out the Map

Add your key influencers on your map by placing their initials in one quadrant on the chart based on their level of influence and the level of interest you believe they will have.

1. **Low interest, high influence.** *Watch* them and provide pertinent info to them at key project milestones. Understand where they may be able to influence, and understand their WIIFM (what's in it for me) to see if their interest may grow. You don't want to be caught off guard if they are able to influence the project but don't really care about it

2. **Low interest, low influence.** *Confirm.* Here, not much activity is required. Monitor on occasion to see if the status changes. Confirm if they are even stakeholders.

3. **High interest, low influence.** *Check* in on them on occasion. Their influence may change. Monitor their status.

4. **High interest, high influence.** *Feed.* Manage these stakeholders very closely, understand what motivates them, and keep them highly engaged and informed with regular meetings.

Do you see a pattern? Are most of your stakeholders highly influential but not likely to be interested? Or the other way around? This is another way of positioning your stakeholders into a category for prioritizing your actions.

If you have stakeholders that have low influence but are highly interested, that could be helpful, but you should look to find those stakeholders that can be highly influential *and* interested. Then you will have greater momentum. Using those four categories, you will interact with them based on the interest and influence of each.

Engage with Your Targeted Stakeholders

Now that you know the interest and influence levels of all your possible stakeholders, and you know how supportive each may be of you, it's time to plan your engagement strategy. You need to confirm:

- What you need from them.

- How they may benefit or be affected by your project (WIIFM).

- When it is best to engage with them.

- What your communications will be to them—and the more important they are to your project, the more important your communications are!

You will engage at the right time with the stakeholders based on where you are in your action plan and what your stakeholder needs are. If you have any stakeholders who are high influence/high interest and are clearly detractors (i.e., not in your corner), your strategy for dealing with them will be different than if a stakeholder is an influential promoter.

No matter their status, monitor them to ensure you are aware if their status as an influencer changes.

During my time at Johnson & Johnson, I was disappointed that I had not received a promotion from director to VP in seven years, although it was under that premise that I had joined J&J in 1997. While serving as executive director at one of the J&J companies (OCD), I was part of a conversation where I was told that the company was technically unable to see its profitability in realtime. They had to wait until February each year to see how profitable the prior year was. I thought to myself, this makes no sense. How will the company know which products are selling with the highest margin? Which customers should we raise the price on versus service better? How does the company know if it is offering the right volume discounts to the right customers who are ordering at the right level? I know the company has the data available. I then remembered the conversation with Karen, my mentor, and I said to myself, "Is this the big, visible, valuable, and impossible project she talked about? . . . Yes!"

I immediately volunteered for the opportunity to help the company remedy its low visibility of key data and to help the leaders see their global numbers. Everyone told me this was impossible because the holdup was with the international division of the company: the stakeholders in Europe didn't want to share their data with "big brother" (i.e., the US team). And if we approached the project trying to get a global data project going the traditional way (i.e., starting with the United States first), we would lose the EU team. Clearly, our European colleagues were important stakeholders for our project. "Impossible? Did you say impossible?" was my question. Hmm. I've heard "impossible" before, and I've learned that what is impossible yesterday is merely inevitable today. "Challenge accepted," I said.

I told my boss, "If the problem is in international, I'll start with Europe and then get the data needed from the United States afterward. That way, the folks in Europe won't feel like second-class citizens or like they're at the back of the line." I contacted our European partners and assured them that we were going to find a way to help them track their profitability and then expand our process to the United States, Asia, and Latin America. I gave them the WIIFM. I worked with a team that analyzed their tools, data, and processes. We gained their trust, and we were able to create an app that allowed the relevant sales data to flow from their system into the app with calculations of profit, volume, and other key indicators. After that, they were able to look at a variety of scenarios, chart customers, and create graphs. The entire outcome was positive, and we helped our international colleagues enhance their profitability and performance.

People around me had said it couldn't be done. They told me I couldn't win. I had to do the extraordinary. Two months after I showed my solution to the company group chairman and the

CEO, I was promoted to VP IT. Working with key stakeholders (the VP of sales ops, the VP of sales, the IT department, and others), looking at the challenges from another vantage point (a non-US vantage point), and embracing the wisdom and knowledge of the team were all critical to my success. I never forgot that, and I ensured I was always aware of the power of stakeholders.

My experience is often known as the "glass cliff"—a phenomenon where someone (especially a woman or a minority) is offered a chance to get a leadership position, but it is offered where the stakes are high, it's very visible, and there's a high chance of failure. So you can jump off the cliff, and if things are not done just right, your parachute may not open and you'll have a crash landing—often fatal for your career! In this case, however, my plan worked for me; my company rotated out the sitting CIO, and I was promoted to CIO/VP IT.

Now you can focus on completing the next column (Column 9) from your plan of action template, which you are already familar with. You can see that I have unshaded Columns 9 and 10 in Table 6.2. Use the stakeholder assessment and stakeholder map you just completed (Table 6.1 and Figure 6.1, respectively), and identify the key stakeholders (or other key resources) you believe will help you achieve that key result and put them into your POA, Column 9.

As you look at those added names and timing, decide if you need to add any action steps for that key result to incorporate the stakeholders you are adding. If so, it is now you would risk-adjust the plan again with any changes to your dates, to ensure you are allowing time for actions you will take to connect with or influence those stakeholders.

Column 10 is for you to use as needed, in the way you will find helpful. I recommend you use it *at least* once every two weeks or upon key milestone achievements to capture your perspective on the status of your action steps. You can add another column(s), i.e., like Column 11, if you want to record even more of your key result and action step status as you go through your Iterate step. We'll discuss that more in Step III.

You may find that you have a gap—the influencers/stakeholders you have access to may not be the right ones for your OKRs, or the

TABLE 6.2   Plan of Action—Status/Comments

ONE	TWO	THREE	FOUR	FIVE	SIX
FIVE Fs Which F will be involved in this objective? Impacts or is impacted?	**OBJECTIVE** What do I want to achieve? (SMART)	**KEY RESULTS (KR)** How will I know I'm on track to achieve my objective?	**KR BY WHEN?** When should this KR be done?	**ACTION STEPS** What needs to be done?	**AS BY WHEN? #1** When should this action step start and end by?

The Five Fs are Faith, Family, Finances, Fitness, and Furthering Career.

SEVEN	EIGHT	NINE	TEN	ELEVEN
HW or TW or FIVE F IMPACT? What considerations matter most?	**AS BY WHEN? #2** Risk adjusted start/end date	**STAKEHOLDERS NEEDED?** Whose help do I need? When?	**1ST WEEKLY/ MONTHLY STATUS/ COMMENTS?** Is the status red/ yellow/green/ complete? Any new steps identified?	**2ND WEEKLY/ MONTHLY STATUS/ COMMENTS?** Is the status red/ yellow/green/ complete? Any new steps identified?

ones you have may not be willing to help you to the degree you need, as in the case of Uma (in Chapter 5), who just knew she had those two sponsors to help get her promoted. Modify your POA to help you account for actions needed to feed, watch, check, or confirm your stakeholders. Columns 2, 4, 6, and 8 are the columns that really truly matter. Those contain the dates you are going after. Make sure those dates are solid, real, and risk adjusted. If you don't hit your dates for your action steps (Columns 6 and 8), you may miss hitting your date for your key results (Column 4), which would impact your ability to achieve your SMART Objective (Column 2).

GETTING THE RIGHT STAKEHOLDERS INTO YOUR SPHERE OF INFLUENCE

Now that you know what the various stakeholder types are, determine what kind of stakeholders you currently have and what kind you need to win when people say you won't. How do you get them? How can you find them, attract them, and be positively impacted by them? If you have the highly influential stakeholder that is not positively interested or in your corner, what do you do? If you have the positive kind that is in your corner, how do you engage? Let's unpack these issues one at a time.

How to address the stakeholder gap? Just as you look at any other situation in your life, you look at your desired outcome, identify what stakeholders you need, and look at what resources and tools you have. The negative difference between what you have and what you need (meaning you have fewer positively impactful or influential stakeholders than you need) means you need to supplement your stakeholders with the right ones, and vice versa. You may not have a direct connection with a stakeholder, but someone you know certainly does.

I am coaching a young entrepreneur, Bantu, a former visual effects guru who worked on major movies such as Thor, Children of Men, The Revenant, Guardians of the Galaxy, *and more. He has a game-changing software, intellectual property, and patents that will dramatically disrupt how we watch videos, play games, and shop. He met with me and asked me to get him ready to meet with VCs and angel investors so he could build up his inventory in the video library, sign on more customers, and scale. The people in his normal tribe were not easy to find, and they were not in the mood anyway to invest, given that much of filming and Hollywood studios were shut down due to Covid-19 in 2020. Revenue was not coming in as fast as it used to in the good old days before 2020. He needed access to new stakeholders to invest capital in his company, and I knew some people I could introduce him to. Some of my direct connections became his, and he was able to continue to generate capital for his business.*

Keep your relationships current and authentic, and keep increasing your exposure to others, being authentically interested in them, and you will not need to know everyone to win; you'll just need to know the people you already know. The people you already know will introduce you to other people you need to know. Just make it clear to your influencers what you need.

How can you attract stakeholders who are interested in you? The demand is there for people looking for people with your capabilities. Make yourself discoverable. We are in the age of the Great Resignation. The senior leaders of companies, hiring managers, and private equity and VCs are all looking for great people, great investments, and great companies. With that said, they will not just fall into your lap, at least not all the time. Be discoverable—on LinkedIn, in blogs you write, on podcasts you host or guest-speak on, in magazines you contribute to, and in events you go to—and drop some nuggets of wisdom that make people want to follow you and know who you are. That's part pushing yourself and part networking. When you do that, people will hear about you, your circle of influencers will grow wider, and you will find you have multidimensional stakeholders that will be able to influence outcomes in multiple areas.

You may go directly to someone who is a role model of yours and let that person know you admire his or her work, or you admire some feature about the person, and ask if you can pick the person's brain on something that you believe he or she knows about; or you may just want to glean some of the person's general wisdom. It may take some scheduling, but that meeting—if you spend time listening to the person's advice in the meeting and following up—can lead to that person being a mentor to you. And mentors can sometimes lead to sponsors.

If you are looking for capital for your new business, go to the SBA; go to the chamber of commerce; or ask friends who are entrepreneurs (surely you have at least one) how they got funded, if they can share their pitch deck with you, and if they can introduce you to any of the angels or VC folks. Your CFO or finance leader will likely know the big banks, which will in turn know smaller banks, which will in turn know companies that may invest in women or Black minority firms.

BUILD YOUR PLAN BY KNOWING WHO IS IN YOUR CORNER

It is said that "not everyone who is in your circle is in your corner." There will be people who may not be supportive of you, but they may be highly influential to your success—or to your downfall. You may not always know their hidden intentions. You will need to know who your supporters and detractors are and ensure that you are aware of where and when they may affect your achievements. That's the nature of competition, capitalism, the Olympics, the stock market. In the struggle to win, to matter, and to be great, there will always be folks on the other side. You will win even when you have people working against you, because you will look at competition and microaggressions as just noise, or as information that you can use to counter with planning, stakeholders, plans of action, and measures of success.

I was one of the highest-ranking African Americans in GE, and even though GE had given me a fancy car (a 640xi BMW), provided me high-profile assignments to lead global teams, and arranged audiences with the top 100 corporate officers in the company (one career level above me), that still didn't prevent negative feedback from my detractors.

Being able to achieve in corporate America took more force, strength, cunning, and strategies for me than my white colleagues seemed to need. I understood that I looked different—I was "leading while Black"—and I had my share of casualties. I am a woman in a male-dominated industry, and I was Black in places where there were not many Blacks.

In one case, I was invited to a meeting with some vendors who wanted to sell me their services for software integration. I was running a bit late, and I walked into the conference room where the men were already seated. I said "Good afternoon, all . . . ," but before I could continue, one of the men said, "I'm sorry, but you must be in the wrong room. We are waiting for the SVP, Daphne Jones."

I said to the gentlemen, "And who do you think I am?" This situation is an example of how it is not always assumed that a Black person will be in a high position of power. By the very nature of some form of privilege, the man (and likely the others in the room) assumed the Black person walking in the room could not be Daphne Jones but someone who was in the wrong room. He didn't ask first and clarify; he shot over the bow and felt foolish later. He didn't know me, but years of supremacy and privilege allowed him to make a purely naïve statement, which let me know he was not "naturally" in my corner. The vendors at the meeting wanted my money, but they didn't think I could have been Daphne. Because of their clear lack of preparation and other key business reasons, they didn't get my business.

Sometimes you have to be willing to be a living example of the opposite of what people believe. Then one by one, they get to understand that not everyone with the same or different gender or race will match the stereotype. I encourage all of you to know who is in your corner so you can win.

I didn't cry racism or sexism at every turn, but for leaders at my company who may have had less education or experience than me, but didn't look like me, they just seemed to have an easier time to get funding, hire more employees, or gain access to key opinion leaders when they needed to. I had mentors, but I believe it was my ability to look at situations and define a plan that would help me through the roadblocks and win.

The need for support from stakeholders will never go away—and help is rarely given too soon. We all need help to win, so don't be afraid to ask for it. No one, not even the president of the company, or the president of the United States, does everything alone. And these people still win.

When I was in college, I needed support. When I was a director in my forties and fifties, I needed support. As a new board member, I needed support. And as an experienced board member today, I still need support. Whether you are moving into middle management, thinking of going back to school, or starting your own company, you should always seek to identify your support system of stakeholders and ask them for their input on your journey.

In order to *Win When They Say You Won't*: Identify and include in your plan the key people who can and will speak into your life, are sincerely interested in your development, and can influence your journey. Planning alone won't get you to the Transform step, though, so it's time to tackle the Iterate step and put your risk-adjusted plan to work. That's the topic of Step III.

ITERATE

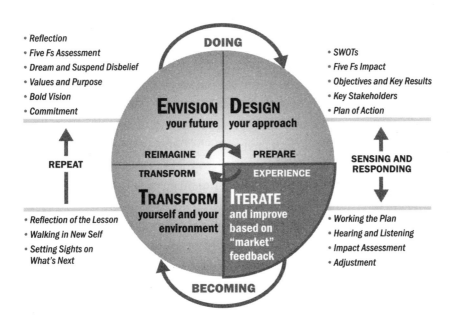

- Reflection
- Five Fs Assessment
- Dream and Suspend Disbelief
- Values and Purpose
- Bold Vision
- Commitment

DOING

- SWOTs
- Five Fs Impact
- Objectives and Key Results
- Key Stakeholders
- Plan of Action

ENVISION your future | DESIGN your approach

REIMAGINE | PREPARE
REPEAT
TRANSFORM | EXPERIENCE

SENSING AND RESPONDING

TRANSFORM yourself and your environment | ITERATE and improve based on "market" feedback

- Reflection of the Lesson
- Walking in New Self
- Setting Sights on What's Next

- Working the Plan
- Hearing and Listening
- Impact Assessment
- Adjustment

BECOMING

By the time you reach Step III, Iterate, you are ready to launch your product plan. This step is where you execute the plan of action you designed and may tweak your actions (go back and forth iterating) in your plan based on feedback from your marketplace—whether that is your boss, your colleagues, your customers, or your family.

The purpose of the Iterate step is to achieve your OKRs by getting feedback from the environment and fixing whatever part of your hypothesis or plan is not working and then trying again, or doubling down on what does work. If your plan of action isn't working (as you planned), you will treat the information you are learning about your plan's effectiveness as just that—information. As my niece Tifani says, "It's not about winning and losing; it's about winning and learning!" Great point, Tif. The learning aspect that is on the other side of winning helps us know how to do things better next time. And the information that we get from our experiences helps us learn. To lose can be a one-time thing, but to learn should be continual: we never want to stop learning.

The consistent action you take as your own product manager is to ensure that your product plan (what we are calling your "plan of action" or POA) remains relevant and accurate in alignment with your vision, OKRs, and stakeholders. If something significant comes up in your professional or personal life after you designed your POA or if more than several quarters have gone by between the writing of your plan and your readiness to execute, you may need to make adjustments to one of three things: your timeline, your resources (money and/or people), or your scope.

In Chapter 7, I walk you through the process of expanding your plans through listening, hearing, and assessing the right feedback. After you learn how to integrate the best feedback, in Chapter 8, you will understand the power of moving from being stuck to unstuck to continue moving forward in your goals. Finally in Chapter 9, you will dive into one of my favorite principles—perseverance—and learn how to keep going when you are discouraged or lose motivation. I view Supreme Court Justice Ketanji Brown as a perfect example of perseverance in this chapter.

Every two weeks or monthly, set aside 30–45 minutes to review your plan and make sure you are executing it, whether you are waiting for a reply from a stakeholder or other resource, modifying your actions and behavior, or modifying your plan in real time. A plan that you don't adhere to or course-correct is merely words on a screen that have no impact. Remind yourself why you are going after your objective and stay focused on it. Remember, you can only change where you are by taking the first step. To drive personal change and transformation takes what I call the Five Cs of transformation:

1. Know your *cause* (this is your vision).

2. *Commit* to your vision (your commitment statement).

3. Have *clarity* on your objectives (your prioritized Bos/Mos/Nos).

4. Have *courage* to execute your objectives through ups and downs (iterate and persevere).

5. *Continue* to learn, grow, and improve (seek continuous improvement by choosing your next EDIT).

By this point in the book, you have gone through the first three Cs and are sitting at the threshold of courage, where you will iterate and persevere (or pivot). This is the time when you will begin to move from merely "doing" what you have always done, to sensing and responding to the feedback from the market so you can "become" what you have envisioned in your purpose.

CHAPTER 7

LISTENING, HEARING, AND IMPROVING YOUR PLAN TO WIN!

I have not failed; I've found 10,000 ways that won't work.

—THOMAS EDISON

This chapter begins the critical step where all the discovery, planning, and diligence you did in Step II, Design, comes alive and you get to see how what you have designed for your personal product transformation functions in real life, not on your Excel spreadsheet. In Design thinking, we therefore call this mode "testing the prototype." Developers use this mode to see if things work as designed or if there are assumptions that may need to be altered. Design thinking is meant to be iterative, discovering and addressing issues just in time, and iteratively. This step is going to be transformative for you. This is the place where you may get tired and wonder if it's worth it. The answer is yes—your purpose is bigger and more important than most challenges you will encounter. Throughout this chapter, you will learn an essential skill in the Iterate step, which is learning to hear, listen, and assess. You will learn how to look at three aspects of answering the question, "How am I doing?"

1. Why feedback is critical, and where it can come from

2. When to get feedback

3. How to know where you stand

EXPANDING YOUR PLANS THROUGH HEARING, LISTENING, AND ASSESSING FEEDBACK

Paramount to your success is getting feedback about your product, your services, or yourself—from people who matter, people you respect, or even those whom you may not respect but who may wield huge influence on your outcomes. Feedback may come from data that shows objectively how you are doing, whether it be a weigh scale or a grade in a class, or it can come from a group of people who are your stakeholders (as discussed in Chapter 6), providing you their take on your performance, behavior, or leadership. It may come from your own perception of how you feel, or an accountability buddy who holds you accountable for meeting your commitments. In the execution of your plan, this feedback is necessary for you to seek the answer to the questions, "How am I doing? Am I winning?"

Your feedback will be either leading indicators or lagging indicators. If you're not already familiar with these terms, a *leading indicator* is a predictive measurement that gives an early idea of how something may go before you actually measure the milestone achievement. Are you likely to hit your target?

For example, in the earlier objective to be promoted to divisional VP in three years, I described several key results that needed to be met to position you as being ready for divisional VP. One of the key results was for you and your team to deliver results two months early and deliver it at 3 percent under budget. A leading indicator in this example will be the percentage of times you as the project sponsor approved out-of-scope or unplanned changes to be done for this project versus the amount of asks. So if there were 100 requests, and you approved 25, then you have a 25 percent occurrence rate of unplanned approved change requests. Every change request has the chance of making your budget run over, so implementing at 3 percent lower than the anticipated cost may not happen, because you're approving one out of four requests. That leading indicator will let you know you may run over budget. But you may also have another leading indicator that shows you are slashing other costs at a faster rate than you are approving new ones. Another leading indicator is the consistency with which you are receiving positive feedback about your 360, or other performance milestones, and that you are being seen more as a VP than ever before.

A *lagging indicator* is an outcome measurement—that is, what you measure after you have reached your milestone. For instance, did you hit your 3 percent target or not? Lagging indicators record what happened, whereas leading indicators can help you see what might happen and can influence change before the fact. If you see your leading indicators are not looking so favorable, you can change something in your approach, and see if improves your leading indicators.

When you change your approach on your project in the right direction, then your lagging indicators should come out more in your favor. Begin to think about what leading indicators you need to know about and measure so you are not surprised at the end of the month or end of the project (which is way too late) and end up way off budget, as your lagging indicators will show when you measure them.

The indicators can come from your stakeholders—the stakeholder list and map you created in Chapter 6 will be important to use here to determine whom you seek to get feedback from—someone who has high interest and/or high influence in your career or life. It may be one person, or it may be a group.

Feedback may come not only from people. Feedback may come through raw computed data, as in the previous example about how many scope changes your team is approving, or it may come from an external market based on a customer trial you are running in support of your objectives. It may come from your family members when they see how you are measuring up to your commitment to spend more time with your children or your spouse or partner each week, because that F was not initially as strong as it could be. Your feedback might come as a result of those postgraduate college applications you filled out for a master's degree program, or from the scale as you look to lose weight, or from your team as you give your first market-segmentation presentation. The feedback you seek will help you know how you are doing as you make your way toward nailing your key results that help you achieve your objectives.

No matter the source, the medium, or the timing, use your leading or lagging indicators and feedback to hear and listen. If you don't
measure where you are, you won't know if there are changes that need
to be made. Are you on track to winning, or are you not? How will you
know? You can't fix what you don't measure, and you can't measure
what you don't see. And you can win when you know where you stand,
because you will make the right adjustments and find a way to win.

Also, knowing where you stand early in your game is important
so that you can address the trajectory you're currently on. You have
defined an objective, so the key results point your actions in a direction
so you hit the objective target. When you know early—for instance,
in the first phase of your project—that you are off target, if you don't
change your actions, reaching your planned outcome will be increasingly harder to reach. Like a ship on the ocean, your trajectory is set
unless you fix it early. Either you'll hit your target, or you could met-
aphorically blow it by 50 miles. You will be able to see the trajectory
you are on and adjust it so you can be closer to winning your objective.

For instance, if you are going to make a sales target of $10 million
for the year, you should probably be hitting $5 million during the first
six months and $5 million during the second six months—unless,
of course, your business is back-end skewed. The sooner you know
how close to or far from your $5 million goal you are, the more likely
you can fix the root cause and hit the target. There are times you may
choose not to hear feedback or know where you stand, because you
are afraid to hear the truth, or you may not accept that you have a
blind spot. Don't let that happen to you. Know what's going on.

*While I was a VP, I was coaching someone in another company
who had a similar responsibility to that of one of my peers.
That responsibility was to drive the IT leadership development
program, which is how companies not only develop functional
capabilities (such as technical prowess), but also drive general
leadership (problem solving, critical thinking, leading others),
so the people who are in these programs will be groomed to be
senior leaders with a leadership breadth and technical depth.*

The woman I was coaching felt she was doing well in her company and was doing a great job of helping the young employees get assignments that focused very heavily on technology skills, but she didn't keep leadership as an equally important area to focus on. Someone in her type of role shouldn't only care about IT but should also care for the business/IT leaders that these young stars would eventually end up working with. Business feedback is essential.

She heard the feedback from the business, but she didn't listen. She didn't realize it, but she had a blind spot: she felt that she knew best and that her business partners didn't know what was best for them.

She finally listened to the feedback, and over the following six months, she changed the program to be more balanced. She did a win-win for her career, for her young recruits, and for the business. The business was more aligned with her, and the young recruits were seen as more valuable with broader and more transferable skills. She continued to drive value for the company.

It is that blind spot that can prevent you from really being your best. In getting feedback, you want people to help you see where you are blind, so you can see what they see, get better, and grow.

WHEN SHOULD FEEDBACK HAPPEN?

During Step II (Design), you identified in your plan of action, an action step for each key result. You will likely go a few weeks in working your plan in Step III (Iterate) to see where best you should get feedback and put that as an action step in your plan. Even if you decided during the Design step where you would get feedback, you can use the Iterate step to adjust your feedback plan if needed.

Your plan of action is not chiseled in granite; rather, it is a living and breathing artifact that you will adjust and change based on the results you are generating or the feedback you are receiving. Like life, it may be messy and imperfect. You will change it from time to time.

That is the nature of designing and iterating. You will seek feedback as part of the nature of your work. Your feedback may come biweekly as you execute on your action steps. You won't act in isolation but with other people. You will know by the nature of your actions how you are doing, and if it is not clear, you will ask and you will go back to your plan and modify as needed.

Five F alert! Part of understanding "How am I doing?" includes checking on your Five Fs. Is your POA having a negative or positive impact on them? *Or* are they having an impact on your plan of action? Checking on them should happen right in the middle of your action steps. You are able to see now if those assumptions or actions about your Five Fs are or are not materializing. Feedback can happen anytime, and the more you know about your POA status, the better your outcome will be. Your Five Fs are still there, and they are just as important now as you said they were earlier. Make sure they are tended to, because your Five Fs are part of how you are doing.

ALWAYS KNOW WHERE YOU STAND

In addition to knowing whom to listen to and when to check on the status of your key results, you should also know where you stand in your pursuit of any objective. One way to know where you stand is via feedback from your stakeholders, the market, or data. However, as the product manager of your product transformation project, you will want to have your own assessment of where you stand and compare it against what you are hearing or seeing in the market.

One of my friends is the CHRO for a $2 billion company. For at least four years, she has been driving the company's diversity mix, to get top talent and have a framework for winning in the market via this transformation. The CEO is skeptical about this work, and he was receiving feedback from his senior leaders that they couldn't find diverse talent. My friend, who is steeped in the *belief that data tells the truth even when others don't, went to work on providing the data to the CEO. In one data point, she found that the company had been recruiting at a Black technology organization annual event over four years and had interviewed nearly 300 diverse candidates. Yet the conversion rate of the hiring was a mere 1 percent.*

Now armed with that data, the CEO knows where his diversity hiring efforts stand (and, in part, his own cultural transformation trajectory); he also now knows whom he can hold accountable (senior business leaders) to drive the cultural transformation necessary to win in the market. The key for the CEO and you is to know where you stand with your key results, identify what you believe is the root cause of any issues, and set a plan to address the root cause and remeasure again in some period of time.

You can use this same approach in your plan by simply asking yourself, "I said I was going to do X by a certain date; am I still going to hit X by that date?" This question is crucial because you want to know if you will be able to honor the commitment you made to yourself (or your family or your team). If you let any part of your project slip beyond repair for reasons that are not acceptable to you, this could have a negative impact on your self-esteem and confidence, and it may impact your desired career momentum.

Use Table 7.1 to see whether or not or to what degree your key results are performing as expected per your POA. Do this monthly or bimonthly, depending on the volatility of your OKRs and whether you will have insights that give you the feedback required to assess.

You must always know where you stand and then determine what to do about it.

TABLE 7.1 Template for Grading System for OKR Assessment

Objectives	Step 3: Objectives (Great/ OK/Poor)	Key Results (KR)	Step 2: Key Result (Great/ OK/Poor)	Action Steps for Each Key Result	Step 1: Action Steps (Great/ OK/Poor)
1. VP 3 yrs	Great	1. Lead 2 big projects	Great	1. Dev plan w boss	Great
				2. Review portfolio	OK
				3. Perf object-ives	Great
2. Lose 50lbs	Poor	1. See Dr. and research	Poor	1. Dr. appt sched.	Poor
				2. Healthy eating blogs	Poor

THIRD: Assess how your objectives are doing right now based on how your key results are doing		**SECOND:** Assess how your key results are doing right now based on how your action steps are doing	**FIRST:** Assess how your action steps are doing.

Step 1. Assess the Health of Your Action Items

The way you will know where you stand overall will be by looking at your OKRs and your action steps (as in Table 7.1) on a regular basis, giving them a grade of sorts that represents how well they are doing based on your plan. The grades are *great, OK,* and *poor.* If you don't look at your progress on the various action steps on a regular basis, you may forget where you are and what is at risk.

Note: The assignment of "great," "OK," or "poor" is subject to your personal assessment and interpretation of where your OKRs stand. The assignment suggestions may not fit your situation 100 percent—and are not mathematically contrived—hence your use of personal judgment will be important.

We know that your objectives will depend on your achieving your key results, and your key results depend on your achieving your action steps. So to determine how your key results are going, you have to look at how your action steps are coming along. You will assign a grade of either great, OK, or poor to your action steps, designating whether they are on track 100 percent (great), slightly at risk (OK), or totally off track (poor).

Key point: These grades *do not* measure how well defined or clear your key results or action steps are; instead, they mean that the level of achievement you wanted either is going as expected or is not. You are to assume your key results and action steps are good, and if they need to be tweaked or redefined, you are always able to do that. But this assessment is on whether or not they are on track. OK? Let's go.

Start with your action steps to assess how they are coming along. Looking at each action step, see if you are on track or not for each one by indicating great, OK, or poor on the corresponding action step line "Status" column of your POA. Go through each one of your action steps using the following guide to depict the overall health of your action steps.

Your action step is doing great if/when the following is true:

- You have achieved or definitely will achieve the action step you have defined.

- You do not need to take any mitigating steps to achieve this action step.

Your action step is doing OK if/when the following is true:

- You have a 50 percent or greater chance of achieving the action step.

- You have confidence there are steps you can take (e.g., add resources, simplify action steps) that will not put your key result at risk.

Your action step is doing poorly if/when the following is basically true:

- You have missed or definitely will miss completing the action that was planned by the planned criteria (e.g., date, cost, people, or other factors).

- You may complete the action step, but it will be of poor quality and virtually not effective.

- You do not believe there will be any mitigating steps you can take to hit your action step's target date or meet other criteria.

Now that you have done this for all your action steps, take an overall look and see how they compare with the corresponding key results.

Step 2. Assess the Health of Your Key Results

Your key result is doing great if/when the following is true:

- You are on track for achieving your key result, based on your action items.

- You have already achieved your key result.

- You do not see anything on the horizon for the next one or two months (or other important time frame) that may put your key result in jeopardy.

Your key result is doing OK if/when the following is true:

- You have not missed your expected milestone, but you may have missed a key action that was required to hit your key result. Yet you feel you still have a chance to do what was expected to hit your key result.

- Action is needed on some or all of your action items, but you are not behind schedule, over budget, or needing resources . . . at least, not yet.

- You have identified a risk that is manifesting itself into your OKR, you may or may not have planned for it—and it could begin or has already begun to affect your project in some way, but it has not hampered the project in a significant way yet.

Your key result is doing poorly if/when the following is true:

- You have missed/will definitely miss your expected key milestone date associated with your key result.

- You have not done all the required actions on your POA that relate to your key result.

- A dependency or outcome you expected to help you achieve your key result is not going to occur.

- A key risk you did or didn't plan for has developed and is turning your plan upside down.

- Missing any of the previous items will result in the key result being late, being more expensive, and/or requiring more resources, putting your objective at risk.

- You probably need to redefine your dates, costs, and/or resources to get back on track.

Step 3. Assess the Health of Your Objective

You will assign a grade to your objective based on the overall health of your key results (again, great, OK, or poor). If all your key results are poor, then it is likely your objective is in jeopardy. If all your key results are great, then it is likely your objective is still on track.

Objectives are not based on a fixed formula. They are based on how well you achieve your key results, but they are also based on circumstances that may be out of your control. Your role is to keep focused on what you and your experienced, influential, and interested stakeholders believe will be required for you to achieve your objective.

Step 4. Now Decide What You Will Do, If Anything

Reflect on what the assessment means to your OKRs and what you need to do about them. Answer these questions:

- Are you on track to achieve your objective?

- How do you know?

- Are the key results that you're focused on going according to your plan of action?

- What is not going to get done as you expected?

- Are the reasons for this slippage within or outside your control?

- If they are within your control, which adjustments will you make to hit your target?

- If they are outside your control, what will you seek to positively influence the cause of the slippage?

- If you are not able to influence the cause of the slippage, what do you need to adjust in your plan of action or your key results so that you can keep moving forward? Your dates? Your stakeholders or team? Your objective?

If your key results in your project are not going according to plan, now may be a good time to get your stakeholders involved again and ask for their thoughts or suggestions. Perhaps a threat you anticipated has materialized and you may simply have to adjust your dates, or you already had adjusted your dates, but you now realize they need to be adjusted more. Sometimes the intervention to get back on track is light; sometimes it's more serious. Your stakeholders will help you assess where you are, because if they are the right stakeholders, they will know, since they've been in tough situations before. When you fall down, remember you've fallen before, and you got back up before. You have to get back up now.

During my time working at a large pharma company I needed help from one of my stakeholders, Betty Gordon. Betty was a board member at a utility company and at my company. She is one of the smartest people I know. I was on the hook for delivering a new SAP enterprise resource planning system (ERP); however, it wasn't approved yet. The SVP of manufacturing had quit. We had obsolete, disconnected systems that didn't talk to each other, and while these systems optimized how their respective plants ran, these similar but different systems across our North American plants were suboptimizing how the entire enterprise would operate from a manufacturing efficiency standpoint.

We were unable to get a complete automated picture of the status of manufacturing, where we could save with consolidating materials and supply chain, reduce back orders across the network, etc. If we didn't do something, our business would suffer, and we would be at a high-level risk of not being able to restore a system if it failed. We were dealing with multiple failure points, and if they were to really occur, that would serve as a perfect storm. The issue is, not many of the business leaders wanted to spend time or money on big enterprise solutions.

This is where Betty came in. I needed an intervention and guidance. I needed to figure out how to ensure the organization realized the enterprise risk at hand, and with Betty as the chair

*of the board's audit committee (where risk management gover-
nance is one of several accountabilities), I had a chance. The
rest of the story is history: by "simply" asking the right questions,
she helped make the enterprise realize that this was indeed an
enterprise issue and made sure there was a joint focus on it at
the board level to help usher past reluctant personalities, and she
got it approved. I didn't know how to get this massive program off
the ground in the absence of an SVP of manufacturing, but my
stakeholder Betty, who had large influence as a board member
and had high interest in the success of this ERP solution, helped
make a positive difference.*

In the moment of anguish and challenge when your key results
are slipping because your action steps are slipping, take a look at the
questions from earlier, and answer them. Whether or not the issue
is in your control, do not let your emotions get you tangled up. Stay
calm, and seek support and advice from whoever is best equipped to
understand the challenge and is willing to help fix it.

YOUR STAKEHOLDERS WILL HELP
YOU SEE YOUR BLIND SPOTS

Your stakeholders will help you get things done, provide feedback, and
help you move obstacles out of the way. None of us has ever achieved
absolutely everything on our own. It's through the provision of products, services, advice, and counsel from others that we have been able
to advance and win when people say we won't. It will be important for
you to communicate your vision and objectives with your key stakeholders, and you should rely on them to provide you with input or
feedback to compensate for any blind spots.

One of the concepts that has helped me see my blind spots
throughout my career is the Johari window, shown in Figure 7.1. The
tool in the Johari window can help you work with your stakeholders
to understand the difference between how you see yourself and how

others see you. The window can help you remove the blindfold so you can see those gifts or challenges that can affect your success, and you can work that information into your plan of action or into how you work and "show up" every day.

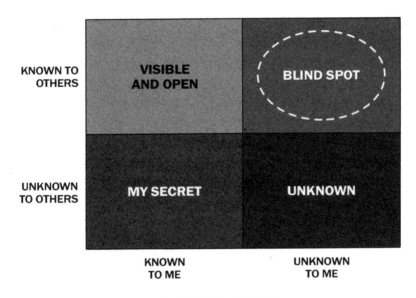

FIGURE 7.1 Johari window

Essentially, the Johari window shows you how you look at information based on the vantage point of yourself or the vantage point of others. We don't always know what other people see. But they react to what they see and perceive of us. When we don't know what they see, we are acting from a position of weakness and are operating in a blind spot. When you are cognizant of how others see you versus how you see yourself, that is the beginning of emotional intelligence. After you are aware of your behaviors and can control or alter them based on the situation, you are moving to a more mature place of leadership and self-awareness. Although we won't be focusing on all the window-panes (just the blind spot), you might want to take a moment and learn about the Johari window to let you see how information about you can be categorized in interpersonal settings.

Here are the four windowpanes:

- **Open.** This pane contains information about your behaviors or actions that is public or known. What do people know about your behaviors that you also know? Knowing is good; being able to control and manage them is better.

- **Blind spot.** This pane contains information about your behaviors that others know but you are not aware of. For example, do you interrupt people while they are talking? You may not be aware of it, but others certainly are. When you have habits, attitudes, behaviors, or mindsets and are not aware of how others assess and respond to you, these are your blind spots. A blind spot is usually a disadvantage. We all have them. The more you know about your blind spots, the sooner they can move to the visible and open section of the window, and you will be at less of a disadvantage than before and can address them. Remember, you can't fix what you can't measure, and you can't measure what you don't see. This windowpane is our focus in the EDIT process.

- **Hidden.** This pane contains information that you know about but may keep hidden from others. These include your ambitions, feelings, political affiliation, skills, and more that you choose to keep to yourself.

- **Unknown.** This pane contains the information, skills, talents, childhood traumas, info about family history, etc., that you may not remember or know about, and neither does anyone else. But these things can still affect how you behave and live.

As a leader in an organization, you should seek access to various tools that help you understand more about yourself and how you are perceived. Some commonly used tools include the 360 review, the DiSC profile (dominance, influence, steadiness, and conscientiousness), Gallup Strengthsfinder, and Myers-Briggs. For example, a 360 review provides you with information about your style, leadership, collaboration, and more from the vantage points of people who see a 360-degree view of you—that is, your boss, your business partners, your clients, your peers, and your employees. Whoever you are to one is likely to show up in a similar way to others. If you are impatient with others, for example—that will show up when you are working with your team, how you express yourself when meeting with your peers, etc.

When under the support of HR, you get an assessment of how people see you, and as importantly, if they see you differently than you see yourself. You learn what your blind spot is, and the tools provide recommendations for how to review those results and take action. For example, if you find out that you seem to be impatient, you will get an idea of what additional development you may need, possibly probing back to earlier career or life drama. If your blind spot is left unaddressed, it may distract people from seeing your winning moves and you won't have the power to change their perception about you.

When I was in my second CIO job, one of my blind spots was that I was a very inclusive communicator—a nice way of saying I talked too much. I had a business partner who sat with me in our leadership meetings, and he suggested to me (privately) that my speaking so much actually caused people to shut me out. I didn't know that, although I felt ignored at times but didn't quite know why.

I had to look at my motivation for this, and after some time reflecting where that habit came from, I surmised it came from my past—from when my high school guidance counselor told me as a Black girl, I would never get into college or successfully graduate from one, let alone become an executive. My talking a lot was my way of showing folks how much I knew, because I felt people (including myself) thought I was too young, too female, too Black, and too inexperienced to be able to succeed in my job. Little did I realize that talking so much ended up proving the point.

My business partner suggested I use an approach called WAIT—which stands for "Why am I talking?"—and to use it whenever I wanted to make many comments. WAIT made me reflect each time I wanted to talk. My blind spot was no longer a blind spot and ka-ching! . . . I had advanced another step up in my move to winning when they say I won't.

Blind spots aren't necessarily negative, though.

I had a Hispanic client who was very strong at giving presentations, but she didn't think she was. Every time she spoke at a conference or meeting, people came up to her to give her great feedback. She didn't listen or believe them and was always the last person who would be willing to do a business review about her function.

Then, after attending Toastmasters, she was given positive feedback, and videos of her talking. She finally believed. This gift of hers was no longer a blind spot, and she began to walk in her gift. As she began to become more comfortable with her speaking ability, and more important, with the positive motivating impact it had on audiences, she decided to turn what was once her perceived weakness into a coaching service to provide to teens who are not comfortable speaking before audiences.

She told me she had been afraid to speak in public for a long time partially because of the ridicule she received when she was in high school by other kids when she did a recitation or read aloud. Her Hispanic accent was funny to some of the kids, and she never got over it. She believed the cruel things they said, and that stunted her desire to speak in public. Being in a business role forced her to speak, but she did it only when she had to! She realized that leadership opportunities come to those who can be comfortable and effective before an audience. Now she specializes in helping kids overcome the same fear she had.

What was invisible can become visible. The intangible can become tangible. If you know now what you didn't know then, you can be empowered to win. Have you ever been given feedback about you that surprised you? That may have been your blind spot being revealed to you! It is said that feedback is a gift. Say thank you!

Use Feedback from Your Stakeholders

Once you know what your blind spots are, you can try to improve as you are working through your plan. When you invite stakeholders into your journey, you want them to provide feedback on your performance and how you are showing up in your environment. You won't win if you don't know.

There are three critical parts to incorporating feedback from your stakeholders, described in the following sections.

Asking for and Receiving Feedback

There are probably a dozen ways of asking for feedback. Before you begin, think about what you'd like to know, and ensure it is related to the performance you are demonstrating either technically or emotionally, socially, and professionally as it relates to your OKRs. Know which people matter the most to where you are in your plan of action. You created a stakeholder list. Not all the stakeholders are important right now, but some are. Know who those are that matter right now.

One effective way I recommend can be used when the stakeholder has firsthand and observable insights into what you are doing and how you are doing it. The idea is to set up regular feedback sessions and use the *start/stop/continue* method. For example, I asked my services business partner Jim up front to give me honest feedback and to focus on how I can be better as a business partner and provider of solutions in the future. He told me to *start* learning more deeply about his service staff needs, *stop* letting my technology team work at odds with his team, and *continue* helping his team understand more of what the external customers pain points were. I didn't want to have blind spots going forward where I wasn't aware of how he was perceiving me or my team. One of the great outcomes—an outcome that resulted from my working with him—was my being appointed to drive a significant and strategic project for GE Healthcare.

Another way I recommend is to ask stakeholders to participate in an anonymous survey instrument—you won't know who said what, but you can get more quantity (and quality) of information with less effort. There is less personal interaction with you and your stakeholder, but you may get more insights in bulk than by spending time in one-on-ones. The survey can have yes/no questions and then ask for comments on your strengths and opportunity areas.

Being Open and Grateful for the Feedback

When you are getting feedback, whether in person or via an instrument, it is important first to be open. This means that your mind has accepted that you can learn something from others about how you are doing, and that you can get better and move closer to your win if you can improve particular aspects of your performance, competencies, approaches, and assumptions.

Go into the feedback receipt with a sense of gratefulness that you are getting what others may not get—a chance to improve, be better, grow, and, yes, win! The amount of information you get is bound to hit on something that may have been holding you back. Take it and get moving!

Determining How to Incorporate the Feedback into Your Plan

When you get all your feedback from your stakeholders, you will want to organize it by question or subject or by starts/stops/continues. But most important, you will want to see the trends, and when you see those trends, you should stop, pause, and reflect on how you could incorporate that information into your daily routine or into your POA. When a restaurant wants to add a new food item on the menu, they don't always start head first and just put the item on the menu. They may create a "today's special," or have a "tasting menu." They will get feedback from the patrons, and if they are swooning over the new entrée, or if they reject it, the restaurant will decide if that will be part of the menu or the entrée should never see the light of day again.

When you ask for and receive feedback from the market, you need to be ready to hear, listen, and act on the insights that are provided (and, no, "to hear" and "to listen" are not the same—read on to the end of the paragraph). Knowing how to be receptive to feedback means that you know how to be a good protégé. If your stakeholders have given you feedback, support, guidance, or perhaps a stern talking to, you will hear what they are saying. Hearing is a natural process or function of our ears, but listening is a choice one makes to give consideration and thought to what is being said. *Hearing is* not *the same as listening.*

When I received feedback during my performance evaluations over the years via my boss or during my 360-degree review, I could see the same developmental areas consistently show up. I knew those developmental areas would hold me back from getting promoted.

One of my weaknesses was that I needed to be more inclusive in my decision-making by including my peers and my business partners. The root problem for me wasn't only that I didn't seek them out; instead, it was that my relationships with some of my more important peers weren't that strong. I was probably shy or intimidated by these leaders, but I needed to build better relationships with them. This was important because at J&J, for example, their culture was more focused on relationships and great outcomes and less on outcomes alone. I was not that great on focusing on relationships—I hadn't really understood the importance of building real professional relationships that go beyond the task at hand and are focused also on the individuals. I certainly learned it, though. The culture had been in place a long time, and if I wanted to win in that company, I had to get with the "relationship program."

I've also gone through feedback conversations where I heard what people said, but I really didn't listen to them. For example, my husband, my mentor, and my HR business partner have all told me how intimidating or strong I can be when in meetings. They told me that because of the way I come across, I have shut down conversations and problem-solving reviews because others were intimidated. I didn't see that—it was a blind spot—because I still looked at myself as a "poor Black girl from P-town," and I didn't think I could ever be intimidating. I also remembered being told or shown that I wasn't good enough, and I took that feedback and sought to toughen up, to get stronger, smarter, better prepared, and, apparently, intimidating.

So from my experiences in various companies, I heard the feedback, but I didn't have the mindset to listen to it, so I didn't address my behaviors. When I seemingly chose not to truly listen to the feedback, I could have potentially ruined relationships (after all, who wants to keep talking to someone who won't listen?), and I might have missed out on an opportunity to advance my personal vision and win. I am where I am because of the continual growth that has come over time.

The mindset needed to "listen" includes (1) being curious, asking questions that help you understand what can be done differently or better for your objective, and (2) having a mindset of choosing to handle the feedback without getting bent out of shape if the feedback isn't what you want to hear. Remember that part of your strength in winning when others say you won't is reminding yourself that when good companies listen to tough or negative marketplace feedback—whether they are seeing lower sales, clients abandoning the company, lower employee engagement scores, lower customer promoter scores, or something else—those companies don't get bent out of shape. They listen, assess the feedback, and strategize to improve their situation. That's what you can also do as you look to create a new version of yourself and launch your new product to the world. Keep listening and keep an open mindset as one of the tools in your toolkit as you look for and receive feedback from your key sources. As you open your mind, you will challenge your old assumptions because you now have new information—from your marketplace. And the marketplace is *always* right.

You can learn to incorporate feedback by hearing, listening, reflecting, and changing your assumptions and behaviors. The key for building trust as an effective leader and getting support from stakeholders is to demonstrate that you can:

1. **Listen more than you speak.** This comes from being aware of your verbal and nonverbal behaviors and keeping them in check. Get feedback from others on how you are showing up, and see if there are times you are talking over people or just talking more than 35 percent of the time. I often tell extroverts (which I am, too) that you should be like a major league baseball player going up to bat. Just as he may have his turn at bat about three times per game, if you are in a meeting for an hour (and you are not the leader of the meeting or have not been brought in as the subject-matter expert), you should talk no more than two or three times in that hour. Talking too much indicates you are not a good listener, and people find it hard to support someone who doesn't probably listen well. Be aware of how much others speak in comparison to you.

2. **Show that you have empathy and that you care about people holistically.** Do this not only for their value to you—what they do for you—but for their value as people. As they see the winner in you, stakeholders want to know that you don't only care about yourself, and you are not merely transaction-oriented—as soon as the job or project is done, you are nowhere to be found. They want to know that you can get the job done, but also recognize that companies are made of humans; that humans need compassion, support, and encouragement; and that you have values that can align with theirs. Stick around after the meeting ends and inquire about the person who was speaking or who asked an interesting question. See beyond the person's title and get to

know how you can be of help to that person. The person may turn around and find out how he or she can help you.

3. **Be consistent by modeling behavior that demonstrates the values and results-orientation of your organization.** Do as you say; do not overcommit and underdeliver. Your judgment, your behaviors, and your values should be aligned with the company's and engender support.

4. **Know your subject matter.** Let your business results demonstrate your value to the organization and appropriately ensure your stakeholders know your role in the wins you are generating how you add value to the organization. Focus on ways to continue to get stronger as a leader.

TAKING IN THE MEAT—AND SPITTING OUT THE BONES

Let me tell you a unbelievable, but true story about inappropriate and negative feedback I received as I was merely "being an SVP while Black." Shortly before retiring as a SVP and CIO, I was at a baseball game with an HR VP. It was early spring, and as can happen in the Midwest, it was bitterly cold, leaving me holding the collar of my fur coat shut against the wind.

"Can I say something?" the HR VP asked as we sipped our hot cocoa.

"Of course."

"You drive a fancy car."

"I do." I was the highest-ranking African American woman in IT in the company. I regularly had dinner with the company's chairman, and I had met with the board on several occasions. I was doing well. I had earned that car.

"And you dress really fancy, really nice."

"Thank you? What are you trying to say?" I asked. I was confused. Where was this going?

"Well, this is the Midwest. We wear khakis—and boat shoes here. And I just want to make sure you do more to fit in, blend in better."

He made more comments—but I was stunned. Over my 40-year career, I had prided myself on representing my companies well and adapting successfully to each new position. Also, I knew that to succeed, whether or not success seems unlikely, you have to solicit and welcome feedback, and listen! Developing technology solutions for businesses is a team sport, and that's how I had played it. . . . But back to the conversation at hand.

I said, "I don't understand. I've been here for four years. Why didn't you ever tell me this?"

He thought for a second and then he said, "I was afraid you'd 'go Black' on me."

That phrase "go Black on me" is something I had heard before, and I knew what it meant, but never in my years in the halls of corporate America had that phrase ever been used, let alone associated with me—an SVP, a female, a pastor's wife, a human being. To "go Black on him" infers that I would have gotten angry, and verbally or physically attacked in a wild manner. It's odd that he seemed to know what it meant, and after working for years together that he thought an SVP would forgo everything civil and resort to attacking.

I have only gotten where I am today because I eventually learned to listen and then act on the feedback, even when I am momentarily disappointed by it, even when it comes with microaggressions or bias. The ability to get feedback from people who matter, whom we respect, or even those who simply wield huge influence on our outcomes is paramount to our success.

Because most organizations only get whiter and more male the higher you go, it is likely that eventually your manager will be white or male or both. Which is not to say that the person can't be a helpful boss or a great mentor. I have had invaluable mentors who looked nothing like me. But people of color seem to work twice as hard to open those channels of timely and honest communication and to foster them once they're forged.

I did not "go Black" on that HR VP that evening, and I believe he thought I would be violent. I don't believe he thought "going Black" meant I would engage in a rational and logical conversation. He knew I was retiring, so he didn't think I would quit. But as I've mentioned before, what we think governs our actions. Our actions determine much of the outcomes that occur. The outcome of not giving me timely feedback was based on his racist "thinking." His silence in my years there meant that I had a blind spot regarding how he and possibly others perceived me. In his mind, also wearing boat shoes would have made me a better leader. As he tried to minimize me, he did so with the veil of being an HR leader, which could have been very effective if he were talking to some other woman.

In situations where you are confronted with a challenge, even if it doesn't appear to be a career opportunity, you can employ EDIT, using the concept of visioning the situation, designing your response, iterating on your design to approach or fix the temporary situation, and then transforming the outcome from what it could have been to something more in line with what it should be.

When I design my response, I use these four Cs whenever I'm given feedback that may not be positive, and may not be appropriate; especially when I'm told to minimize myself, my voice, or my strength:

1. Get *clarity* on the issue at hand. Who is my behavior (or dress) affecting? Everyone or just one person?

2. Confirm *cultural* fit. I had to understand if the culture or situation was truly as described and whether I fit in the culture.

3. *Choose* my action. What will I now do about the feedback? Reject it or accept it?

4. *Confirm* impact. After I make the changes I decided to do, did they change the narrative about me?

I engaged with him in the conversation and iterated back and forth on my perspective versus his perspective as I suggested to him that especially employees of color, women employees, and under-represented voices need feedback in a timely and respectful manner. Not four years after the fact! I shared with him that there is power in "knowing early" so people can adjust their behaviors, where appropriate, so perceptions and performance can be adjusted.

We all have blind spots. Feedback shrinks them. So, I advise, seek feedback from people whom you respect, who have a vantage point to see your performance or behavior, or who are successfully charting a course that may mirror where you are headed. And when you get feedback, be slow to do a knee-jerk reaction, but quick to listen and appropriately adjust your behavior or your plan.

In order to *Win When They Say You Won't*: Remember that assessing your progress is key to achieving any objective. Find out for yourself how it's going, and see whether or not things are lining up as expected. Understand the status, and respond appropriately, utilizing your stakeholders if and when needed to uncover your blind spots. As you continue moving on your key results, there may be weeds in your way that might try and stunt your growth. Let's figure out what to do about that next, in Chapter 8.

CHAPTER 8

FROM STUCK TO UNSTUCK

KEEP YOUR DREAMS MOVING

*An excuse is a way of promising ourselves today
that we will have the same issue again tomorrow.*

—HENRY CLOUD, CLINICAL PSYCHOLOGIST

Understanding the process of the Iterate step and perseverance is one of the most relevant and important sections in this book. In addition to people not having sufficient mental and time commitment to achieve a bodacious objective, getting discouraged in the midst of the journey is another key reason why people do not advance. Just when you think it's safe to go outside, another internal or external distraction tries to take your eye off your prize.

This chapter reviews the distractions and foibles that can get in your way on your path to winning. These things can make you freeze with fright or be doomed due to your doubt. I want you to know you have to keep it moving. You should dream, claim your intention, never give up, and surround yourself with people you can depend on—people who are in your corner, not just in your circle. This is a book about winning—and in order to win, you have to be very clear on some of the things that might cause you to lose!

I'm a gardener, and at different sections of this chapter, I use the idea of weeds in a flower garden as a metaphor that demonstrates how weeds can be a distraction growing side by side with your lovely flowers, in your beautiful garden, disrupting your garden's growth and beauty. The lovely flower garden in this case consists of your OKRs.

ELIMINATE THE DISTRACTIONS
THAT CAN DELAY YOUR WIN

When you are going through the process of growing and changing, creating and achieving, there will be challenges that can cause you to slow down, become discouraged, or even quit. As complex human beings living in a VUCA (volatile, uncertain, complex, and ambiguous) world, there are unpredictable forces inside and all around us. We want to do as much as we can, as much as we must, to minimize the negative impacts of those forces, and we have to ensure that nothing will stop us from achieving the objectives we set. You are at the stage of your project where you are starting to see whether your POA is working as you designed it, and you may be seeing things crop up that you didn't think about. Old habits come back to challenge your faith in your plan, as you are deep in the throes of your POA. I want to put a name to some of those for you and give you perspectives of how to navigate through common challenges and get help.

I think of the issues or forces that stand in our way to win as weeds in a flower garden, which get in the way of progress and can destroy your garden's ability to have sustainable flowers and a successful existence. Weeds can deprive your flowers of sun, of nutrients and all the things needed for your flowers to thrive. There are external forces that, when left unchecked or unanticipated, can cause damage to the garden, such as harsh wind, hot sun, frost, rabbits, and other factors. There are also forces that come from the inside that can wreak havoc in a garden, such as weeds, disease, etc. The three most common weeds I have seen stymie the growth of my protégés, peers, and even myself that we need to watch out for are:

1. Excuses and procrastination

2. Fear, uncertainty, and doubt

3. Analysis paralysis

Let's take a closer look at each of these.

Eliminate Excuses and Stop Procrastinating

There are times when it is difficult to get started. Think back to yesterday or last week and reflect on how many things you said you were going to do: When you said you were finally going to catch up on all your emails, schedule new monthly customer engagement meetings, or redo your LinkedIn profile. When you said you would go back to school and get your next degree. Whether your goals are important or unimportant, what we want to accomplish will not happen without you taking the first step.

The weeds of *excuses* and *procrastination* can cause your progress to stop in its tracks, because you make excuses. These excuses are justification for our inaction and possibly a crutch you now have that may encourage you to put off taking action or fixing issues. We don't normally procrastinate without a reason or an excuse. We may not know exactly why we are procrastinating, just that we are. A few key reasons I've seen why people procrastinate are as follows:

1. Fatigue or overcommitment. You cannot complete your commitment because you are busy and didn't do a good assessment of what it will take to do your key results or action steps or didn't weigh the required time or resource commitment against already existing commitments.

2. Fear of failure. This journey is new to you, and you're concerned that you may fail or that you are not good enough. I shared with you the need to suspend disbelief and think about your vision as if you would not fail. Remember that as a person thinks, that's who he or she becomes. Suspending disbelief was important in defining your vision, and it's important now as you execute your plan of action.

3. **Fear of success.** You may believe that when you win and achieve a success that your life will change. Friends may change. Time with your family may change. Expectations about you may change, and on and on. You may want to hold on to the status quo.

4. **Lack of understanding of the target.** Your OKRs may not have been specific enough. Go and review them and make sure they are SMART. Then adjust your action steps to allow for the changes in your key results.

5. **Other factors, such as your Five Fs.** What sounded like a cute idea to become VP has now changed the dynamics of the family. You're taking courses now, and you are spending less time taking care of your fitness than you ever have. Sure, you risk-adjusted your plan to know that you may have to sleep one or two hours less so you can keep your fitness going, but it's more a challenge than you thought. In my case, I gave up living with my husband full-time for several years while I moved to the Midwest for a larger job. I committed to the arrangement, he committed to it with me, and we were able to do it. If you thought you could do that but find that your family F won't really allow for it, then you change your objective—or you change how you will go about it. Relocating may not be the only way, as it was for me. Go back to your commitment and ensure you are still committed and what you are willing to give up to achieve it.

Of course, there are consequence for when we do something and for when we don't. Two key consequences for procrastination are:

1. You don't get to ring the bell of victory. Your victory will be delayed as long as you are sitting on your hands waiting for things to happen. What are you waiting for? Is what you're waiting for more important than your objective?

2. You are delaying your own personal transformation. As a product manager, you defined your vision of what you wanted your product to be to your market—in order to achieve that transformation and remain relevant, useful, present for your family, etc., you cannot wait. You don't transform when you procrastinate; you don't get to be a new version of yourself.

At the end of the day, your reputation, as well as the perception about what kind of person you are, is reflected in how many or how few excuses you make along your life's journey. You must take accountability for your actions when you make a commitment and don't follow through.

Monique was one of my peers at J&J and wanted to get promoted to director. There were many opportunities to get promoted at J&J, due to the sheer number of companies within the enterprise. At that time, director and VP roles weren't normally posted but rather were discussed, so you had to hear about it from your network, not from a job board per se. After hearing about an opening, Monique applied for the position. Then she started to update her résumé, including the quantification of the value she created for the company and her strengths, interests, awards, etc., and then she stopped.

A few weeks went by, and I thought I'd hear how she was making progress, but she said she didn't keep pursuing it. I asked her why, and she said she got too busy. I responded, "You weren't too busy three weeks ago to apply for the job. So what's really going on?"

She didn't answer me right away, but after time passed, she told me she didn't think she was good enough. She thought she wasn't ready. As we discussed it, I did my best to share with her what I saw in her, and told her that I thought that she was more than capable. She was already doing much of the job for her current director. That is why she was also too busy for the earlier opportunity.

"Not being good enough" is something I—and many women—feel, and we tend to believe this narrative when it comes at us. This conditioning started when we were little girls. Little discouraging comments about us and math, or us and science, or how we measure up to some impossible standard of beauty. Then those little seeds of negative direction grow into a full grown tree of imposter syndrome.

Women believe we need to be perfect for the job, while men believe they are perfect, when they are often less than 100 percent capable. She decided to go after another director job. Her excuse about the first one caused her a delay in her promotion, but when she went after the second one, she got it. Her win, along with her transformation, was delayed, but not permanently denied.

How can we eliminate this weed? When you find you are procrastinating, here's what I recommend you do. First, look at your commitment statement. Do you still want what you committed to? Do you believe your OKRs are still valid and achievable but for the little doubt in the back of your mind? If so, your mind is already there. Then how you act must catch up with your mind.

Second, identify the reasons for the procrastination. Is it one of those listed on the prior pages? You need to know what the cause is, so you can treat it. Just like in our garden, you need to be aware of what is killing the leaves on your particular flower, so you can treat the problem, or else the damage will continue. Flowers don't die right away, but when you keep ignoring the source of the attack, they eventually will. So, too, it is with your objective—it won't be snuffed out immediately with the first delay, but after time, you will have to start over again and redefine your OKRs.

Third, what do you think is the remedy? Based on the cause, you then have to actively take steps to counter it. For my garden, I may put a barrier around the sick plant so the others don't get sick, and then I treat the plant with Ortho spray or whatever is right. I may uproot it and put a healthy one in its place. Talk to your mentor or stakeholder to see if he or she has insights. But you must want to stop procrastinating and then put your plan in place for what you need. Your situation may have such a strong hold on you that you may need counseling. Be careful what you commit to, so you don't leave room for excuses and procrastination. Let your yes be yes, so you don't have to make excuses later for why your response should have been a "not now" or a "no." I learned through others that if I were to continually make excuses and not take accountability, my reputation would be damaged.

Overcome Fear, Uncertainty, and Doubt

This is often called FUD. We are often afraid of things we don't understand or don't know. Fear is having a dread or apprehension about something. On the other hand, fear, uncertainty, and doubt can sometimes be lifesaving. FUD can protect you from squandering money or taking unnecessary risks with your life.

When I refer to FUD, I'm not speaking of fear as a result of any serious mental condition. I'm referring to the fear you feel when you are not able to make a move toward your objective—a feeling of being stuck or paralyzed. Do you sometimes feel like you are "stuck in a rut"? There is a battle that is waging inside each of us. It's truly a battle for our mind. When I talk about the mind, I don't mean your brain. The brain is a physical organ that commands and manages your body: it sends messages to your body that the body will carry out. It is the "command center" that receives information. It is the motherboard that controls how the rest of your computer (aka your body) works. Then there is your mind, which is a higher-level part of your brain—that is unique to all of us. It is where you source your feelings and thoughts, your personality and human consciousness. It is where your will, motivation, and resolve come from. Your brain will cause you to learn consequences of behaviors, but it is your mind that judges whether things are right or wrong.

When you are unsure about going in a certain direction or going to the next logical step in your tasks that can move you forward toward your objective, your brain receives the information, while your mind decides what to do with it.

What I'd like you to take away from this part of Chapter 8 is that FUD is not a product of your brain, but it is your mind that makes the decision to be afraid. It's the same mind that decides to be optimistic, to have faith, and to trust others. Your willset drives your mindset, which opens your mind up to embracing the toolsets you can use to win. (You'll learn about willset, mindset, toolset, and skillset in Chapter 11.)

> *Early in my career I worked with one of the most analytical leaders I know, Chuck Masters. I spoke briefly earlier about having a growth versus a fixed mindset, and how that influences what actions we then take. In a similar vein, Chuck introduced me to a concept of TAR—thoughts, actions, and results. As we worked together, he helped me and others understand that whatever we* think *will determine the actions that we take. And that the* actions *we take have consequences, also known as* results. *The enlightening part of this is that in* The 7 Habits of Highly Effective People, *Stephen Covey reveals that he advises the reader to "begin with the end in mind." In other words, you start with having your mind reflect and decide on the results that you want to achieve, and then you determine what actions are needed to accomplish that objective. Here is the sticky part. Our minds can get in the way of us taking action that generates the results. So we must use our "will" to manage our thoughts and our minds to foster the right thinking, so we can act and get results.*

Again, there is healthy FUD that saves your life, and then there's unhealthy FUD that holds you back. You need to know the difference. Sometimes we need to be reminded that it is OK to be afraid—it's a natural part of life.

Fix your mindset to eliminate irrational fear. Reach back to where you were successful before in your career or in your business ventures, and recall why you were successful. Because you did only what was familiar? Because everything was without risk? If that was the case, you never got promoted. You don't advance when everything stays the same. So know that fear is normal and natural, and the purpose of fear is to help you eliminate or minimize the causes of danger, which could hurt your career. But you don't want to use fear to stop you from growing.

Know that uncertainty is part of our lives every day. Uncertainty is normal. There are degrees of uncertainty, but regardless, being paralyzed by uncertainty is not helpful to you or those who depend on you. The world didn't foresee Covid, or the war in Ukraine, or the massive supply chain issues, or the massive fires in Texas, until, of course, they started to manifest. But as the product manager that is driving your personal product transformation, you are to be nimble, and you must tell your mind that whatever comes your way, you will win because (1) you have past career experience, (2) you have a plan that can be adjusted to make way for the new reality, (3) you have stakeholders who are or will be there to help you, and (4) you know how to work through issues. You just need to engage your POA regarding headwinds and tailwinds and the Five Fs to mitigate those things that are most uncertain.

Confronting Analysis Paralysis

When you are busy trying to figure out the meaning of information you are receiving, you can get so caught up in the action of overanalyzing that you are paralyzed from moving to the next step.

If a high degree of analysis is needed in order, say, to ensure patient safety when it comes to a new drug, or to prevent a nuclear reactor explosion, we must analyze and test a lot of information. The level of scrutiny must be equal to the importance of the objective and line up with the risk of what will happen if we don't analyze. "The juice must be worth the squeeze."

Analysis paralysis is often used as a stall tactic by someone who indicates that he or she is still analyzing an issue. My mother always reminded me to "measure twice and cut once" when she was sewing, because you don't get a second chance if you cut off too much fabric. Although it is a good principle, eventually, you have to cut! You've got to make a decision and move! Analysis paralysis is like procrastination. Decisions and actions are being delayed; therefore your results may be delayed. But know that sometimes not making a decision is still a decision. Make sure you are studying a situation for an extended period only because it is necessary. Then set a goal or a target of what you need to learn, so when you hit that threshold, you'll know it's time to move.

As an executive, I have spent time with my team to focus on data—about customers, employees, products, market, and other areas—basically using analytics capability. With analytics, companies can have the information/data to help them understand patterns and make decisions—decisions, for example, for their internal efficiency or for customer fulfillment. Companies with analytics now can actually predict what a set of customers may do, when airplane engines will need maintenance based on the type of weather they fly in, or when an MRI machine may next fail so the service folks can set a date to do preventive maintenance. In short, analysis and analytics are a good thing.

However, there's a case where one of my former companies had a division that was underperforming. The company had the data about sales, profit margin, timelines, quality, and other factors, and it had information on whether the root cause was the leader or whether the business was just not good. The company still chose to not make the decision to divest the division or fire the leader.

How much money could the company afford to lose each quarter while the division continued to be unprofitable? How many quarters of business results did the leadership and CEO require to make a decision? At what point is the analysis enough, and it's time to cut or make other moves? While the leadership waited to make a decision, the market was still moving and beating this division. Making no decision still results in an outcome—except you have less control over that outcome, because you stood still while the world was moving and your situation got caught up in the move.

When you find yourself trying to analyze your action step, or quantify the success of your key result so you can give it a grade and move on, ensure the following:

1. Define what are you looking for—what metric, what leading or lagging indicators, will you need to capture that will tell you if you are successful or not?

2. Know the date by when you need to make a decision so you can move on to your other action steps. Watching is good for a while, but watching cannot be indefinite.

3. Understand what may occur internally to you, the state of your OKRs or your Five Fs, for example, or externally to your department, your team's morale, your boss's perception of you, etc., while you are analyzing and not getting your project moving.

HOW TO WIN WITH INTERNAL POLITICS

While we recognize that FUD, analysis paralysis, and other weeds can slow us down or stunt our growth, there are other things that can happen in our business lives, and we should take accountability in how we respond to those things and respond in a way that is truly helpful, productive, and emotionally intelligent, for you and your company.

I've had situations where I was talked over in meetings, was misconstrued as being someone much lower than an SVP, was ignored as an SVP, became a zero on Friday, when I was a hero on the previous Monday. How do we handle these things? Let's explore.

First of all, know that things will happen. Be prepared for something. There will be people who, through their own conditioning, will say things or do things in certain ways that you will not find respectful or appropriate (i.e., my HR leader). Sometimes they intend to be rude; other times they are simply not empathetic and have no idea they are being rude. You cannot look at these affronts and take them personally, even though it is personally happening to you.

Look at these incidents as you would look at data or information. When a competitor steals one of your best leaders, what do you do? Drive to that company, pound on its front door, and demand the employee back? No, you take it as information, and as dispassionately as you can, state the facts and make decisions—the employee is gone. Do I need to backfill? Is there a successor in place who can take over, or do I hire outside? Why did the employee leave? Was she running from us (because our culture, or norms, or salary, or something else was not favorable to her), or simply running to another company because she likes where its headquarters are located and needs to move for family reasons? Do we need to change how we manage our teams? Etc.

Second, most things in life that are important need a strategy or a plan. If you are looking to be promoted, or be considered a high-potential employee, or get assigned the best projects, you need to be intentional about how you position yourself to be that person. Many aspects of our career require planning, proactivity, and support.

Finally, what you actually choose to do depends on your personal style, so let's take a few of these political challenges one at a time.

What to Do When Your Promotion Is Given to Someone Else

First, breathe. Be calm and carry on. Clear your head. You will be no good to anyone if you start charging into offices like a bull. The promotion has been announced; the person who made the decision will not rescind it. So it's done. The horse has left the stable.

Be clear on why you believe it was *your* promotion and not the other person's. Did the CEO or your VP say it was yours and then give it to someone else? Or did you merely *believe* it was yours and it seems it incorrectly went to someone else?

Although this is a time for reflection, as mentioned above, your reflection could have occurred proactively prior to the promotion happening. Here are some points to consider:

- Identify if some part of your PIE was at fault here (remember performance, image, and exposure, discussed in Chapter 6?). Do you perform OK? Or great? Is your image intact? Do you take initiative? Are you late for meetings? Do you often complain?

214

Do you have the right exposure to the decision makers? How do you know?

- Think about your relationship with your boss. Is it a great, so-so, or poor relationship?

- Bosses can also be sponsors: is your boss your sponsor, and does he or she support you a lot more than others? If not, there's still an opportunity for the future.

Use these reflections as things to discuss when you talk to someone. Identify whom you want to talk to about it. I would start with your mentor or someone in a business role whom you trust. This person may be able to help you with your reflections. Don't talk to the bartender or to your swimming teacher, unless that person is a retired executive or someone who understands corporate politics.

Then meet with your boss, and don't talk about the other person who did get the promotion, but rather talk about how you can start now making yourself the obvious choice the next time a promotion that seems right for you comes along.

Show emotional intelligence and congratulate your colleague, and ask if you can help him or her in the new role. That should go a long way to show your maturity and company-first mindset.

What to Do When Someone Talks Over You in Meetings

This is one of those situations you may not be able to anticipate until it happens to you. Here are a few ways to handle this situation.

If the person is not letting you finish your thoughts in the meeting, and if this is the first offense in the middle of the meeting, say, "Sandy, I wasn't done with my comments; please let me finish." Or say, "Sandy, I wasn't done, but if you'd rather express your point before I finish mine, please go on." Chances are, Sandy will back down. If you choose this second alternative, only do this one time. Sandy doesn't get a pass again.

In contrast, if this is *not* the first time this person is not letting you finish, then (let' say the person is male) go to him privately and let him know what he is doing. Maybe he's doing it to others in the meeting, and if so, let him know. That shows you are not taking it personally, but rather trying to help him show up better. Also, if your mentor or sponsor was in the room when this happened (especially if your mentor or sponsor is male), ask privately what the mentor/sponsor recommends that you do.

What to Do When Your Comment Is Restated by a Man Who Gets the Credit

This has happened to me many times. Here's how I handled it. On one occasion, I said something like this: "Jake, you captured and restated my point very well; let me build on my earlier suggestion/observation and make another point." This type of response gives "Jake" credit not for the idea, but for the articulate restatement of it. Then you take the idea back to your ownership by adding another point onto it.

In other situations, if the same person kept doing this, or if multiple men did it, I would nod to a close colleague (sometimes the SVP of HR) to indicate that my comment had just been repeated. My colleague then would say, powerfully, "Guys, I think we are repeating ourselves. Daphne just made that comment, so let's think of new ideas."

This approach may not seem as forceful as the previous approach because it may feel like you need an ally to speak for you. But your colleague was not speaking for you really. He or she was giving you credit for the thought but was more concerned about productivity and not repeating comments (which just so happened to be your original comment).

What to Do When You Are Asked to Be the Scribe or Notetaker

Believe it or not, this still happens—at least, it happened to me, and on more than one occasion. I often found myself in a room or subcommittee full of men, and whether there was an old-fashioned flipchart or a notebook or laptop, I was often the one singled out and asked to take notes. Admittedly, this happened more in pre-Covid times.

Old stereotypes die hard. And as a former secretary from back in the day, I had issues of being stuck as a secretary, and I couldn't go back there. I bit my tongue every time. I got out of the assignment or of being considered by saying, "Guys, I have lousy handwriting, and no one will be able to read my writing." Or "I'm not a good typist. I hunt and peck on the keyboard."

What to Do When You Don't Get Timely Feedback and Are Surprised by Your Performance Review

Although this should never happen, it should, at most, happen only once. Your job is to make sure your boss knows how good you are, every day. (Well, not every day, but often.) And that what you are doing is making your boss look great. The boss cares about the quantity of results; quality of results; people leadership; process ownership; results achieved or results overachieved; things that you did, though not asked of you, that made a difference; business partner support; client supporters; client feedback; etc. And all these factors should be measured against your performance plan.

Your development plan should be linked to your performance results as well. Your development plan helps you and your boss know what your aspirations are and what it will take to get there. Getting there usually starts with performance (PIE), so your performance plan and performance status each month or quarter should be clear that it's all good.

If your boss is not the type of manager to meet with you and discuss your performance monthly or bimonthly, then you should either set up time for that so you are on her calendar or provide a written document that shows how you believe you are doing, including metrics, client or customer or peer feedback, and stoplights (red/yellow/green) for projects that are works in progress.

During your one-on-one meetings, take ownership and bring up your performance documents; ask your boss if she has any questions or feedback, and what you should start/stop/continue doing. If she never read the document, she'll start reading it now, because she knows you will be asking that very deliberate question that requires more than a yes or no.

The bottom line: Own your situation, call your own plays, and choose your response. Choose your response with your key mentors or stakeholders, and choose wisely.

FOCUS ON YOUR DREAM, NOT THE DISTRACTIONS

It's OK to feel challenged as you are working through your plan of action. This may be the first time in a long time that you worked on *you* and planned your actions to drive an outcome that only you dreamed was possible. It's natural to feel challenged or overwhelmed when you are balancing your career, your home, and your personal and community responsibilities. However, if this feeling becomes paralyzing or unhealthy, you need to take a serious look at what is overwhelming you. You can ask yourself, "What is causing me to be overwhelmed?" or "What is causing me to tip over the edge?" This will also be a good time to get feedback from your mentor or close family member to help you to see through a blind spot.

Don't Be Distracted by Naysayers

Focus on the outcomes. You need to become like a football team that is focused on getting that ball in the end zone. You can't be distracted by the people who seem to be "coming after you." Even though you will be aware of the naysayers, the haters, those who will try to drag you down, don't focus on them, but merely calculate how you will go around them or through them to get to your outcome and goal.

My oldest sister, Millie, always wanted to be a doctor, specifically, a surgeon. When she and my other two siblings came home from Jamaica to live in the United States, I often found her dissecting frogs or snakes or whatever she could find, to inspect their internal organs and understand how they functioned. Unfortunately (tragically, really), she was told—at the ripe age of influence of about 15—that she would never be a doctor. For a young Black girl, that is devastating to be told (as I was similarly told years later) that she could not be what she had a passion for. Her naysayer stunned her with that "insight," and she gave up her dream of becoming a doctor.

Instead, she went to a tech university and stayed true to her dream of being in medicine. Did she become a doctor? No, but she got her bachelors degree in biological sciences and she studied medical technology, becoming a certified medical technologist. And after graduation until she retired, she worked in a lab managing blood analyses. I'm proud of how as a teenager going into adulthood, she stuck with her passion for medicine, even if it meant that the naysayers got to her at 15, before she could resist and ignore their distraction.

It is important for you to always remain focused on the outcomes and not focus on the distractors—they are doing their job of distracting and discouraging you. Do your job of winning and taking the long view. Look beyond the naysayers and see the end zone.

Believe in Yourself and Never Downsize Your Dreams

You have to believe in yourself. You have to know you have an advantage over your circumstance because of your gifts, your passion, your grace, and your experience. You have superpowers—and you have purpose. When you have life experiences behind you, you know that you have accomplished many things—and you are capable of achieving even more. There will be times when things won't go your way. In fact, you may get hurt by a company's M&A, the dissolution of a division, or personal calamities that may not have been avoidable. Remember when I shared in Chapter 3 that I was downsized by IBM. I was downsized, but I refused to downsize my dream.

After my downsizing, I reflected on what my former branch manager, Tony, told me about who should make the relocation decision (as discussed in Chapter 6, in the section on mentors), but I didn't listen to him in deciding about the move to Atlanta. Instead, I let my husband make the decision to relocate to Atlanta. So we moved, and during a marketplace financial downturn early in my move there, I was one of the many that IBM decided to let go.

That horrible experience of being told I was no longer needed in my job—how that probably catalyzed the breakup of my marriage, how that affected the security of my son, and how it dashed my dreams of being a named leader in an organization—was debilitating. At first.

Yes, I went through the stages of grief. And I felt discouraged, but then I realized what I had accomplished in my life and how far I had come, so even though I was downsized during my time there, my dreams weren't. My dreams leveled up. My sister Pam, who was with me at the time, continued to encourage me daily. As Pam was one of my stakeholders, I was able to go to her—not for a job, but for life-sustaining words.

The same should go for you. You should never downsize your purpose, and your vision is not up for debate. In whatever moment you feel disappointed, stressed, or hopeless, you have to say to yourself, "Even though this is a lot, I'm not going to downsize anything. I'm not going to erase what I know is in my gut." You need to focus on playing the long game. You must be courageous. You should look fear in the face and not blink, because you and only you were perfectly created for your purpose. You may have gotten delayed, but your purpose has not been denied.

My niece Alexis is not even 13 years old yet, and she is clearly not a woman in business, but when I asked her about winning, she told me she can see already that her friends who look like her and those who don't look like her have started listening to what society says is a winnable way to be and what is not winnable. She has learned that she needs to set her own course. What struck me about this young girl is that she is learning from her mom and dad, and she actually used the phrase "perseverance and persistence in the face of adversity to win against all odds." I mention this here as an example that it's not too early for mothers and fathers and aunts and uncles to recondition and teach their girls to not give up but to persevere, so that at a young tender age, they already have their mental trajectory set up to win.

DON'T LET WEEDS STUNT YOUR GROWTH

I had a garden at one of my former homes. It wasn't an especially lavish garden, but I designed it; I bought shrubs, trees, bulbs, dirt, and mulch, and I tended it, especially in the spring and summer. In the back of the house, we had evergreens that were eight feet tall, separating the neighbors' properties from ours, using the bushes as a natural barrier instead of a wooden, iron, or chainlink fence. My small garden in the back framed the pool and patio on all sides.

The more I worked in my garden, the more I came to realize that there's something very similar about how we garden and how we set out and achieve objectives. There are things that can hurt our progress or stunt our growth, just like FUD, procrastination, and analysis paralysis can. Those come from inside us, but sometimes weeds come from around us as well.

I envisioned the gardens I wanted to have by looking at magazines or other people's gardens to get ideas for what I wanted for my own home.

Next, I designed my garden by drawing the outline of the garden and marking where each shrub or tree would go. I did a SWOT analysis of each part of the garden: I asked myself questions such as, Where did it have good exposure to sunlight? And was there a risk of deer or rabbits that could hurt the garden?

Then I risk-adjusted my design plan based on my SWOT analysis. Finally, I hired someone to help me to dig and install the garden.

Using stakeholders (including neighbors, my husband, my sister Millie, who is now a master gardener, and others) helped me iterate on the garden as I used their feedback, adding something over here, taking away something from over there. I kept iterating as time went on, adding more color or replacing a shrub that died.

The result was that my garden had transformed from one that looked barren to one that was lush and colorful. That became my Version 1.0 garden. I enjoyed my garden as I worked to build on this beautiful oasis, . . . and then I began to envision again, to consider what I would do next year to take my garden to Version 2.0.

As I went through the process of transformation, watching my flowers grow, there were several things about weeds that became clear to me. Some weeds can create a pretty flower—and if you believe that weed is a flower, you might make the gardener's mistake of not pulling it up because you see a flower and think it is not a weed. Every living plant blooms and grows—it can be a tomato plant, a culture in a Petri dish, a flower, or a weed. And like plants, both good situations and bad situations can blossom and grow.

Find the Weeds That Camouflage Themselves to Look Like a Valuable Flower

It can be easy to be deceived by people, organizations, and other things that may be beautiful on the surface, but they can be camouflaged and cause you to lose your way. Look at people who seem to be part of your challenges. They may or may not deliberately set out to hurt you, and they appear to be your friends. You've known them for a long time, so they couldn't be that bad, right?

222

Yet they may be blossoming in some unhealthy ways with unhealthy habits or mindsets. Those habits work their way into your life, and you take them on as your own. They hide and commingle with the flowers you are trying to grow, and they confuse you into thinking they are a good plant, but they may not be good for you.

Find the Root Cause of Your Weeds

It takes a lot of energy and effort and strong intervention to get to the root of the weed. We have all heard the term "root cause." It is important for us to understand the root cause of the problems we have. Why do we procrastinate or make excuses that cause us to lose our way toward our goals? Why do we associate with the people who are not good to us or good for us? The root cause is what you look for when trying to answer those types of questions.

When you remove the root, you remove the weed. When you remove the root, you remove the issue from having an impact on you. Look at the "root" cause for why you have the habit or escape mechanism in your life. You will attempt to pull up and eliminate the weed, but like a cancerous tumor that needs to be cut out of the body, unless you get to the bottom of the very deep root and possibly pull up some good dirt as you dig, you can never be sure you got it all. And if you didn't get it all, it will continue to grow and will eventually be visible above the ground in a few short weeks. You have to work hard to get rid of your weeds at their roots.

Exterminate Your Weeds

They're outta here! You will have to be creative in order to exterminate certain weeds. Some weeds require extra focus or resources to eliminate them. Sometimes we make excuses for acts or people that may be growing and flourishing in our lives but should not be. Those excuses we make can be a mechanism that allows the inappropriate situation to continue to exist. Examine your circumstance and see if there are things going on that seem to be protecting the weed. Whether you put on gardening gloves to pull it, get a garden shovel and spike to dig it out, or spray weed killer on it, you need to be willing and creative to exterminate the weed that is destroying your garden.

When my high school counselor told me that my career would consist of being a secretary, he represented a weed in my life—a weed that was dressed as a flower. He was someone who seemed to have my best interests at heart and who was paid to give advice and guidance to students so they could become contributing members of society. I trusted my counselor, although I will never know if he was using all the information he had at his disposal and truly believed that a secretarial career was best for me. I don't know if he was racist or sexist (or both) and gave all girls or non-white people the idea that their role in life was limited to whatever he thought they should be. Either way, his advice to me was really a weed that had a bloom on it, and I mistook it for a valuable flower. I couldn't change him or his way of thinking at that time, but what I did was change my response to his vision of my future, and I removed that weed from my life. Well, actually I graduated and moved on, but it was also his words that remained a weed in the garden in my mind, long after I left high school. I had to remove the weed by infusing myself with information, achievements, self-reflection, mentors, and other activities and people that allowed me to have faith and belief in myself. From there I knew I could win when the counselor said I couldn't.

There will be plenty of challenges, and having a strong network is key to success. There are times when you listen to the wrong people, sometimes in spite of your own gut and in spite of the data. As noted, in the garden of beautiful flowers, there are also weeds that disguise themselves as flowers, that will rob the nutrients from the dirt, and that wrap themselves around the real flowers, constricting those delicate and beautiful flowers of leadership, collaboration, customer service, teamwork, etc.

As the product manager of your career and your current product transformation, you will need to be agile, responding with emotional intelligence when situations go wrong. Take risks when the outcome might be worth it to your company, but know that you can't risk-adjust for everything that can happen. Sometimes bad things may happen to you, to your project, to one of your Five Fs. Know that you have access to your stakeholders, your accountability buddies, and your plan of action to focus you back on modifying the bad situation so you can get back on track. Do as a company would do, and when things happen to you—or your project, your Five Fs, or your areas of interest—just use the tools provided, be dispassionate, and ensure you employ the strategy to change your plan, change your behavior, or change your team!

I was a high-ranking leader at a corporation and had broken the concrete ceiling as one of the highest-ranking women of color to sit on the leadership team. I was in the midst of building my team, setting strategy, and getting ready to drive results. But early on in my stint as CIO, I had hired a consultant who was in my circle (and I thought she was in my corner) to assess what projects were behind and not performing per plan and to identify what issues were burning—such as, was there high employee turnover? Were there morale issues? Did we have a good reputation for delivering projects that add value? Did we have a vulnerable infrastructure that would put the company at risk of cyberattack, or were our processes immature and unreliable? Were we really a well-oiled organization that required only a few tweaks?

This consultant understood where my organizational weak spots were and knew what was needed to bolster the organizational capabilities of my team, and she recommended a special and strong leader to be on my team. After interviews with this candidate—who would be on my CIO leadership team and would potentially rotate to be a VP in the finance part of the business, as part of executive development—I decided to hire the candidate. I had a few inklings in my gut that something was odd about her, but I ignored them.

But from the first moment she joined my organization, trouble began. From being insubordinate to driving subtle dysfunction and infighting across my team, the new leader was a challenge. Disrespect, noncollaborative behaviors with other leaders, backbiting, and more were aspects of this person's M.O.

Complaints across the organization came in, and I had to do something about them. I needed intervention from the SVP of HR, because I wouldn't be able to fire this person on my own because of her high level. I met with my mentors and got their feedback, and I listened to the guidance that made the most sense relative to where the situation was. As soon as I got HR involved, the individual was terminated and walked out. The consultant was also quickly let go.

Later, I learned that there was collusion between the two of them—if this new leader had been able to be promoted or moved to another high level role in the business, the consultant would have received money that would surpass what I was then providing her in fees. It was a perfect setup—the weeds were disguised as flowers, but a weed eventually shows itself as a weed.

I had to win even though they thought I wouldn't. I hired a new leader to take the place of the fired one, and fortunately, over time, the organization was able to heal.

There will inevitably be weeds in your garden. Here's what you need to do:

1. Spot them early. Those weeds are people, thoughts, attitudes, distractions, disbelief, procrastination, stagnation, your personal mindset, and FUD that are not conducive to the healthy achievement of your OKRs. Trust your instincts on whether you are dealing with a weed or not. If you are not sure if the situation is good, check with a stakeholder you trust. If you are not making progress on your OKRs and action steps, it's likely a weed is trying to steal away nutrients or deflect the sunlight from your key results so they don't grow and materialize into your objectives.

2. Understand the root cause so you will know what brought the weed around you or your project, and what you will need to do to prevent it from coming back. Your mindset of suspending disbelief and knowing that you have made a commitment to achieving an objective will help keep your environment from being conducive for weeds to develop. If you keep the ground hostile to weeds but open for a good mindset and leadership, the weeds will not be successful and will not thrive.

3. Eliminate the weeds by creating a positive, forward-moving, growth-oriented, metrics-based environment that will that keep you focused on your objective so there is no room for weeds to grow.

In order to *Win When They Say You Won't*: Embrace the fact that you were built for this moment. You are working your plan and are aware of those challenges that could stunt your growth. In order to complete the Iterate step and continue working toward your objectives, you should identify those challenges. Understand root cause so you know how to eliminate the weeds and ensure you don't create fertile ground for them to come back and feel welcome to destroy your dream.

You will continue in the Iterate step, and when needed, you will either persevere or pivot for the win. Chapter 9 talks all about that.

CHAPTER 9

PERSEVERE

YOU ARE A SEED

I really think a champion is defined not by their wins
but by how they can recover when they fall.

—SERENA WILLIAMS

There are times during a project that you reach a point where you discover your hypotheses or plan assumptions were not 100 percent perfect. You wanted to go after a VP job but ended up focusing on a senior director job because the company restructured. Or you had some personal issues; for example, a CEO friend of mine retired so he could take care of his sick wife. Although you know where you stand regarding your POA, you get distracted by focusing on those daily tasks and emergencies that come up. In fact, you can become so distracted that you may keep your eye off your objectives or actions, forgetting that you are supposed to be moving through the EDIT process toward a key milestone. Without a clear SMART plan, you will not easily know if you are making progress or if you are appropriately managing your moves through each step in the EDIT process. You need to know if you are on track or are at least gaining some ground.

This chapter looks at how to put into action the feedback you received from your stakeholders or your "market" in this Iterate step, as you may need to alter your journey. As you are iterating and working your plan, you will likely come to a point where you will have to do an adjustment, just as when you change the thermostat in your home if you are feeling too cold or hot or leaving for vacation, or when you ask your team to cut some of its discretionary spending so your budget can get back on track. By using the tools and discussions in this chapter, you will have a firmer idea of how to continue iterating on your plan as you prepare to move forward to Step IV, Transform.

SETBACKS ARE A SETUP FOR A COMEBACK

There will seldom be a stage in your progress that you will skate through a large project at work or a piece of your vision without setbacks. I have learned that although it may not feel like it in the moment, you can use a crisis as a catalyst for innovation, collaboration, and better outcomes.

Remember my story about how I needed to get the mostly white male plant leaders to work with me as part of my supply chain IT role at Johnson & Johnson? I was intent on ensuring they knew I had their best interests at heart and that I was going to help them win. Only when they won would I then be able to add another notch win on my career journey belt. After about a year or so of working on some of their smaller, individual plant challenges, I worked with several p... ts together to create and present a manufacturing execution system (MES) strategy. Having an MES is a complicated capability for the plants to drive product quality and profitable manufacturing and requires more collaboration of certain plants working together versus how they were currently working, in silos. Our objective was to define the best approach and technology for the right data to come to and from the plant floor equipment, to be funneled up to the various managers in the plants and then to each of the five plant managers across the manufacturing network.

When this supply chain deliverable was completed, the data would also be consolidated across all plants to my business customer, the SVP of manufacturing, Rob. The MES strategy includes the information that MES strategies have—that is, the vision, strategy, tactics, problem definition, SWOT, hardware/ software, suggested manufacturing plant rollouts, risks/mitigation, costs, quantitative and qualitative benefits, and plant implementation phases.

My team's task—to consolidate and harmonize data across disparate systems and get multiple machines that didn't use the same language to talk—seemed impossible, but I've heard that word "impossible" before. I had a plan.

Rob frequently questioned my approach, my findings, and my thoughts, and he made me feel less capable, and, yes, like an impostor. I said to myself, "I'm really the secretary who should have stayed a secretary." I began to feel like I was never going to successfully get through the process of building the MES strategy. For example, when he and I reviewed one of the prototypes of the potential future plant reports together, he noted it was focused on the wrong issues that were not a priority to him. And of course, information is used so leaders can make decisions. But the data he saw wasn't good.

Rob knew that I didn't have deep manufacturing experience, and he didn't put out much support to help me up the curve. The goal of most plant managers is to keep costs down and quality high, while simultaneously ensuring they can deliver as promised with quantities the sales force needs to supply to its customers. My job was to help him to do that through technology. At J&J Corporate, I was considered a high-potential leader. When I got to J&J Consumer, I was anything but that. (If you're unfamiliar with this term, a "high potential" refers to a leader, no matter what level you are, who has the potential to make it to higher levels in the company.) Even as a hi-po, it was still a dangerous project for a manufacturing rookie. If I slipped off this glass cliff, my career would crash with a dull thud.

I was discouraged, and I could feel my FUD starting to creep in. I'd seen other hi-pos who didn't look like me get major support to help them succeed. Me? I received skepticism where support should have been. It felt like I had to come fully equipped and should have gotten my development somewhere else. But this was a development assignment! Outside of school, where else do you learn about manufacturing except in manufacturing?

But I didn't quit. I said to myself, "Daphne, you are 'high potential,' and the way you demonstrate your high-potential capability is simply going to be different from someone else's. But you are still awesome!"

The goal of delivering a win to the business, and therefore to my career, was more important than the embarrassment I was going through! I knew I had the ability to choose my response (response-ability) to this situation, so I chose my response to be one that would use the setback as a setup for a comeback. The energy being expended should be targeted, focused on the long game, with the belief and knowledge that you will not fail. You shake off the delay and keep on moving.

When you have an approach or plan of action that you thought would work one way, but the assumptions you made did not quite pan out the way you thought, and your results that you are measuring are off target, you can do something called a "pivot." A pivot is when you need to change something about your assumptions and actions (without abandoning the vision) to see if you will get better and more predictable results, as was expected when you began to execute after making the change. You don't quit when your project is off track; you just pivot.

My meeting with Rob let me know that I had not fully understood his needs; as a result, I needed to change the team's approach to better appreciate and deliver on Rob's prioritized needs. We were not going to be successful if we did not pivot to this more focused approach. We had to switch it up, pivot, and take his needs more into account. We went deeper into the investigation of what the plant leaders really needed, while also putting great priority on what Rob, the actual potential MES project funder, was thinking. This would ensure we took more into account his needs—what he needed to win—and not just the needs of the plant managers.

The opposite of pivot is to persevere. You may not have the high numbers you wanted, but you're getting some. You may simply need more time, or more customers, or more money, but generally things are going well. When you don't change anything because you have a strong belief, insights, and data that prove what you have done is likely on the right path, then you can persevere.

I went back to my stakeholders, which included my team, a mentor who was the former president of a division of another manufacturing company, the software vendor, and my plant managers who were on the MES team. We altered our approach and focused on the top three issues Rob felt were standing in his way of the win. After reviewing massive amounts of data from the lines and the teams, we deconstructed the presentation into more granular points that would cover a different set of objectives. We reimagined how to present the solution, mustered up courage, and presented it, and fortunately Rob signed off, with some follow-up action items. But I was able to win when he and I both clearly thought I couldn't.

Sometimes it takes a lot to get to a win, when faced with challenges, but the victory is sweet because it gives you experience that you can use again for the next opportunity; you can also use that experience to help mentor and coach others on how to use their setbacks as a setup for a comeback.

The victory you earn not only shows you that you can win; it also puts another data point or lesson in the minds of those who may not be supportive of you or what is possible from those they doubted. That helps you pave the way for future women leaders or people of color, who to this day may receive more skepticism than support.

In my previous story, I shared how I pivoted in the middle of a project. However, when you are driving your plan of action and you get a rejection or tough news, if you feel in your gut and believe in your marketplace data that you are on the right track, you should persevere. Use disappointment as fuel to help you prepare for what the next thing is that will use your skill. It's just a matter of time before the world sees and knows your capability.

Let me share how my colleague Monica Caldas decided to persevere. Monica and I have worked together at GE. I admire her deeply, and she is one of my go-to thought leaders around leadership and technology strategy. It was years ago, and she envisioned getting her first opportunity for an executive role. She was eager and excited to apply for this new job. She had been given a lot of feedback from her mentors that this job would be a great fit for her skills. But even after going through several interviews, she did not get the job. Her first reaction was grave disappointment, but she leaned on her family and faith to guide her.

Ultimately, she reflected and concluded that the job she didn't get must not have been for her. She realized she needed to continue to push forward and persevere to keep trying for an executive role, and she needed to be willing to take risks.

She went right back and applied for a different executive role, even if this particular one carried risk to one of her Five Fs—family. She would need to relocate, she had a one-year-old baby, and would be going to a place with no family or friends to support her and her husband. Plus, the job was in a business that was going through a difficult financial period. Yet she interviewed for the job and got the offer. She took it. And because she persevered and didn't give up on her vision to find a new executive role, it positioned her for other bigger, future opportunities. She has since left GE and is now EVP global deputy chief information manager at Liberty Mutual.

WHEN TO PIVOT AND WHEN TO PERSEVERE

As you iterate through your plan, you will execute on an approach to make progress on your OKRs. You will see what the result is and make adjustments accordingly, like doing a prelaunch demo before fully introducing a new product to the market. Was it perceived well? What were the comments? Were they catastrophic—e.g., "The solution doesn't work consistently," or "It doesn't meet most client needs," or "The design could be greatly improved"? Or were they merely cosmetic, such as "Change the screen color or font size"? If catastrophic, the team will most likely need to pivot. If cosmetic, then no major change is needed to your approach, your platform, or other parts of your solution, so you would persevere. Make some tweaks here or there, but nothing too serious. Keep on going. This is an example of what is called "build-measure-learn-repeat" cycle of continuous learning. You execute your plan of action, you measure how the results are stacking up as, and you learn real-time lessons based on the feedback and leading/lagging indicators you are getting.

Unless you have an epiphany, your objective remains the same; you will just decide if your approach is working (persevere) or if you have to change it (pivot). This allows you to keep your product relevant, timely, and contemporary. You don't keep hammering away at something that you can tell will not yield the outcome you expect. No matter which direction you choose, it is important that you assess at key points of your project if and to what extent your reality is matching your assumptions or expectations. Your expectations are mostly coming true. Or you can see with the current trajectory that they will not or they mostly are not.

WHEN YOU NEED TO MAKE AN ADJUSTMENT, CHECK YOUR MINDSET

A few months ago, my husband and I met a young woman who shared with us that she was going back to school to learn how to be a radiologist who specializes in brain imaging. She noted that the program will require seven years of study. I said, "Wow! That's quite a commitment of time. What made you want to focus on this particular specialty?"

She said, "I was looking to study breast imaging, but I discovered that brain imaging is a field that will continue to grow by 11 percent every year for the next 10 years. I definitely saw this as an opportunity because this area of imaging will have demand growing at a pace faster than certain other imaging, and I want to go where the action is."

Here is someone who was pursuing one career specialty, but then she saw a more lucrative opportunity, and she chose to pivot from her current plan so she could have a greater outcome. She can clearly see that there will be more career opportunities and most likely a higher salary by specializing in brain imaging. She didn't abandon her objective to go into imaging; she just pivoted on one aspect of it—the type of imaging.

She sounded excited and motivated by her decision, and I hope that she and readers like you will always leave room for adjustments for better opportunities and for unexpected curveballs that life can throw your way. We don't want to jump around from objective to objective, but rather continually learn, research, and check assumptions throughout a career project. This young woman used her research and confirmed she could commit to sustaining a long trek through brain imaging training before she decided to pivot versus persevere.

In the programming world, agile development is a way of designing the programming effort so that the team that is working on the digital solution can get feedback from the market or clients "in real time" and "in the moment." This enables the team to easily correct or adjust the solution before it gets baked too deeply into the core software and before it's too costly and time-consuming to make changes. As you make room for adjustments, both major and minor, ensure you are not relying only on your personal experience as you continue to iterate on your objectives. Include your stakeholders or resources in your discussion as you pivot and persevere into a new level of your career or vision.

One of my favorite sayings is, "If you don't like the fish you're catching, change your bait." Let's look at persevere versus pivot again. Your bodacious objective (BO) is to bring three fresh trout fish home for dinner by 5 p.m. Your key result was to (1) secure the fresh-trout-catching bait, and gear, (2) find the best river or lake for trout, and (3) go fishing and catch it yourself (of course, you had action plans around getting the bait, driving to the lake or the river, etc.). When you saw that the time was approaching 5 p.m. and you caught only one trout you assessed that you now had to catch two trout in 30 minutes, even though you had caught only one trout the last five hours. You have to decide to pivot or persevere.

Persevering is when you keep on fishing (probably with new bait, further up river), while pivoting is when you change your approach, by giving up the fishing rod, going to the fish market, and buying some fish. You didn't give up on your objective of bringing fish home for dinner, but how you got there was a different path. As you iterate, you will change your behavior, your resources, or your plan, but you will not give up on your BO that is in line with your purpose.

When you persevere through the challenges and triumphs of your plan of action and you're getting the results you want, you will achieve more and more over time, and you will begin to win. You'll make incremental improvements in your life or on your career path, and you'll keep checking back and/or modifying your plan of action to make sure you continue moving toward your vision, your OKRs, and your action steps.

Every time you choose to persevere, and even if you choose to pivot, you are still committing to your purpose and vision. You are owning your plan, and you are willing to do what is required to get you through the process. If your vision is truly important to you (you've made it to the Iterate step, which is the third step of this process, so I know your vision is incredibly important to you at this point!), you will keep your mind open and recommit to your vision. How you think about your vision will determine how you're going to act, and that action will then give you your results. You should persevere or pivot, but not quit, while being aware of these basic principles:

1. **Be resilient.** You will encounter issues as you go through the Iterate step. You can't always avoid a setback in your life or in your network, but with good focus, you can recognize it for what it is, a distraction, and be resilient as you work to neutralize it and get back to executing your plan of action.

2. **Understand the secret life of weeds.** As you continue engaging with your stakeholders throughout the Iterate step, you will know the enormous value of having the right ecosystem of colleagues and friends. You will learn to recognize that some of your friends, families, or colleagues may actually be weeds in your garden and are essentially snuffing out your dreams and passion.

3. **Stay focused on your performance, image, and exposure (PIE).** No matter what is going on at work or as you work toward your personal vision, you must always be aware of your performance, your image and brand, and your exposure (i.e., whom you know and who knows you).

4. **Understand and maintain control of your emotional intelligence.** Not only is iterating on your plan of action about *getting* an objective achieved, but it's also about how you achieve it. You want to ensure that you are executing your plan with self-awareness, self-control, empathy, and good communications.

5. **Evaluate thoughts, actions, and results (TAR).** If you don't like the results (fish) you are getting, you need to change how you think (your bait). Your thoughts determine your actions, and your actions generate results. EDIT means *change*. So if you need to change your mindset, do it. That will change your behavior, which will change your outcomes. Your mindset needs to be agile and growth-oriented so you can be agile and growth-oriented when it's time to act. Pivot or persevere, but don't quit.

A dear colleague of mine was sexually harassed by eight leaders of her company. Yes, eight. Not only were they leaders: they were senior leaders. She was very shy, and perhaps like people who have been abused, she didn't feel she had power to say anything or do anything. After all, they were the leaders of the company. She threw up every day before going to work because she was so upset. After the head of HR of the company actually put his hands on her in a sexual way, she mustered up the nerve to take it to the CEO. Immediately, two men were fired, one was demoted, and then a few more were fired later. She could have quit several times during and after the attacks, but she persevered and decided to ride out the storm while she sought justice. Unfortunately, because of the incidents, she was also let go. In other words, although she was the victim of harassment, she also became victim of being wrongfully terminated after her attackers sought revenge.

After her firing, the company said that she hadn't been fired and that she had actually quit. Her unemployment money was in jeopardy. She'd had more than enough pain, and she decided to sue for unemployment and for the damages brought on by her harassment. It took her nearly two years, but she hung on, she persevered, and she won. They tried to bury her, but she was a seed.

STAY CONFIDENT AS YOU ITERATE

People or circumstances may try to bury you, but always remember that you are like a seed. A seed is "born to be buried," but more important, once the seed is buried, the seed doesn't just stop there. It gets its strength from its resources: its stakeholders—the sun, the soil, and the water in the ground. The seed will rise up above the ground and will throw "shade" on those that buried it. While it is able to throw shade, it also produces fruit or vegetables, or in your case, your seed will produce new leadership, great market growth, or new innovation and strategies.

The Covid-19 crisis has shown how many companies, people, and relationships were buried by this unprecedented global health pandemic. We know that women have borne a disproportionate and inequitable brunt of the Covid unemployment consequences. Many of you reading this book had parents who were sick or children at home to care for at the same time. You have had to choose between your kids and your careers—and perhaps all your Five Fs were affected at the same time, and perhaps you were not able to handle multiple crises at one time.

You cannot let this current situation (or any situation!) cause you to doubt yourself. Seek your resources—your mentors, your coach, your family, your accountability buddy, your spiritual book of teachings, and your experiences. Use them to help you dig deep into your roots so that you will eventually be able to stand above the ground stronger than before. When others say you won't win, you must tell yourself that you will. Better yet, show them: you will be a role model for your children, your mentees, your team members, and your community. As you execute on those new behaviors and activities, you will continue to iterate and finally transform.

DON'T GET DISTRACTED; PLAY THE LONG GAME

I stood there shocked, my mouth agape; then I sat down and held my head in my hands. I finally lifted my eyes to the heavens as I reflected on what I was watching on social media and TV: the process and spectacle that is now known as Ketanji Brown Jackson's Supreme Court confirmation process.

But I held my head in my hands only for a moment. Because I remembered the experiences of a woman, especially of a woman of color. We are required to jump hurdles that others don't, and it is something I've lived through, read about, heard about, and witnessed throughout my life.

That is why I wrote this book. A leopard doesn't know how to change its spots. It doesn't know how to do anything but what it does every day. But the prey needs to outthink, outstrategize, and outperform the predators, lest the prey be captured and devoured.

We have been targets for a long time. We have had people talk to us any way they choose—and with little to no consequence. We have been shown that what works for the majority gender and race won't work for the minority. The "great" gentleman senator Thom Tillis, in essence, told candidate Ketanji Brown Jackson how hard it must be for her during the hearings. After all, it was eleven Republican senators against one nominee. And he acknowledged that those senators have more power in the hearing room, because "it's not like you can really come at us."

Why are there no consequences? Didn't prior Supreme Court nominees yell, scream, cry, and threaten the Senate? Didn't the candidates "come after the senators"? If Mrs. Brown Jackson had stood up for herself, she would have been an angry Black woman. Yet when the white man stands up for himself, he is rewarded with applause and support.

The final public show of disrespect was at first startling, but all I had to do was remember that if it walks like a rat, and talks like a rat, and looks like a rat, then it most likely is a rat. So don't be surprised when the rat behaves like one. In fact, get ready for the rat to act like a rat with you.

One by one, many Republican senators turned their back on confirmed Supreme Court Justice Brown Jackson, and they walked out of the chamber during the applause that erupted when the final count came in and she was announced as the newest Supreme Court justice.

Let's extrapolate the very public behavior of the senators turning their backs on Supreme Court Justice Brown Jackson and walking out to the likely private situations in other settings in America. Can we imagine the real possibility that exists behind closed doors, where bosses are turning their mental and professional backs on their women, gay, Black, Hispanic, Asian, etc., subordinates? Where raises and promotions are delayed or denied? Where healthcare providers turn their backs on certain demographics of patients and don't provide optimum care? Where judges turn their backs on lady justice and issue harsher sentences to a person of a minority race than to a person in the majority who commits the same crime? The public display of disrespect and prejudice is often echoed in private meetings and private hearings.

And so we have it: this book was written to equip you to not fall for the trap that presents itself when you get a less-than-great performance review, even when you know you had a great year; you were denied a promotion, even when you and your peer who received the promotion were tracking at the same pitch; or when you are told you're not good enough, even when management gives a "developmental opportunity" to someone else who isn't "good enough" either.

You will find that sometimes those who are set against you simply cannot take the real truth when it is contrary to their statements and beliefs. Those senators couldn't take the truth; they couldn't take Mrs. Ketanji Brown Jackson's power, her capability, her superior achievements. So they did only what they could do and turned their backs on her and left.

You know how to win, and you know how to play the "long game," just like a business does, and as calmly and dispassionately as Mrs. Ketanji Brown Jackson did: assess the situation, decide your outcome, design your approach, execute your plan, persevere when you can and pivot when you must, and transform your business, your family, your team into a reflection of your capabilities and leadership.

Remember that you are smart. You have brains. You deliver, and you execute. You improve. You build up. You inspire. You persevere. You empower. You win.

HOW TO KNOW YOU ARE READY TO PROGRESS FROM ITERATING TO TRANSFORMING

That's a very personal decision because your purpose is personal to you alone. Your OKRs were made by you for you, and others cannot tell you when you have reached your objective, unless they are empowered to know your success. It is your call. If you suspended disbelief in Chapter 2, and if you created a bold vision and a risk-adjusted plan of action in Chapter 5, you may not go into the Transform step until you have achieved that significant OKR you went after. That could take some time. Right now, you've been toggling between the Design step (where your plan was created) and the Iterate step (where you work your plan, and measure feedback, applying it back to your plan). Did you achieve a major milestone that has changed your life in some significant way? Or that changed your family significantly? Or that changed your responsibilities?

You may have defined a small OKR that allowed you to test the EDIT in a small way before you went after your purpose. If learning how to use the tools in this book in a disciplined manner was a major step forward toward greater discipline, that in itself is a transformation! Again, that's a personal decision—you know how far you've come. What feedback is your product getting in the market? Your product will either delight or disappoint. You may have promoters that rally around your new product and capability, or you may have detractors that don't. Most likely you will have both. You have the opportunity to decide based on the outcomes you as a product were looking for if you have transformed enough and your product is ready to be stamped with a "new version number," or not.

You have embraced a new mindset, and with this book, you have a new toolset, and it is my belief that as you apply these tools, you will have new skillsets that will allow you to continually advance in the direction you choose. In transforming, you will sit with the change you've achieved and get ready to set a new vision. If you haven't achieved a change that is transformational, you will still be in the Iterate step, working your plan and deciding if you should pivot or persevere, make some changes or stay the course.

You should go into the Transform step at the achievement of a significant OKR. If your OKRs were very significant, then the milestone you achieved may be transformational and you are probably more than ready to go into the Transform step.

In order to *Win When They Say You Won't*: Commit to do the following every month:

1. Track where you are versus where you wanted to be (actual versus plan).

2. Understand what strategies or assumptions worked and which ones didn't. Seek stakeholder support.

3. Be willing to change your plan, resources, and behaviors and keep moving, learning, and growing.

4. Decide on your move—you can choose to pivot or persevere.

When you have achieved a significant key result or objective from your plan of action, you are ready to enter the fourth and final step of EDIT: the Transform step.

TRANSFORM

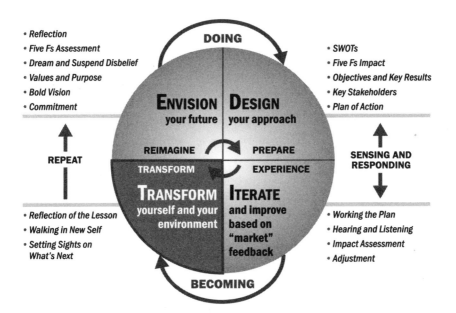

- Reflection
- Five Fs Assessment
- Dream and Suspend Disbelief
- Values and Purpose
- Bold Vision
- Commitment

DOING

- SWOTs
- Five Fs Impact
- Objectives and Key Results
- Key Stakeholders
- Plan of Action

ENVISION your future

DESIGN your approach

REIMAGINE

PREPARE

REPEAT

TRANSFORM

EXPERIENCE

SENSING AND RESPONDING

TRANSFORM yourself and your environment

ITERATE and improve based on "market" feedback

- Reflection of the Lesson
- Walking in New Self
- Setting Sights on What's Next

- Working the Plan
- Hearing and Listening
- Impact Assessment
- Adjustment

BECOMING

The fourth step, Transform, is akin to your product fully being in the market! You've been iterating, testing/learning, and getting feedback from your marketplace. You've been improving your results and making continuous improvement. You are transformed, and you will begin to transform your environment around you. You will now sit and work with the changes in your product. Because you are not quite the same person (or product) who started your journey and if you don't take time to adjust your identity to your new role, you could backslide. So here is where you reflect on your accomplishments and decide what you learned and will do differently next time you seek growth—because there will be a next time. While you want to stay with this feeling of triumph, you never want to feel like you are done growing and learning. So you will end where you began by deciding where you will set your sights next.

In Chapter 10, you will take a moment to reflect and absorb what you've achieved, how you did it, and what you've learned—just like the replays athletes use to see how they performed in their last competitive encounter. You will want to apply your learnings the next time you go through your EDIT or while you are learning your new situation.

Chapter 11 helps you learn how to sustainably walk in new shoes so you can focus on what's ahead of you, design your strategy for how you will initially learn about your new situation, and then transform the situation. Staying confident in your achievement, while staying grounded and humble so you can learn and contribute, can be daunting. I will cover how you can do both.

Chapter 12 is a special chapter that addresses some realities of how to "win while Black." To be authentic or to assimilate is a daily challenge for people of color while delivering on commitments. People of color should not take the negative feedback and behaviors personally, but should take them strategically instead.

Chapter 13, the last chapter in the book, reveals how there are times that life will happen, and no risk-adjusted plan can predict what will happen or when. I will discuss how I handled a major setback and how we all can keep improving our product to become the next better version of ourselves.

ARRIVING
ON THE PODIUM

If you can't fly, then run. If you can't run, then walk.
If you can't walk, then crawl. But whatever you do,
you have to keep moving forward.

—MARTIN LUTHER KING JR.

This chapter starts the Transform step by showing you how to reflect on your EDIT process journey. In the Iterate step, you took on some initiatives that worked, and I hope you created and celebrated your incremental successes along the way. You may have focused on other key results that didn't work as well and slowed down your progress toward your anticipated objectives and milestones. At the end of my team's projects, we would do a postmortem, reflecting on how our project went, what we learned, and what we would do differently in the future. As a new product, you will do the same so you can "understand" how your product will move forward in the market, what attributes of it are working as intended, and how some aspects of it may need to be tweaked. This chapter focuses on reflecting and journaling on your OKRs—the way you managed and dealt with headwinds and tailwinds, the status of your Five Fs, and the way your performance, image, and exposure have changed.

You will spend time with a reflection chart, which will enable you to address three key questions:

1. What to start?

2. What to stop?

3. What to continue on your next journey in the EDIT process?

I mentioned the start/stop/continue approach briefly in Chapter 7 as a way to get more meaningful feedback; this chapter shows how to use it.

The EDIT process became clearer to me when I was promoted to be executive director of Ortho Clinical Diagnostics (OCD), one of the Johnson & Johnson companies. While I didn't call it the EDIT process at the time, I began to reflect on the steps that brought me to that long-anticipated promotion. As I started to think back on this step in my career, I could see the following:

- *I was becoming stronger, as I wasn't as easily distracted by the headwinds of racism, sexism, and my own doubts.*

- *I became laser-focused on delivering my metrics and deliverables; I discovered that regardless of what anyone thought of me, when I delivered the numbers, results, and key milestones, my work spoke louder than any opinion or perception of me or my character (although having a good brand is truly an accelerator—remember PIE).*

As well, I consistently asked myself and my team reflection questions, such as these:

- *Did our assumptions prove to be valid? What did we assume that we should not have? How can we do better?*

- *Did our projections meet or exceed our budget? Why or why not?*

- *Was our change management planning effective?*

  - *What should we have done better to prepare the organization for the change?*

I took time with my team at the end of every go-live—whether it was a manufacturing system or a business analytics pilot—or at the end of key presentations, to review our work and see what we had learned together.

The lessons, challenges, and victories that I achieved at OCD eventually led me into my next EDIT of becoming a vice president for the first time in my career. What a great celebration that moment was for me!

Before you picked up this book, you might have been in a toxic, unsatisfactory, or negative situation that without reflection may have gone unnoticed until you lived your entire life and looked back with regret—saying "If I woulda and coulda, then I shoulda . . ." You might have shown your dissatisfaction by criticizing others or blaming others in your pre-Envision step. But when you started doing the work of the EDIT process, that gave you an opportunity to look at your state of doing and your state of being. Success isn't about other people; it's about how you respond to situations—you can either stay so you can win or leave so you can win. Your Five Fs always existed, but in the Envision step, you intentionally and consciously defined their importance and their impact. Your commitment statement to yourself made it clear that you were serious about your transformation journey. Now that you are in Step IV of this process, you can look back with new eyes and see that you aimed to be something or someone different that is more in line with your purpose.

The Transform step is an opportunity for you to step back and holistically view your plan of action and reflect on how well you did against your OKRs, so as you move forward into your next EDIT cycle, you will appreciate where you are and what you have learned, and you will be ready to apply those learnings in the future. Your learnings don't go to waste; they are in your mind to be used in the future as needed. You clearly achieved some key milestones, or else you would not be in the Transform step. You may not have gotten on a for-profit board, for example, but you may have gotten on a not-for-profit board— that's a milestone! Your future EDIT could then result in your getting appointed to a paid board. You may have been promoted to the role you wanted or maybe to a different role—that's a milestone! You may have improved your public speaking, or have done a great job leading a project team, achieving very key objectives—that's a milestone! You achieved some or all of your OKRs.

This reflection during the Transform step is slightly different from the reflection you did early on during the Envision step. In the Envision step, your reflection was akin to looking at the windshield to define and envision where you wanted to go, but not forgetting the past as you looked into your rearview mirror. The windshield before you in the Envision step was large and expansive, allowing you to dream and envision seemingly without limits. You could look miles and virtually years ahead.

This reflection in the Transform step is where you will look more in the rearview and side mirrors to assess and reflect where you came from, during the entire EDIT process, and let that inform what and how you will envision as you go through another cycle of EDIT.

You should take this reflection time to ask yourself questions such as these:

- What tailwinds spurred you on?

- What headwinds hindered your progress?

- How did your Five Fs factor into achieving your objective or contribute to missing or achieving any of your targets?

- Were you able to prioritize your Five Fs to ensure that the key F remained or became healthy and whole?

- What did you learn about yourself during this process?

- Who were the best stakeholders and friends you could call on? (Who was in your circle *and* your corner?)

- Are you more resilient and stronger than you thought you would be? How do you know?

You won't necessarily do anything with these reflections except to learn from them and remember them when you walk in the new Transform step and tackle the next EDIT. You will remember what worked and what didn't. You will be grateful for the progress and feel good that you are once again in the winner's circle!

My friend and buddy Kristen Lamoreaux, founder of Lamoreaux Search, reflected on how she created SIM Women (SIM is the Society for Information Management). She essentially transformed how women in technology (who are rare breeds indeed) can find each other, connect and engage with each other, learn from each other—and grow. As she reflected on her vision to start SIM Women, she identified her headwinds—there didn't seem to be enough critical mass to really start a tech woman's group. She had gone to an IT event, and during a midmorning break, she saw there was a long line for the men's room, while there was no line at all for the women's room. She and the two other women there laughed at that, and then cried out, "We need to do something about the lack of women and women leaders in IT!"

Her tailwind was catalyzed by a colleague who was the national president of the IT organization. He gave her permission to leverage the organization's national logo to drive credibility and gave her support to create a women's interest group. The next IT event had 22 women out of 300 attendees. Based on the answers to surveys of those women and others nonattendees about mentorship, benchmarking information, and such that showed the need for a women's networking org, she designed SIM Women.

She learned that there were women who had questions and other women who had answers. What if she could help both get together and share with each other? Her learning also revealed that the time was ripe for this group: more women were going into IT than before, but there weren't enough to make them confident in being a force or in showing their development gaps—even to the men in the same company as they were. That became known as the "confidence gap." Some women would rather spend hours looking for a woman outside their company who had an answer to their question than ask James down the hall who knew the answer. They said, "Oh, no! I can't be perceived as 'not knowing the answers' to the men." On the other hand, there were other women who would seek out whoever had the answer. Those two mindsets needed to meet and learn together.

Kristen had her first conference call with six women and later expanded SIM Women to three dozen chapters across the country and into Canada inside of two years. As she reflected on her Five Fs, the main one she focused on as she took on this extracurricular activity was her health (fitness). She'd had some health challenges in the past, and she needed to ensure she kept up on her health-maintenance regime.

She knew she needed a champion, and her biggest champion was the head of the national IT organization, a man. He was in her corner, supported her vision, and was influential while she kept her eye on her objective. When I asked her about her resilience and what kept her going, she told me, "Daphne, if I don't do what's in my mind to help women, no one will." To this day, Kristen's battle cry is "Do Something—Don't Quit—Do the Right Thing!" Kristen has built on her victory and has since built up her business, using her learnings and mindset to win.

You will use the learnings from the rearview mirror to take a new-and-improved look through the windshield as you move forward. I believe you will be able to look further and see differently about what is possible. While you look in your rearview mirror, it will help you see and learn how your environment, stakeholders, and assumptions matched your reality. You will be smarter, your blind spots will have been uncovered, and your expected or unexpected headwinds will be more familiar to you. As you plan to go forward to another objective, you will do so understanding the possible challenges and accelerators that may be waiting for you, using all the resources needed (such as your windshield, mirrors, and side window), with your eye continuously on your bodacious objective.

Focusing on reflecting first during the Envision step and again during the Transform step is not to say that you will reflect only twice—in the beginning and the end. You also reflected, assessed, and monitored your progress as a product manager throughout the middle of the EDIT process. The major reflections in the beginning as a product manager help show you where you've been and where you as a product want to go; in the middle, reflecting on your product transformation project helps you know where you are and how your project is doing; your reflection in the Transform step helps you see how far you've come and where you're going in the next EDIT.

At the end of the EDIT process, in the Transform step, you will have outputs of your journey—what you've done and what you've achieved, and you will turn around and use those learnings as input for your next EDIT.

REFLECT AS YOU LEARN

Are you learning, earning, and returning all you can? Truth be told, it's hard to imagine that you are only in one season at any time, but you do have a preponderance for one over another. Even though someone might be in college full-time (learning), this person is still working part-time to make money (earning), and he or she may volunteer at a food bank (returning), but the person's main focus is learning.

As the product manager of your transformation, you need to continually be in learning mode. You did some things that worked and created small successes along the way. You also did some things that didn't work or may have slowed you down a bit. It is always good to reflect on the lessons, because when you transform, there's always a lesson to learn.

When you take on a high-level role, that means high accountability and extreme visibility. You have to learn to watch, anticipate, measure, and respond. For example, remember my story in Chapter 8 about the consultant I hired who went behind my back? The next time I hired a consultant to help me in the organization, I didn't cut any corners: the candidates were vetted better and with improved performance metrics.

As you reflect on your achievements, you will know who was there for you, who wasn't, and who was helpful in your walk. Just because someone wasn't needed in your first EDIT cycle does not mean that person will not be needed in your second EDIT. But if someone who may have been influential in your first EDIT chooses not to be in this second round, he or she can be part of your reflection. As you either redefine your objective with more clarity or dig deeper on your OKRs in your next EDIT, you will review your stakeholder team and assess who is influential versus interested, or both, or neither.

What to Look for as You Reflect

The primary tool you will use during the first part of the Transform step is a questionnaire that will help you reflect on how you went through achieving your OKRs. You will ask yourself some questions about your journey, and then you will decide at least three things as a result of your reflection—what to *start*, what to *stop*, and what to *continue* as you begin your next EDIT, or as you sit in your role and perform at the next level. You will get feedback from your stakeholders to see if perhaps you missed a key objective that was important for them, or if you have a special gift that showed up brilliantly, and that when used more, will help propel you to a new level.

In this reflection questionnaire, these are the key areas of focus that will help you know what it may take (start/stop/continue) for you to prepare for the next EDIT:

1. Objectives and key results achieved

2. Controlling for headwinds and tailwinds

3. Watching over your Five Fs

4. Improvements in PIE

In the sidebar that follows, review, reflect, and answer the questions that cover those four areas. What will you start/stop/continue?

QUESTIONS TO REFLECT ON

- Did you achieve your committed *objectives*?

- Did you achieve your *key results*?

- Did you have to *iterate on your plan*?

- If so, what did you change as you iterated? Your objectives? Timeline? Resources? Something else?

- Was there any leading/root cause *headwind* that slowed you down?

- Did your *risk-adjusted plan* include the headwind?

  o If not, would including it have helped you anticipate the risks?

  o Could you have known about the headwind?

  o Was the headwind within your control? Outside your control?

- Were any headwinds within your control?

- Which tailwinds helped you along?

- Which, if any, of your *important Five Fs* were impacted—positively or negatively?

- Did you identify and utilize your *stakeholders* effectively?

- Did you *pivot or persevere* on your objective? Which one? Why?

- Look at your commitment statement. How far have you come to honoring your commitment to yourself?

- As you look at your overall PIE (performance, image, and exposure):

  o **(P)** How was your overall performance? Did your performance reviews improve over this time period—e.g., from a 3 (*meets*) to a 4 (*exceeds*)?

  o **(I)** Did you seek out and get a 360-degree feedback? If it was not your first one, did it improve? Are there still blind spots that were uncovered? Do you show empathy for others more, or are you demonstrating awareness and control of behaviors that may have needed improvement before? Do you role-model trusted leadership behaviors?

  o **(E)** Do you now have a sponsor and a mentor? Are more key executives aware of your leadership, and would they spend political capital on you?

  o Has your network improved? Does it have a stronger presence and awareness from your business partners about your capabilities and more support from your business partners than before? If so, how can you tell?

From these data points, you will understand that you more than likely have hit some key results, or you are closer to being and achieving where you wanted to be. To set your sights on what will be your next EDIT, you can contemplate your answers to the following questions.

What Will You Need to Start Doing That You Didn't Do During Your First EDIT?

At this point, you likely have identified things you didn't do that caused you to have less than desirable results. Could you have gone further faster if you had done something that you didn't do? For example, perhaps you should start thinking and behaving at a level higher than what your title may indicate, because you now have the maturity and experience in your career to do so.

> *My friend Jackie has always been scrawny and stayed away from sports. As she envisioned, designed, and transformed her career into a chief legal officer and board member, she discovered that she needed to start getting involved in sports, her fitness. But she had to break the cycle in her family where the girls mainly focused on cooking and doing house chores, while the boys were outside playing basketball or learning how to golf. As she was iterating in her career, over time she realized she needed an outlet to let off some steam and improve her muscle tone and overall strength. She found that as she strengthened her body, her character, team camaraderie, and other attributes also grew stronger.*

What Do You Need to Stop Doing?

Maybe it's a bad habit that caused you to alienate your team or your boss. You may have been overly aggressive for the culture you work in. You could have also not demonstrated good emotional intelligence and improperly read the room during a critical meeting, resulting in less positive response to you. Take the time to think through the actions that you need to stop to get a better idea of what not to do moving forward. This is where feedback from those who saw you in action will be invaluable. Remember the Johari window and blind spots (discussed in Chapter 7).

What Do You Need to Continue Doing?

What has really worked well for you during your EDIT? Using your collaboration skills? Thinking like an entrepreneur? Being a bridge across silos? Maybe you should continue communicating and motivating your team during these times of the Great Resignation, or continue aiming for a 10X performance of the team? Chances are, the list of what you should continue doing will be longer than your start and stop lists!

> *When I was new to Hospira, as SVP, it was my first time working in a pharma company. I was successful in my EDIT of becoming an SVP/CIO of a company, where I was the top-ranking leader in the IT organization. Little did I know I would be the top-ranking woman in the company—that was a bit more than I was aiming for! However, as a person new to the company, I was in the early Transform phase of my job. As I reflected on my start/stop/continue of my career project to be enterprise CIO, I realized that what got me there would keep me there. So I felt my "continue" would be to stay focused on speaking the language of the business (a lot of people in the IT function tended to do "techno talk," which is not comprehensible nor helpful to the business side). I would continue to connect with business partners in the business, as I did during the interview process, so they would know I understood their challenges. That is what helped me win and stay as SVP/CIO there for five years.*

When you go back to design and iterate your next objective, you should review your completed reflection chart in tandem with your start/stop/continue assessment. Then those conclusions will be used to help you for your next EDIT. They should show up in your plan as a more conscious action to take into your risk-adjusted plan of action.

In order to *Win When They Say You Won't*: After you achieve a key milestone, reflect on what you achieved versus what you didn't. Before you get back in the game, what will you start doing, stop doing, or continue doing? Commit to it and ask for help from your tribe of stakeholders. As you get ready to walk in a new pair of shoes—in Chapter 11—you will need to be aware of how you can continuously improve.

WALKING
IN NEW SHOES

If you always put limits on everything you do,
physical or anything else, it will spread into
your work and into your life. There are no limits.
There are only plateaus, and you must not stay there,
you must go beyond them.

—BRUCE LEE

Now that you have reflected on where you are in the Transform step and what you have learned from your journey, this chapter helps you learn how to "walk in new shoes." So many personal and professional self-improvement programs treat attaining your objective as the finish line—but in my experience, attaining an objective is really just the beginning of a new race. Beyond the finish line is a new reality that you must navigate as savvily as every step you took to get here—or this will be a short-lived success. For Olympiads who achieved the first gold medal in their lives, their post-Olympic lives will be very different from before they won. There will be media, endorsements, book deals, extra-heavy attention and temptations, deeper scrutiny into their personal lives, money, and fame! When you win, you don't want your talents to take you where your character and discipline can't keep you.

There are times that you will hit a truly major transformational milestone in your career. Each major step I took—from director of

IT to vice president to senior vice president and corporate officer—
required that I had to get a new pair, a bigger pair, of virtual shoes.
Every time you reach a milestone or plateau, you will need to assess
where you are, design how you will adjust for the change, adapt to
the new and bigger reality, and then thrive. For me, as I moved up, the
responsibilities were greater, the risks were higher, the visibility was
larger, the expectations were relentless, and the ripples through my
Five Fs seemed instantaneous, good and bad.

To teach you how to walk in these new shoes, first, we will get
familiar with being in learn mode—first you *learn the job, then you do
the job, and then you transform the job.* All three of those are critical for
the win. Then we will cover how to assess the critical success factors
(CSFs) that need to be addressed to thrive in this new position, i.e.,
"our first 90 days."

*When I became a board member on my first board, it represented
years of results I had worked toward. Ascending into a board
position was a reflection of the value that companies see in people
with my background and skills. But I wasn't sure how I was going
to execute in this new role. I started my corporate career at IBM
in 1979, and for nearly 40 years, I was accustomed to being an
operator. I wondered if I would be able to sit in a room for hours
for two to three days and only listen to the business activities
versus acting on them. Would I be able serve in this new capacity
as a board member, asking questions, governing, and providing
oversight and perspectives, instead of designing and driving what
was happening, as I was used to doing? The answer had to be yes!
Or else I wouldn't be on the board of directors for long.*

*In order to walk in new shoes, I had to go into learning mode.
I took a four-day board director class at Stanford, joined the
National Association of Corporate Directors, read books, and
sought out mentors. Then I reminded myself of my value propo-
sition: since the board members had selected me, they must have
appreciated the critical skills I would provide to the board and
the company. As I became clearer on how I would fill any gaps on*

the board, I could be sure to set myself up to provide value, which led to more board opportunities.

The data about diversity on boards is clear and is getting more compelling. Anna Meyer reported in *Inc.* magazine in July 2021 that companies with more than 30 percent of board seats occupied by women delivered better year-over-year revenue in 11 of the top 15 S&P 500 sectors than their less-gender-diverse counterparts. Moreover, 54 percent of these gender-diverse companies delivered positive year-over-year revenue in 2020 compared with 45 percent of the companies with lower gender diversity. The best-performing sectors for gender diversity were retail and computer software, whereas transport and energy were the poorest performers.

My serving on a board is a highlight of my life, and being a Black woman with a background in STEM, it is my honor and duty to provide value for each company on whose board I serve, and the data is on the side of women and women of color that we are and will be good for the companies.

Although you are now moving through to the end of your first EDIT, as you become accustomed to moving through more EDIT cycles while you continue to transform your life, you will likely hit a truly major transformational milestone in your career or with your overall personal objectives. It's bound to happen. I am now serving on three boards, and joining each one required new shoes and higher degrees of transformation.

Board service may not be on everyone's radar, and it may not be something you achieve even if you want it. But if you want it, don't deny yourself having that in your vision. And if it doesn't happen, you will have still reached and arrived at a higher place than where you were because the skills and capabilities you will develop along the way will be higher than where you were.

Every time you reach a milestone, your virtual shoes may not be bigger, but they may fit differently. What happens as you go through the various challenges is that you continue to develop those muscles that you have always had but may have been underdeveloped or never used. And like the seed that you are, you are more than equipped to handle challenges and produce more fruit.

It is said that we are a product of our environment, but I believe that our environment should also be a product of us. As we respond to the environment, the environment responds to us—whether that be through our winning teams, our loyal families, or our individual breakthrough performances. As you continue to work within the EDIT process, each micro or macro achievement will enable you to be stronger and more powerful in how you impact your environment. Each achievement of your key results and milestones will put you closer and closer to having your major transformation. Your EDIT will continue to help you cycle through greater achievements in your life, allowing you to make bigger impacts on your company, family, and community, as well as on yourself. So not only have you transformed into a new version of yourself, your transformation will have an impact on others in your environment. You will lead differently and you will use tools that you used in your own transformation to help your company with its transformation. You transformed your body by getting healthier, and you now can help others do the same.

While you are walking in your new shoes, there are three steps that I believe are critical to note as you get comfortable with this new level in the organization.

1. **Leave whatever you now own better than when you found it.** To ensure that you are setting yourself up to win continually, focus on achieving where you want to go; then walk in that achievement, stretching your mind and imagination, and transform what you found—making it better. For example, if you helped your business reduce labor costs, what else can you do to reduce other costs or drive greater productivity? How can you take the achievement you just made and increase it 3x, 7x, or 10x? You can transform the culture, the competencies, the performance, and the strategies of the business.

2. **Know your worth and value.** This may be a moment when you hold your head in your hands and say "I can't believe I did it" or

"What have I gotten myself into?" If you ever have that feeling of "Now what do I do?" and self-doubt, and feel impostor syndrome creep in, remember you are perfectly made for this time. You would not have had the vision, passion, and capability to achieve your objective if you were not built for it. Remember that at one point you disbelieved, and you had to suspend that disbelief and charge forward with your vision and true north. Remember—*you are the real deal.* Put one foot in front of the other and keep moving forward.

3. **Ensure you have the right stakeholders in place.** Sometimes you have to change up your stakeholders. Don't throw the old ones to the curb, but rather strategically include newer stakeholders that now reflect where you currently are in your overall journey. You may have outgrown the earlier ones, or they may not need to play the same role in your life as they did before. The new ones you may seek may not have been right for you before, but now that you have made a major transformation, you still need mentors or coaches to help you traverse the new and bigger landscape.

Sometimes you need to walk in your new shoes longer than you may like or feel is necessary. When you walk in them longer, you have a better feel for the needs of the business over time, and you can also be there to celebrate when the tactics you deploy generate results.

When I was at J&J, I was continually intrigued at how people would be in a new job for only nine months to a year and then would get promoted to another job. They were barely in the new job to make any significant difference. They appeared to be on a fast track to somewhere and had to "check the box" of this current job so they could move on to the next job that was seemingly part of their fast-track career transformation.

When this type of rapid movement happened, the risk was that the leader in that position would make decisions that may have a short-term positive impact for which they would get credit, but the mid- or long-term impact was unknown and might be negative, or it could be positive. It was difficult for the leader to take the long view because by the time the "long term" came around (often two, three, or more years later), that leader had moved on, and the impacts of their short-term decision now had to be owned by someone else—not the original leader who drove the department to where it is.

After seeing more short-term thinking and fewer favorable long-term results, Johnson & Johnson realized that a leader needs to spend at least two to three years in a new role before being promoted to a subsequent role. The company decided to change the leadership road map.

As a leader myself, it was clear to me that for people to be successful in a role, they first have to *learn* the job they were promoted to do. Hard to do that in nine months. Regardless of the type of role one goes into, they need to hypothesize and seek to understand the following:

- What does success look like?

- What are you accountable for?

- Who is your customer?

- Who is your customer's customer?

- What are the short-term and long-term company or department goals?

- Who are the people on your team?

- What collective skills are required to successfully deliver results that were expected?

- What commitments are behind schedule? What issues are burning?

- What can you do to exceed expectations? Is anything ripe for disruption and innovation?

- What will your servant leadership strategy be to both support and drive your team?

- What are your beginning thoughts on a blueprint you may use to make a difference?

If you think again about the PIE model, with the focus on performance, as you are learning the job, you come to an agreement with your boss regarding your performance plan based on his or her objectives, along with the accountabilities you will own to help drive the attainment of his or her objectives.

After you *learn* what it takes to win, then you *do* the job. You put one foot in front of the other, and you begin to use your own 90-day plan to execute on your blueprint. Part of the blueprint is meeting with people who have a point of view through which you can confirm the hypotheses you made when you were in the early stages of walking in your new transformation.

For example, if your company's sales are lagging behind where they should be, you probably have an initial set of reasons why you think that is. You will need to have that as a priority to focus on not in the first 90 days, but likely in the first 90 minutes! But when you begin to *do* the job, you will seek and acquire more information from your team and from the other leaders in the organization, and with the multiple data points you will come to a more refined conclusion on why sales may be lagging. This may confirm or conflict with your original hypothesis, but in either event, you will *do* with your team what you feel is most appropriate to address the disappointing sales. It may involve only your direct team, but it will likely involve other teams across the value chain. You will apply some action, and you will see what the results bring you.

Doing the job is something that will take some time as you learn the culture, politics, metrics, and relationships, and are able to determine the effect of the actions you're taking. You will also understand what types of decisions will generate short-term versus long-term results.

Finally, after you are able to *do* the job successfully, you start setting your sights on how you can fix any systemic issues that may help accelerate your team's performance. This is when you are beginning to *transform* the role. You no longer are just doing what is expected or what the leaders thought was possible. You are exceeding expectations in ways that your boss or organization may not have anticipated or considered.

This learn/do/transform process is another one of those life cycle processes, similar to the EDIT process, that help you look at a goal or role from a systems standpoint for ease of planning and execution. If you know there are three steps to doing well in your job—learn/do/transform—it gives you clarity to take each step, one step at a time. Once your EDIT transformation has happened:

1. You *learn* and understand what is needed to sustain your change and transformation,

2. Then you *do* what it takes to make your plans come to life, and think of how you can improve,

3. And then you *transform* it for sustainability and long-term greater impact.

4. And you rinse and repeat!

Let's go to another level in this thinking. You have read throughout this book about these terms "willset," "mindset," "toolset," and "skillset." They apply in learn/do/transform concept as well. The transformation that you have gone through and will go through again via the EDIT process happens because your "willset" allowed you to make the decision that you were going to win, and that you were going to become what you envisioned. Your mindset opened you up to *learn* via a growth "mindset" (versus a fixed mindset). Once you were open to learning, you then had to *do* what was required by using "toolsets" in this book or other tools that were at your disposal to drive change in your life, your career, your relationships, etc. It was through the application of the various tools, such as Five Fs, OKRs, stakeholder assessments, etc, that you have acquired a "skillset" that empowers and enables you to *transform* and improve not just once, but continually. Transformation will happen continually because your skillset will be applied again in your next EDIT.

> *As a board member, currently serving on three boards, I am still learning, while in "do" mode—doing what I can to help make the companies better and drive stakeholder value. That includes my helping ensure there are strong internal controls via the audit committee or reviewing executive compensation plans via the compensation committee. It may mean helping senior management understand how to navigate relating to their employees during the murder of George Floyd and the subsequent racial reckonings throughout the country and the world during the summer of 2020 and beyond; or it may mean how to drive more effective digital transformation strategies and how to ensure protection and resilience against cyberattacks.*
>
> *My role as a board member will* transform *as I set the stage for my personal continued growth as a board member, including teaching other senior executives how to get ready for board service.*
>
> *To continue moving forward in the Transform step, the key skillsets I had to cultivate included self-confidence, emotional intelligence, intellectual curiosity, and the willingness to continuously improve.*

You need to remember that you made it through to an outcome that mattered to you, in spite of roadblocks—and you can do it again. You will learn from your experiences, and you will seek insights on any areas of your current role to help push you through any doubts or fears so you remain on track to achieve the next bigger or better thing toward your purpose.

UNDERSTANDING YOUR CRITICAL SUCCESS FACTORS

Your will and your mind enabled you to get to this step of Transform. But even though you suspended disbelief, and you dreamed big and aimed for the moonshot, there are times when fear, uncertainty, and doubt can creep back in. Where your mind is, energy will follow. There are affirmations and critical success factors that you can embrace to help you keep moving forward to learning, doing, and transforming the space and getting ready to take on your next EDIT.

The following four CSFs will be helpful to use so you can stay both grounded and confident in wearing your new shoes for your first 90 days:

1. **Acknowledge.** Declare where you are, and define (in a sentence or two) what you have achieved. Determine if what you have achieved is the same as or different from the commitment statement you created in Chapter 3. Confirm the state of your Five Fs and acknowledge the work you did to ensure your critical Five Fs remained healthy was worth it. If your Five Fs have taken a negative hit, then acknowledge that, too, because without acknowledgment, the issue with them may fester. You may need to spend part of your first 90 days repairing or at least focusing more on the F that was negatively affected.

2. **Be grateful.** Now that you are standing in your transformation, you can say, "I am grateful for what I have achieved, the people who helped me get there, the obstacles I overcame, and the lessons I learned." In Chapter 10, you reflected on the lessons you learned and the actions that you will start, stop, and continue, and now is your time to be grateful for the work that you've put in thus far toward your objectives.

3. **Affirm.** Some of the affirmations you should keep in your heart and mind are:

   ○ "I didn't get here by accident. I executed my plan of action, was agile, persevered in times of trouble, and am at a place better than where I was."

   ○ "I will continue to choose solutions over problems, courage over fear, and action versus inaction."

○ "I know my purpose and will pursue it relentlessly on a daily basis."

○ "I will continue to seek feedback from the market, my mentors, my team, my family, and my buddies, and I will use it to grow."

4. **Set your sights high.** You had bodacious aspirations in this EDIT. How will you ensure you will continue to have them? Let learning, doing, and transforming be your mantra in this season you are in.

In order to *Win When They Say You Won't*: Learn to walk successfully in your new shoes by staying in your continuous learning and improvement mode. Don't stop improving now. Remember, you got to this place because of your worth and value. And also remember to ensure you assess your stakeholders to see if you need to add to or change your tribe.

CHAPTER 12

WINNING WHILE BLACK

ASSIMILATE OR AUTHENTICATE?

A winner is a dreamer who never gives up.

—NELSON MANDELA

A s a Black woman in corporate America, I grew into seeking and appreciating feedback from the "right" mentoring or coaching sources and not be afraid of it. All feedback is not harmful. I had to find a way to get balanced feedback. I realized as I got higher in my career, the great accolades were harder to come by. But I needed to get feedback to know how I was perceived and performing.

Having good coaches and mentors as a woman or person of color will pay off if they can show you which circumstances you should assimilate into your company's culture or when you can remain authentic. The goal is to help the company win, and in so doing, you also win. But at what cost? There's a trade-off and a constant battle between *assimilation* (i.e., when a minority group or culture comes to resemble a society's majority group or take on the values, behaviors, and beliefs of another group or organization) and *authenticity* (i.e., the quality of being genuine or real, being oneself and not trying to be like others.) This chapter explores the challenges of being a person of color in a corporate space and strategizing how to win in these places when others say you won't.

When you assimilate, you seek to minimize the inherent obvious or subtle differences between a subject and an organization. In doing so, you minimize the aspects of *your* culture, your beliefs, or your authenticity that may be distracting or uncomfortable for those groups you are seeking to assimilate into. For example, if a person is different in her skin color, her gender, her dress, her ideology, her behavior, and her religion, and if we believe that people feel more comfortable around those who are more like them, then we have a person who is different in six ways. Each of those six ways (or combinations of any of the six) in which she is different will likely cause her peers to be curious, distracted, and disrupted and may display other sentiments that may not help the organization focus and win.

But if that person assimilates, then although she cannot change her skin color or gender, if she modifies the other four aspects of herself to be more mainstream, or to not have those aspects be as visible or known, then she will likely be *more* accepted and can work more easily with others. But, yes, in truth, she is giving up some part of her true self to fit in. And even then, it won't be 100 percent.

I'm a member of the Delta Sigma Sorority, Incorporated, one of the first Black women's sororities in the United States, founded in 1913. Before I could join the sorority, I had to go through an induction process (pledging); however, to be allowed to go through that, I first had to go to a tea where the members meet all the prospective pledgees. I tried so hard to be the person I thought the actual Delta members were when I first showed up to pledge. They were sophisticated, so I tried to show up as sophisticated. They were confident, so I tried to show my confidence. I overdid it, instead of just being me.

They rejected me the first time, because it was clear I was not authentic, and they couldn't connect with me. Here I was, trying to join a group of women who looked just like me, and

I pretended to be something that I naturally wasn't. I tried to assimilate based on what I thought they wanted to see, and I failed. As Black people, we try hard enough to assimilate in the larger world. Why would I try to assimilate into a group of other Black women? Duh.

The following semester I came back and was my authentic self, and they accepted me into the pledge group. I've now been a Delta for more than 40 years.

I believe you should seek to be authentic as much as possible and not change out the core of who you are, but rather improve the core of who you are for the better—for being of service to others, for helping others, for driving your company higher in the market, for developing leaders, etc.; you have a superpower and gifts, and they should be shared with your marketplace. But just as we individuals need to improve our core, I also believe the organization should seek to improve the core of its culture—to train its leaders and employees and ensure its practices and policies drive better diversity, equity, and inclusion (DEI) so the burden of what becomes "extreme" assimilation doesn't rest on the woman of color's shoulders, or be the only way for a woman or employee of color to survive. People of color (POC) are fewer in number as it is and are already feeling vulnerable. When people are not being themselves, they are not thriving; they're pretending. When you are not honest with who you are, you are out of alignment with your spirit and your mind. Creativity is suboptimized, the free exchange of ideas is not really free flowing, challenging the status quo is rife with negative consequences, etc. and when an integral part of the organization is suboptimized, the entire organization is suboptimized and is not hitting the market with full strength.

We hear about the challenges Black men face in incarceration, healthcare disparities, more severe charges for the same crime as a majority male commits, gangs, murder, etc. In our church in Syracuse, there are far fewer men in the congregation than there are women. In corporate America, you see the same thing. You will more likely see a Black woman sitting on the board, being CEO, or filling any number of leadership roles than you will see a Black man. Black men and women in general tend to be less groomed for financial or profit and loss (P&L) roles, which are natural successors to a CEO. So when we go out looking for a Black male CEO for a board seat, or for a Black male for a CEO position, the same people get tapped on the shoulder repeatedly because the pickings are few and the investment in seeding a more diverse CEO/board pipeline is insufficient.

I call that the case of the "missing senior Black male leader." I've seen the burden of assimilation or the requirement to fit in the culture and be successful seemingly fall on the few Black males that may make it into senior leader roles. I believe they are an endangered corporate species, to put it mildly. The question becomes, how can an organization hire, develop, retain, and promote those who are at risk in society? Even though diversity and inclusion are business issues, what society does and teaches has a social impact on availability and perspective about Black men. I have seen organizations discuss the dismissal of Black men leaders far too casually and not notice the corporate pattern, as if their performance is only on the shoulders of the men themselves and not a shared responsibility with the organization. Like me, Black men are often given the glass cliff opportunity—a nearly impossible job, that if the Black man didn't do well, at least the company "tried" to bring in diversity.

But the focus on DEI should not be defined in merely a social context. It is truly a business issue. Many data sources exist on this, but an article by Moira Alexander in *CIO* magazine (September 3, 2021) shows that inclusive teams perform up to 30 percent better in high-diversity environments. Cognitive diversity is estimated to enhance team innovation by 20 percent. With diversity come multiple perspectives. When team members bring together a variety of backgrounds and cultures, they are likely to solve problems and be innovative. When companies really care about winning in the market and ascribe a zero tolerance to letting the corporate culture continue with the less-than-diverse status quo, they will win.

STRIKING THE FINE BALANCE OF AUTHENTICITY VERSUS ASSIMILATION

When you choose to be authentic and therefore different in certain obvious ways, you are telling yourself that you matter and *your* individual expression is important. Be aware, however, that if you choose to express your authenticity way beyond the norm—to where it may appear disruptive and distracting and where the culture hasn't been prepared to receive your authenticity—that may create challenges. Extreme authenticity may show others that you believe your authentic self-expression is potentially *more important* than the team's culture, shared values, or objectives. I believe you need to be authentic with who you are, while being aware of the written or unwritten guidelines regarding the company's values and culture. Every company has its own values and approach. Know yours and ensure you live those values—if not, why are you there?

If you look at your cultural fit in the organization and you see there is a gap between what you are willing to assimilate to versus what the company expects, you have several options: (1) you can try and be the catalyst that inspires a culture change—knowing that will take time away from your job, and will likely require you to enlist leadership to join you in this quest, (2) assimilate to what the company expects because this job is truly the one you love, or you have other rationale, or (3) move on and find a company where the cultural fit really fits if that is a critical factor in your peace of mind.

Being authentic does bring challenges, as does assimilation. It is a horribly difficult balance to strike, but it is one that I had to strike. However, when you strike it and you win, you will change the organization just that much more.

> *I had to decide how much of my identity, culture, beliefs, and inequities I could share with others without seeming like I was protesting the non-Black culture in the office. How I looked, how I dressed, which conversations I had about my race and gender that would not frighten or intimidate people who didn't look like*

275

me. Before MLK Day was an official holiday, I had to make a decision about whether or not I would take the day off on his birthday, which depended on how supportive of DEI I thought the company I worked for was, how visible my absence that day would be, and how that might affect my boss's perceptions. Would I appear too rebellious? These are things people of color and those that manage them need to think about. Why? Because until we embrace DEI in our corporate culture, the focus will be on gathering of those whose culture/diversity is outside the norm. Our corporate culture goal should be to get to a place where DEI isn't a special business metric, but that DEI represents how companies win in the marketplace.

It would be disingenuous for me to talk about transformation without acknowledging what this journey means for me as a Black woman and what *winning when they say you won't* looks like specifically for people of color, from my vantage point.

As Black people, Black women, or people of color, we have been told we will be required to be overprepared and overqualified and will need to overdeliver and achieve at such higher standards just to be recognized as merely minimally qualified. It appears that the very first Black female Supreme Court justice has qualifications that when compared with those of the other Supreme Court justices are double or triple theirs. Is that required of a minority in order to achieve at a higher level? Two or three times as qualified? Why the double standard? It appears the only thing Judge Ketanji Brown Jackson has not done in the field of law is build a courthouse from scratch with her bare hands. The mindset of the majority culture has continued to view Black people, Black women, and other people of color as inferior and incapable of meaningful achievement. When we do achieve, it is viewed as an aberration or is because we are unicorns. My goal is that we will use tools that are twice as good to win and not have to work twice as hard or be twice as good, unless being twice as good gets us to go twice as high as those we are competing against.

I was asked recently to lead a talk at a major university, and while the leader of the university and I were preparing for it, he told me I was a "unicorn." He proceeded to share that he didn't know any Black people who had my combination of capabilities. I didn't feel like asking him where he had looked; I decided I didn't have time to get into teaching at that moment.

Then, before he took the time to listen and learn the skillsets of this unicorn, he continually attempted to dominate the planning process for this event. He finally calmed down and let his micro biases or presuppositions take a back seat to the reality of my expertise. I was able to lead the planning meeting for the talk I was doing. And the event was a hit!

Many women and women of color live with this *every single day* and endure even more outrageous actions and reactions just to their very presence in the room. This occurs whether they sit on the top leadership team of their company or are on a project team as an analyst.

Even the female justices of the Supreme Court have been talked over while they are speaking, both by their peer justices and by male lawyers who are petitioning the Court. The Supreme Court has made changes in the process to address this disrespect. But you can appreciate that fact that disrespect really happens, no matter how high in organizations women may be. We cannot afford to take these things personally. Some of the men don't know better, and we have to teach them through our actions that we won't get upset at how women are treated. Rather, we will take the their actions and use them as data, then follow a business approach like EDIT, and no matter who is saying what to or about people of color, the strategy has been defined for how to deal with the bias—not by taking it personally, but by taking it strategically, and personally executing one bodacious objective at a time.

IF YOU'RE NOT AT THE TABLE, YOU'RE ON THE MENU

It is said *if you are not sitting at the table, then you are likely on the menu.* If we are not able to be in the room and at the table—where decisions are made about policy, the succession pipeline, procurement, pay, and other issues—it will be difficult for us to be able to influence those decisions to represent the values of all stakeholders more appropriately. We need to be at the table. Not for social reasons. Not for fairness reasons. Not for equity reasons. But for business reasons. The diversity of the input, when done correctly, will improve the quality of the output. If diversity isn't at the table to craft strategy, then diversity will be "optional," and will be carved out of the business strategy.

As a Black woman, I look up to Harriet Tubman as one of my long-time inspirations, motivations, and role models. When I look at how much she accomplished versus how much she was *supposed* to accomplish, I find pride in her achievements. I was given limits and labels by my high school counselor when he told me that I would be nothing but a secretary. She was given many limits and I-can-only-imagine so many labels. What I call her "push-and-pull" process was highly effective. She pushed forward into new and dangerous situations every single day, carrying not much more than a shotgun and a lantern and few things to sustain herself. That was nothing short of courageous and would be to me an example of overdelivering. She pulled the slaves along with her, led them, mentored them, and coached them to freedom. With few resources. Think of how much more people can do when equitably given proper tools, training, resources, and support.

In business, when there is an expectation of you and you do not deliver on that expectation, whoever had that expectation (your boss, your family, your client) is typically disappointed and dissatisfied. This can be expressed in a simple formula:

Disappointment = where expectations > delivered results

When there is an expectation and that expectation is met or exceeded, your client (or boss or family) will typically be delighted and highly satisfied, which can be expressed as:

Delight = where delivered results > expectations

Like Harriet Tubman, you can win in whatever your industry is, in spite of the odds, and you have an opportunity to delight, surprise, and satisfy those who don't expect much. Men don't expect much from women. My high school guidance counselor and society didn't expect much from me. So when I delivered over their low expectations, it was almost a cakewalk. It actually would have been a cakewalk, except not only were expectations low for me, but people went out of their way to make my life harder and results more challenging to reach. I'm OK with folks having low expectations, but sabotage is unnecessary and wrong.

But it is in the surprise and achievement of objectives that we win. It is in having a businesslike approach to situations that may appear personal or targeted against us that we win. It is in having strategy, OKRs, plans of action, and the ability to be resilient that we win. Anytime I surprise people with my performance, I win. And so do my people, my gender, my family, my company. So prepare to win, not complain. Prepare to have a plan, not anger. Prepare to show your superpowers, not shrink into the wallpaper.

I don't believe in "getting in where I fit in." If I do that, I don't stand out. And to win, you need to pull away from the competition and lead. If I don't rise to the top and stay there, I am like a crab in a barrel, or marbles in a jar, and I will not be in a position to lead. If I do that, I won't be in a position to speak truth to power or to empower the disenfranchised, because I would be one of those disenfranchised people trying to fit in, blend in, be invisible. As women, we need to put on our big-girl pants and remember that "no one said it was going to be easy, and no one was right!" The victory comes from achieving what no one else said we could, and it comes from helping others win when things around us may be failing. Our contribution lifts others up so they can follow our cookie crumbs we left, and be better, badder, bigger winners than we ever were.

DO MORE THAN JUST HANG ON—WIN WITH PERSEVERANCE!

There's a saying that "when you get to the end of your rope, tie a knot in it, and hang on." As a Black woman in corporate America, I continually felt like I was at the end of my rope. I was discouraged, and I was continually questioned about how I achieved my level of success. I was told that I looked too young to be a senior vice president. Even when I was asked to lead a team of leaders on how to define the digital DNA for GE in my last position at General Electric, I was often talked over or had my suggestions take a few minutes too long to be accepted, while other suggestions, from those who didn't look like me, as crazy as they were, got nearly instant consideration. Corporate America isn't designed for people like me to win. When businesses started with men like Carnegie, Rockefeller, etc., they didn't envision women or Blacks sitting in their office. So how they work has been exclusive from the start. It's been a setup from the beginning. Some of my former bosses, HR leaders, and even the head of diversity at various points in my career seemed not to understand why the focus on diversity or inclusive leadership was important for business. Power at nearly all companies is reserved for the SWGs (same white guys). I give a high five to the many white male and female CEOs who have reached out to call members of the Black and/or POC community not to ask for what white people can do, but rather, how they can learn more. But hanging on to the knot of the rope was a skill I learned, and as a Black woman, the following three things really helped me stand tall:

1. **Remind myself of my achievements.** My achievements were real. The hundreds of millions of dollars my team and I saved companies over my career were real. The improved productivity, market share, and customer net promoter scores were real. The implementations of impactful solutions to drive predictive maintenance for in-field equipment were real. My awards were real. Developing leaders who became VPs was real. My comments, articles, and recognition in *CIO* magazine, *Forbes,* and

Savoy magazine were real. The recognition and the acknowledgment I got from industry peers and organizations were real. The requests I received to facilitate a panel, or keynote an event, or speak at numerous organizations, schools, and clubs were real. At the end of the day, I rested in the knowledge that I was the real deal. No one could take away my accomplishments, or my brand, from me. I knew the value I had, and I continued to learn, do, and transform. Remember, "first they ignore you, then they laugh at you, then they fight you, then you win."

2. **Maintain a strong growth mindset and toolset and deliver.** I was so blessed to have been sent to leadership development training, new manager orientation, second-level leadership development, Harvard Business School, Smith College, Stanford, etc., for numerous classes, technology development seminars, IBM business fundamentals, and strategic planning courses. Because of the amount of learning I did, and the infusion of strategies, tools, and approaches, I knew as much as if not more than, the people around me. That knowledge kept me on my feet.

It is said, "In the land of the blind, the one-eyed man is king." In our case, the one-eyed woman is queen. Having great knowledge, excess capacity, and energy also kept me on my feet. I wasn't the smartest person in the room, but I knew a lot and was able to share wisdom, experience, and knowledge clearly and empathetically. More important, I knew I didn't know everything, but together with my team, we knew a lot. And what we didn't know, we tried to have a continuous learning mindset—lest we stagnate.

As product managers, we have to always seek to improve our product and if our mindset about our product says it's perfect and complete, we will then begin the erosion to obsolescence. We must keep our mindset toward improvement and growth, so we stay relevant and useful.

3. Fortify my life with my faith. Even though knowledge kept me on my feet, my faith and humility kept me on my knees. I relied on my relationships with various pastors, and no matter what city I was living in—in Milwaukee, it was Pastor Monica at Mount Zion Temple of Healing; in Miami, my friends Pastor Keith and Chanel Moore; in Syracuse, it was my husband, Pastor Max—I never forgot who I was and whose I was. Sometimes you have to pull from a place that is stronger than you, bigger than you, and more divine than you. My F for faith lifted me up when I was down, and it helped me realize that I didn't know everything, and that I didn't need to know everything. My faith and God's grace were sufficient to see me through, put the right people in my corner, and help me stay humble.

These three things are what I do. If you believe in them, then ingrain these three concepts in your life and create more truths about yourself. Control the narrative about you; don't let anyone else do it for you.

Sometimes as people of color, it can be very easy to blame "the man," the justice system, or whatever political party that's in power. Far too often, we can get into the bad habit of pointing fingers at someone outside of us as the cause of where we are, or where we are not. Being a victim is rarely how anyone can win. When you are a victim, you get pity, and you may get a handout or a court settlement. But as a woman who is determined *to win when others say you won't,* you don't want a handout. At most, you want your turn at bat. You want the same opportunity that others have, and you want an opportunity to show your strength and capability to help the team win.

Also, it isn't only about you winning; it's about how you help other people win and achieve their objectives, while you achieve yours. *We are not here by ourselves, and we are not here only for ourselves.* We are here to contribute to life and let our environment be a product and recipient of us—our gifts and our presence. The question is not "What do we want out of life?" That will provoke the wrong answer. Our answer should describe "What will life get out of us?" It is the answer to that question that keep me going to my next EDIT.

But oftentimes the protagonist is us. It is the history of women being raped. It is our history of minorities being assaulted. It is our history of coming from a motherless or fatherless home. It is our history of low self-esteem that has forever been suggested by people who don't look like us. Far too often, we embrace these lies and misperceptions that have been fed to us, to keep us in our place—and we wear them like a mink coat. Similar to what happens when we face the bitter winter winds of Chicago or Milwaukee, we seem to pull that coat of lies closer around us because it's familiar, and therefore we figure it must be helpful.

I have lived a life where I didn't believe I was good enough, and at times, in truth, I still wonder if I am. I can easily think of 100 reasons why I may not be good enough. But then I put on my big-girl pants, speak to my mentors and friends, and realize there are 110 reasons why I am.

Even through the negative cues I received in my life, and my feeling that I was anything but an authentic winner, I had to tell myself that my purpose and my desire to win was greater than any negative crap that someone had thrown at me. When people threw crap at me, I had to muster everything I had to not throw it back at them, but to be more resourceful, more business-minded, cooler, and more resilient so I could win in the larger game of business and in my life.

You have that opportunity now to choose your response to what life or people throw at you. My fundamental belief is that your will-set and mindset are where it all starts. If your will is broken and your mind is closed, you will have a hard time achieving and transforming, because you won't believe you can.

In order to *Win When They Say You Won't*: Remember you have superpowers that make your diversity especially needed and powerful in your organization. You have the ability to make your environment a product of you. But you should determine which aspects of the organization's culture align with your authenticity and build up from there, striking the right balance. Know that you are strong and valuable, that you have a growth mindset for which you will discover a myriad of tools around you to help you move up to a new version of yourself. With the toolsets you use, learned in this book and in others, you will have a skillset that you can now use repeatedly. You will be in the land of continuous improvement. You will not just be a success; rather, you will be successful—full of success—and you will own your victory. You will win when they said you won't.

CHAPTER 13

GET READY FOR WHAT'S NEXT

The key to realizing a dream is to focus not on success but on significance—and then even the small steps and little victories along your path will take on greater meaning.

—OPRAH WINFREY

You are here at the end of the Transform step of the EDIT process because you have achieved a significant level of success meeting your objectives and obtaining your key results. This chapter will help you set your sights on your next objective. Whether or not you hit the bull's-eye for where you wanted to be at this point, you are set up for what's next because you reflected (in Chapter 10) on the lesson of where things went off the rails and celebrated where you actually did things right. You are poised to do more and to be more because of what you learned and how you will apply it to your next cycle.

Rarely did I do everything perfectly, and rarely did I completely fail. No doubt, you could say the same thing. I hope that by this point in the EDIT process, many circumstances in your life are different (and, I hope, better!) than when you started. Now is the moment to see and celebrate all that you've learned along the way in your EDIT, and it is time to chart your next course.

No matter which category of achievement you find yourself in, you should never, ever stand still. When I think about water that stands still, it is quiet and stagnant. Standing water breeds bacteria, mosquitoes, and other undesirable things we don't want. When you sit still, you atrophy, much like your muscles if you haven't moved your legs or arms in a long time: muscles get weak and are unable to carry weight. But remember, these are the same muscles that you had earlier, and through the EDIT process, you rediscovered that you could use them again to drive forward on your objectives.

If you stop now, the gain you achieved in your journey will likely stagnate. You'll be stuck in that zone between where you were before you started on your EDIT and what you now see as possible—your major transformation. It's only through continuous improvement that you get to where you want to go. I've come to realize that you can't always prescribe or define precisely where you will go in your life. As you move toward an objective and key result, you will find that life happens. When life happens, it creates an unexpected input into what you had tried to expect, and it is in that moment that the magic of your willset and mindset will manifest.

As I look to drive continuous improvement in my life, my next EDIT will be not only to continue helping the companies on whose boards I sit, but to help other people who may have been overlooked, undervalued, or underappreciated and use my experience to help them strive for and do things that are higher than themselves. My next EDIT will comprise coaching, teaching, and helping—after all, I am in the "returning-all-I-can" phase of my life. I have much to do, and even if life takes me in an unexpected direction, with EDIT, I'm always ready to win.

Let's talk about unexpected direction. In mid-2020, I decided to seriously pursue becoming an author, which had been a dream of mine for more than a decade. It fit in the return-all-I-can phase I had been anticipating. I had been retired for three years; I was happily serving on three boards; my son was grown and off in the world pursuing his dreams; and my husband was happy to have me close by at home in New York. There was no better time than now to Envision, Design, Iterate, and Transform my ideas and my platform by publishing a book to better serve the world. While I was excited by this new burst of energy to further my purpose by becoming an author, I could not have imagined the EDIT that was in store for me before completing this book.

When I was ready to put my dream of being an author into high gear, I drew on my connections. First, I recalled that one of my colleagues, whom I ran into often at conferences and networking events, had written a book that had been published. John generously introduced me to an editor at a Big Five publishing house, who in turn introduced me to several literary agents and ghostwriters. John was my stakeholder, and through his referral, I was able to meet my agent, Lucinda, and she helped me find a ghostwriter to help me write my book proposal.

My proposal was presented to a few publishing houses, and near the end of 2020, my agent received quite a bit of interest from several notable publishers. As 2021 dawned, I was excited to see how my publishing journey would unfold, and I just knew that I would seamlessly move full steam ahead into my dream of becoming an author—until I had my routine physical in January 2021.

"Mrs. Jones..." I can't perfectly remember the rest of the phone call I got on January 8, 2021, but I remember it had something to do with the biopsy and breast cancer. My husband had to repeat back to me what he thought was the gist of the conversation.

Meanwhile, there was still a book I was determined to find the right publisher for and deliver to the world. I had to pivot for a moment and find a way to first win against my cancer, and then persevere onward to get my book completed and published. While breast cancer was an unexpected headwind, there was no way that I could have created a risk-adjusted plan for that! My Five Fs were nearly all affected, and I had to call on my faith when I needed it most. But I kept moving forward in the process by answering emails and taking Zoom calls and phone calls with potential publishers, while still fulfilling my various board duties. I had two surgeries to remove the tiny, noninvasive tumor; then three days after my second surgery, I accepted a formal offer from McGraw Hill to publish my first book.

Unfortunately, I needed yet another surgery and a round of radiation before my doctor confirmed I was and always had been at stage zero with a 98 percent prognosis for a full recovery. A 98 is an A+, and I'll take it! Now that I was able to put my cancer in the rearview mirror, I began working on writing this book. Before I could finish it, though, I faced more tragedy: one of my only two nephews was in a horrible car accident, and two days later, he succumbed to his injuries. Tragically, that same month, my husband lost his older brother.

I share my journey of becoming an author with you, first, to let you know that nothing is impossible if you have the will, the mindset, and the tools to bring your objectives to fruition. Second, I want to illustrate that anything that you are willing to EDIT—from your relationships to your health to your career—will come with its own set of challenges, both expected and unexpected. There was no way for me to predict that when I said yes! to the call of becoming an author, I would face breast cancer and the loss of my beloved nephew and brother-in-law.

Fortunately, I remembered the purpose of this book. I began thinking, "God, you gave me this incredible book platform to speak to people about winning when others think they won't. They have to win, but first I have to win. I believe that you want me to win and you want me to be a testimony to people about how no matter what happens in your life, whether it's a bad boss, a bad marriage, or an unexpected cancer diagnosis, that you can still win."

Focusing on this book gave me the reassurance that God was not done with me yet. I knew that my purpose was bigger than anything that happens to me. My purpose is so deeply embedded in me that I know that I've got to get things done. Unless my brain is damaged or something physically stops me, I know I have to keep on moving forward.

I knew that worrying about my cancer diagnosis would not be productive. FUD—fear, uncertainty, and doubt—would be distractions and weeds in my life. I knew that feeling sorry for myself would not move the ball forward. Instead, I started focusing on what would work and what I could do to keep on winning. Eating better was going to work. Meditating and having quiet moments were going to work. Getting a good night's sleep would work by helping me have the energy and stamina I needed to achieve my goal. Focusing on writing my book was going to work. Imagining myself as a bestselling author with a book that impacts the world was going to work.

More than anything else, however, it was these words from my late nephew that firmly anchored me in my purpose about why I wanted to write this book in the first place:

> *Right now, we have the ability to make decisions to be the greatest version of ourselves. No one can take that from you. If you have a goal, don't let anyone take it from you.*
> *IT'S YOUR DREAM.*
> *PROTECT IT.*
> *—Andrew Glen Lawrence*

You will not face the exact same challenges I faced. Yet you will face *something*. For example, when most of us began 2020, we couldn't have had the foresight to see Covid-19 ravaging the world and disrupting life as we knew it. I know that risk-adjusting your plan to think of what could go right or wrong is important. But there will be times when you will not be able to predict everything, even something like cancer or Covid-19. While cancer may have slowed me down, my purpose to complete my book was bigger than the pain, bigger than the problem and disruption that cancer presented in my life. I was delayed but not denied. Becoming an author was not impossible . . . it was inevitable.

When you have the will and the mindset to win, short of death, nothing should stop you. While we have no idea what life will bring us as our world continues to evolve, at this point of the Transform step, my big question for you to consider is this: What are you willing to take on to achieve an even bigger dream?

CREATING VERSION 2 OF YOU!

I'm especially excited for you as you journey through EDIT, because you can perpetually create a new version of yourself, enabling you to not be only a one-time success, but to be "successful"—that is, *full of success*—as you continuously improve.

As discussed before, I modeled EDIT after the development life cycle that software programmers use to develop a new technology software solution that will solve some problem that people have in the world. Like the iPhone, or WAZE, or an e-commerce app, etc., developers use development cycles of "plan, build, run, and maintain." That's similar to Envision, Design, Iterate, and Transform. At the end, whether it is software, cars, or our careers, we end up with something that is transformative or that has transformed. In software land, people refer to each new transformation as "versions." As I write this, iOS is at Version 15+. As I reflect on my personal journey over the years, I assert that I am at Version 6+ in my life. This is a totally subjective and personal assessment. There is no formulaic blueprint for my version assignments; I simply felt it important for me to define my various milestones, my current version, and assess if, when, and how I will move to a new version in the future. Here's how I assigned my versions:

- When I advanced from student (Version 1) to professional at IBM, that was a version change to V2.

- When I added to my role as professional to include wife and mom, that change moved me to V3. Major EDIT!

- When I went into senior management as a director, then executive director, and then VP, I believe I iterated through mini-transformations to become V4: I labeled the mini-transformations as V4.1, V4.2, and V4.3 as I grew in my career.

- When I made a huge transformation and became an SVP and corporate officer, that moved me to V5.

- When I retired and began serving on three corporate boards, I jumped to V6 of my life.

- And as I began to set my sights on what was next, my current EDIT is what you are all witnessing firsthand. I realize I can become an author, a CEO of my own company, and I can do motivational speaking, coaching, and board training. I'd say I'm on my way to V7. And in continuous pursuit of my purpose—where my capability and passion meet.

The question you should be pondering is what product version of your life are you currently in, and what version is next for you? What have been the versions of your life so far? How are you as a product being perceived by the market? Is it changing? The numbers aren't as important as the recognition that you have moved, advanced, and grown. Use EDIT to continue getting to the next and the next and the next version of your product. You will continuously improve, your life will be powerful, and others will be empowered and transformed because of you! Speak it, claim it, and do it.

BECOMING FULL OF SUCCESS

As you get ready to move forward from your current EDIT and take on your next objective, remember the following lessons to help you set your sights on what comes next:

- **Be clear on your current life stage.** Knowing what stage of life you are in will help you understand what matters to you most right now, and that will shape your vision. You can mostly learn, mostly earn, or mostly return in your current stage. Those stages are not mutually exclusive, but there will likely be a more dominant stage you are focusing on right now. Are you focusing on achieving those things that align with the stage you are in or a stage you are going to?

- **Define your own concept of your next win.** Winning is not merely creating a high-power career or amassing millions of dollars in your lifetime. Winning may be seeing a community thrive because of your love and dedication. Winning may be helping a school in another country where women are disadvantaged. Winning may be having a family whose members love and support each other. Winning may include being the role model that women look to for courage and strength so they, too, can climb a corporate ladder.

  To me, winning happens when I can walk in my purpose. As mentioned in the beginning of the book, I believe our purpose can be found where our passion and love for something intersects with our capability that we continually build on and nurture. If we are merely passionate and don't have the innate skill or capability that will help us realize our passion, we are not likely looking at our purpose. And don't let someone own or define your win. Define your own win.

- **Honor your Five Fs.** By now, you know there is so much more that matters to you than simply furthering your career. You also have your family, your faith, your finances, and your fitness—your emotional, mental, and physical well-being. Your life is an integrated system of various components. When you pull or impact one component, it is likely to impact another. Understanding what components are most important in this season of your life will help you protect them while you go after your transformation.

- **Move beyond limits and labels.** No one should define what you can do or how far you can soar. I had limits and labels put on me over the course of my career. I had to understand that I had *response-ability*—the ability to choose my response to those limits and labels. Either I can go with the label and limits, or I can choose to ensure that my purpose is clearly seated in my mind. From there, I can define myself on my terms. I choose the latter!

- **Suspend disbelief.** Do not use logic in your aspiration. Your logic will put a lid on how high you can go. And wherever your mind is, is where you will be. Whoever has your mind, has *you*! Take the lid off the jar and continue to imagine what you would do since you know you will not fail.

- **Be diligent in setting your objectives and executing your plan of action.** All objectives are not created equal. Set your product objectives and decide which one or two you will go after that are most in line with your purpose. Don't oversubscribe to too many. Prioritize. Find your BO! Once you set your prioritized objectives, you will create your OKRs that will be part of your plan of action to help you get closer to your objective.

- **Own your product journey.** As I have encouraged you throughout this book, *you are the product manager of your life.* You defined how you—the product—will transform and what you will become, how you will add value to the world, continuously improve, gain virtual market share, and be more valuable than before. You designed and iterated on your product transformation plan, aka your plan of action, calling the plays, setting due dates, measuring status, pivoting or persevering and cultivating resources. You were not a bystander but rather an active participant and manager. You are and will always be empowered to drive outcomes that will get you closer to your purpose and your objectives.

- **Keep good stakeholders around you.** You are not on earth by yourself, and as such, you cannot achieve everything in life by yourself. Know who is in your corner and whom you want in your corner as you continue moving forward.

- **Don't quit.** When others try to bury you, remember you are a seed. Seeds don't quit. They get to work. Find your support system of stakeholders who will become the soil, the water, and the silt below the surface to strengthen you at your root. You will now have the power to burst your way back through the soil so you can stand up, produce fruit, and throw good shade on those who tried to keep you down!

In order to *Win When They Say You Won't*: Know that to be a success is to achieve an objective. But to be success*ful* (full of success) is to continually achieve objectives. Decide that you are ready for what's next and you will be.

ACKNOWLEDGMENTS

First, to God.

My mother never got a chance to advance or improve her station in life. Her job was to clean bedpans and change linens at the local hospital. But she wanted the best for us and expected the best from us. I think even though she wouldn't achieve certain levels of success herself, she would still win through us. She showed the determination that many immigrant parents have: "I will live in the United States, sacrifice much, so my children will be able to win . . . ." I mention Mom first because she was the driver of the family. Dad was our family's spiritual leader, a gentleman, and showed us unconditional love, but it was Mom who made things happen. She saw our report card, she took care of our health, loved us, disciplined us; she not only fed us food, but also fed us aspiration, expectation, and consequences. Mommy, because of you, I rise, because of you, other women will win.

As I reflected back on how my book came together, it dawned on me that the book was written by a woman, ghostwritten by another woman, is about women, and is for women. Published by a woman, edited by women, promoted by a woman, and my brand is being accelerated by women. Having a book tribe of all women wasn't intentional, and I'm sure if I had tried on my own to make this book 100 percent women induced, it wouldn't have happened. So there you are.

Thank you to all the wonderful winning women named, pseudo named, and unnamed in the book. You made EDIT real through your stories, experiences, and triumphs. There are many women who suffer in silence, who from a tender young age are told that the answer is no. Not them. Not now. Not ever. I know that by ourselves we are just individual drops. But when we come together, we become the ocean. Powerful. Unstoppable. Energy creating, life sustaining. I hope that this work touches you and lifts you up to reach a place you never thought you could reach. And I hope it inspires you to reach back and pull others along, creating a powerful movement of women who win continuously, don't seek permission to prosper, and transform their environment as they are also transformed.

Lucinda and Connor, my wonderful, ever present literary agents, you educated me about the process, and although I don't know a lot about being a writer/author, you pushed me along with your sage advice, a few "Daphne, calm down" moments and connections to some great people in the business. It was you who said there are probably two books in me, and you thought I had something worth sharing.

Leah Lakins, my ghostwriter, thank you for sharing your gift for words with me. Because of you, I was able to more deeply find mine.

Donya, you read my proposal and then gave me the most meaningful and life-changing "thumbs up" I've received in my life. As a woman, you clearly felt my story even better than I wrote it. As a publisher your instincts always came through as you helped me make numerous decisions about the book, its promotion, its audience, and its tone. Although it was tough, I must thank you for the editing process!

Mr. and Mrs. Fred Jacobie—you were my first job ever, as you owned and operated the local family dry cleaning and rug cleaning business. You taught me customer service, honoring commitments, focus, and what running a business looked like.

Max, you are the partner I have always needed. You lift me up when my heart is heavy. You tend to me when I am ill. You keep me riveted with your entertaining stories and hold me steady with an unfailing love. Although I'm still a mystery to you in some ways, you have learned how to lead me from the front and how to lead me from behind. Thank you for unending support and for praying with me, while writing those checks to help my dream come true.

ACKNOWLEDGMENTS

Jared, you are my motivation, my gift from God, and it is for you that I keep reaching. Your kind heart and gentle spirit is evidence that there is a God and he's in your life. Tilly and Maarz, you bring me joy and happiness, and proof that love for self, others, and our planet will always be what is most important.

My sisters, Millie, Pam—you are also my best friends—and I know you only want what is best for me. Thank you for being there for me in every way imaginable.

My brother, Al—my eternal love goes to you and the family unit! Bernie, my ride or die!

Nomi—we have a very old friendship that is only a few years old. You treat me like I'm a part of you, and I hope I always will be worthy and show you the same love.

Kaye Foster, Barbara Bowles, Monica Price, my dear Janet Thompson, Monique, Pat, Maggy, Audrey, Monica, Cindy, Nichelle, Dana, Chanel, June, Marla Jo, and Dawn. You all are my core and it is from you I receive love and support to help others.

To Jamaicans and all my sisters and brothers of the West Indian Diaspora—Jamaica is still my "one love." Much of what I learned came from its roots. Everyone has a reason why they are special . . . mine is my Ja.

Drs. Khandheria and Zaremba, Amy Alms and team Aurora, thank you for saving my life so I could finish this book and the next phase of my life.

Sorors of Delta Sigma Theta Sorority, Inc., you demonstrate the epitome of professional, authentic women, focused on education, community service and lifting all women up. You showed me the ideals we are all striving for.

Cal Hunter—in our time together, you have taught me much about the book (and bookstore) business. Thank you for letting B&N Fifth Avenue be "my house" and for advancing the cause of helping women authors win when others say they won't!

Not least, but last—*Win When They Say You Won't* is dedicated to my late nephew Andrew G. Lawrence—'Drew, you always found a way to win in life, and you are now continuing to inspire others to do the same from heaven.

Let's Go.

INDEX

ABOUT THE AUTHOR

DAPHNE E. JONES has 30 plus years of experience in general management and executive level roles at some of the world's most recognizable companies: IBM, Johnson & Johnson, Hospira, and General Electric (GE). At GE, she served as SVP for Future of Work; SVP and Chief Information Officer (CIO) for Product Engineering, Imaging, and Ultrasound; and as Senior Executive & CIO for Global Services. Her responsibilities as CIO covered a $13 billion segment of GE Healthcare. Jones currently serves on the board of directors for AMN Healthcare, Inc., Barnes Group Inc., and Masonite International Corp., and is CEO of a company that teaches others how to be prepared to serve on boards. She is also the recipient of numerous domestic and international awards. She has dedicated her life to enabling, empowering, inspiring, and instructing those who have felt stymied, stuck, or discouraged from ever feeling they had the power or capability to win. She wants to help people—including women and people of color—to win earlier, better, and more impactfully than she did.

She is a wife, mother, and grandmother and lives in Miami Beach, Florida, and Cicero, New York.